# Grit in the Oyster

# Grit in the Oyster

Mike Keeble

Published by The Elm House Trust

A CIP catalogue record for this book is available from the British Library.

ISBN 978-0-9928867-0-7

Cover design by Trixie Walker of Tradewinds Design & Printing, Leyburn

Prepared and printed by:

York Publishing Services Ltd
64 Hallfield Road
Layerthorpe
York YO31 7ZQ

Tel: 01904 431213

Website: www.yps-publishing.co.uk

*Dedicated to the memory of Margaret Ritchie (1920–1999)*
*whose archive of family papers this book is based upon.*

All profits will go the Elm House Trust and the Vocational Learning Trust

# Contents

# Acknowledgements

*Mike Keeble took on a considerable challenge when he agreed to condense documents filling a whole shelf of a gentleman's wardrobe into a readable record. I am most grateful to him for doing so with patience and good humour and for making the enterprise so enjoyable. The catalyst was the legacy left to me by my Cousin Margery which included 1½ gaits on Middleham Moor and so led to my meeting Mike at a Middleham Moor Gait Owners' meeting. The legacy was also the catalyst for the building of The Work Place at Newton Aycliffe and the setting up of two charities: The Elm House Trust and the Vocational Learning Trust with the help of charity lawyer Ros Harwood, now at Gordons in Leeds.*

*I hope that I have edited out any factual errors, but if any have inadvertently slipped through, they will be corrected in any future print run. My mother only left the odd snippet of paper noting some of her references as she carried out her research and these have been listed at the end. Except for the last two chapters, the book reflects my mother's collection. Beyond a visit to the North Yorkshire County Record Office to look for Cousin Margery's great grandmother, limited further research has been carried out. So the end result is an archive set in its historical contexts. My own memories of what I was told by my parents, Cousin Margery and others have been woven in and I have added a spattering of footnotes to Mike's text. The last two chapters reflect my own records, scrapbooks and memories and the building of The Work Place.*

*I am also grateful to the following:*

*Nadina Alexander – Amy Armitage's grand daughter*

*Fiona Ligonnet née Chapman-Purchas for help with information on Henrietta Mabel Lister*

*The late Anthony Chapman-Purchas for copies of several family trees he gave to my mother and me*

*Caroline Gardiner – daughter-in-law of Sylvia Thornton-Berry*

*Alastair Broadwith for his help with the photographs*

*Christine Baker who helped me sort and catalogue the archive on its return from Mike so that it can in due course be lodged with the North Yorkshire County Record Office*

*Philippa Gray and Tim & Bernie Ritchie for reading the draft and for their helpful comments*

*Trixie Walker of Tradewinds Design & Printing, Leyburn, for the design of the cover*

*The North Yorkshire County Record Office*

*York Publishing Services Ltd.*

*Cardale Asset Management Ltd. for sponsoring the book launch*

Jane Other Ritchie

February 2014

# Introduction

Jane Ritchie had three reasons for commissioning this book:

Firstly, to keep a promise made to her mother to tidy up her papers after she died. Secondly, to give her nephews and niece a readable record of their family history to pass on to their heirs. Thirdly, having done so, to use the sales of the book to increase the funding for the two charities she has founded: the Elm House Trust and the Vocational Learning Trust.

I was lucky enough to be commissioned to work with Jane to assist her in achieving her objectives. I had access to a comprehensive set of archives, collected by her mother, which were not catalogued. My main occupation, as a farmer living in Wensleydale for 50 years, has been breeding cattle ultimately for profitable dairy and beef production. It is, I trust, therefore both understandable and appropriate that I have approached my task in the form of a genetic investigation which tells an intriguing story while explaining the links, good and bad, between the two leading players. To justify my role in producing this account, I should add that another side of my life has been writing and broadcasting.

The composite family came together in mid-Wensleydale during the late 17$^{th}$ and early 18$^{th}$ centuries with some coming from the far south west of England, Wales and northern Scotland via London and Gloucestershire, as well as from mainland Europe via the United States. Most were from agrarian communities at the time of the birth of the industrial revolution which offered huge opportunities to the intelligent and hardworking entrepreneur. There is a strong thread of military service which includes the horror of the trenches and the "biggest bang of WW1" on the Western Front and the hell of Dunkirk in WW2. A family member helped to repair the bodies of war torn soldiers during the Great War in the infirmary at Highclere Castle. Another sought escape from an English marriage in South Dakota during the days of the Wild West. These incidents provide the backdrop to a story set mainly in Wensleydale, which remains the hub of this extended family. But it is not a simple tale of genealogy for it tells of the social and financial upheaval of the time, of love, greed, suicide and divorce.

Most of the players settled in the area between the market towns of Leyburn and Hawes over a period of 200 years. Jane Ritchie and her second cousin twice removed, Margery Freeman, are from families that played an influential part in many of the developments and changes that can be seen in the Dale today. This story demonstrates, how over two centuries, national shifts in the structure of populations from rural to urban, from labour intensive to mechanised, and the growth of a large middle class have changed every community in the country.

Mike Keeble

East Witton, Wensleydale

September 2013

# Chapter 1

## Setting the scene: a brief history

The Roman invasion of Britain saw the beginning of the countryside as we know it today for they brought with them sophistication, organisation, innovation and discipline. Before their coming, the people of these islands led crude simple lives, only leaving lasting traces in the form of ruined dwelling places, defence ditches and burial sites. They were pastoral hunters who domesticated wild cattle, sheep and swine to provide a basic diet of red meat and roots. From carcasses they took hides for clothing and bones for tools, and they painted blue woad upon their bodies to scare their enemies. The Roman Empire occupied the country for 450 years before departing leaving sophisticated buildings, a road system, a wall dividing north from south and settlements with social and civic structures. Gauls, Saxons, Vikings and Normans all invaded our shores. Some stayed, while others pillaged and left. Each race had a lasting influence on the genetics of the British people. Monks from mainland Europe made their mark, especially on the rural economy. Arriving in small travelling parties, preaching their religion, they eventually settled to build strategic abbeys around which communities of converts gathered to establish agricultural and mining enterprises.

The Pennines are the backbone of England dividing the wetter land in the west from the drier flat lands to the east. Running from them are valleys, or dales, formed by the rivers of melting ice of past Ice Ages. The River Ure, or Yore, carved out Wensleydale, eroding away the limestone to the north and millstone grit running away to the south. For centuries, these uplands were regarded as bleak and unwelcoming by many people despite yielding considerable mineral wealth. The monastic influence ensured peace in their surrounding communities thus escaping the unrest from which many other parts of the country constantly suffered.

In 1156 the Earl of Richmond proudly declared Jervaulx Abbey, the main abbey in Wensleydale, complete. Built by Cistercian brothers with slabs of millstone grit dragged down on sledges from Witton Fell, it stood beside the Yore, and along with its sister community at Fountains Abbey, became the centre of an international wool trade supplying the skilled craftsmen of Northern Europe. The monks shepherded and sheared the vast flocks roaming the hills to the west and south and trained local people in their art and craft, in time delegating the care of the flocks to them.

The yearly wool clip formed a major part of the early British economy. The 'Golden Fleece' became the most valuable export from ports such as Boston in Lincolnshire, going across the North Sea to the spinners, dyers and weavers of northern Europe. The sheep also produced lambs and milk in the summer months to feed the communities in and around the monastery. Surplus milk was made into cheese and stored in subterranean ice houses, or sold to raise valuable income for the monks and lay brothers. The annual wool clip was however the primary product, and when unproductive or old sheep were killed, their meat was eaten, the skins used for clothing and shoes and the bones for tools, with surplus fat rendered down to produce fuel for light and heat.

The sheer size and influence of the abbeys across the north of England enabled the Cistercians to control the countryside and provide the social and 'professional' services that developing communities required for their sustainability. Religious Houses attracted men of considerable intellect able to develop and practice law and medicine, who undertook research into such things as cheese production, metal working and building techniques. The labouring lay brothers hewed stone from hill side quarries, felled timber and then hauled these materials on sledges to building sites where they levered huge stones and timber to great heights using pulleys for which they had to spin the rope and manufacture the wheels.

In the autumn of 1538, the Dissolution of the Monasteries moved into the area bringing labouring gangs, supervised by troops, to destroy Jervaulx Abbey. The plate and coinage were taken away directly to the dwindling royal coffers of King Henry VIII. 356 tons of locally produced lead were stripped from the roof to which a further 34 fodders[1] were added to be transported to Lord Cromwell in London. He was informed however, that he would have to wait for summer before the lead and the bronze bells could move along the muddy tracks leading out of Wensleydale to Leeming Lane, the Romans' Great North Road, to be transported south. The mud was so deep that pack animals could hardly move.

At the top of Wensleydale lay the Great Parish of Aysgarth, 18 miles long, running from Lunds on the Westmoreland border to below the village of Aysgarth to the east, covering roughly half the length the valley. It is in this ancient parish, and in the small Parish of Middleham[2] that many of the family settled. After the Dissolution, Wensleydale fell into disarray as the professional and social roles of the monks came to an abrupt end. Their grazing land became overstocked with sheep in an attempt to meet the burgeoning demand for wool in Northern Europe where washing, spinning, top making, dying and weaving were established trades. The monks had borrowed large amounts of money to expand their flocks and as they departed and the flocks became owned by the shepherding farmers, an epidemic broke out caused by overstocking and a proliferation of ticks in the sheep's fleeces. These lurked in bracken and scrub waiting to drop onto other sheep to feed from their blood, then to infect and kill. The result was a financial disaster which had a lasting effect.

Land ownership became complex as the nation matured. After William the Conqueror's invasion, large tracts of land were allotted to noblemen in exchange for feudal commitments for the provision of horses, armed men and food to fight in future conflicts. Subsequently, they divided the land still further between selected army commanders and lesser nobles in exchange for commitments of loyalty to ensure money and troops were always available to control local populations or to fight invaders. The monks and their successors were graziers without title. It could be argued that the true freehold of land remains to this day with the Crown, and that modern landowners, the heirs of original titles, actually hold the equivalent of seemingly endless leases.

---

1    A fodder is a unit of volume of unused smelted lead.

2    2118 acres.

In the years following the Battle of Hastings, large acreages became owned by institutions such as the Church, hospitals, scholastic colleges and corporations. At the top of Wensleydale thousands of acres remained in the hands of the Crown until the reign of Charles I. In order to avoid re-calling Parliament to Westminster to discuss and debate raising taxes to fund the mounting costs of running the nation, Charles quietly sold this land to the Corporation of the City of London. Enormous wealth had been accumulated through dues and taxes from the Port of London which the Romans had established as the country's main trading harbour during their occupation. The City divided the Wensleydale land into smaller lots and sold them at a considerable profit. Sheep and wool remained the backbone of Dales' farming and gradually cattle appeared, but it was not until the late 16th century that numbers rose substantially. Lead, copper and coal deposits were exploited in the hills and the extensive timber cover was gradually felled to make room for farming. Prime timber was sold for shipbuilding and that of lesser quality was sawn up as pit props or used for building, the poorest being used for shelter and fire wood.

As the 17th century dawned, after years of conflict at home and abroad, the country became confident and well organised with growing ambitions for empire building. The variety of immigrants that had arrived and stayed created a hybrid society of intelligent, artistic, creative and hardworking people, but the majority lived lives of rural subsistence with neither time, nor inclination, to exploit their abilities. They were a peasant class through no fault of their own, victims of circumstance. By the start of the 18th century, the Industrial Revolution was underway, and, in parallel, a similar revolution began to take place in the countryside. Rural folk started to move away from their peasant lives to the growing industrial communities near mineral ore and coal which, combined with water power, drove the iron and steel works. Manufacturing was established alongside these heavy industries as a growing tide of humanity arrived in haste with little planning for their welfare.

The landed class dominated both Houses of Parliament along with a few military victors from battles successfully fought and others largely drawn from the Church or Courts of Law. These were the people who saw investment opportunities in expanding industrial centres who borrowed against land holdings to invest and retain control. However, there were some rural newcomers who quickly understood the new industrial way of life. They worked hard and long to build their own finances, usually as managers, creating a new wealthy industrial class which emulated their peers by buying land. Rural Britain gradually became a nation of smaller estates with land let to farming tenants, who in their turn employed the remaining peasant class to till their acres. Some of these successful tenants, especially those close to intensive industrial populations requiring constant supplies of fresh food, made sufficient profits to eventually buy their freeholds thus becoming yeomen and qualifying for the vote. The social balance was changing.

The 2nd Viscount Townshend,[3] Squire Coke of Holkham, and the Duke of Bedford were just three landowners who researched and developed new farming techniques while village blacksmiths, such as Jethro Tull, invented implements to improve the growing of crops and the reduction of labour. Even King George III, 'Farmer George', ploughed up part of Kew Gardens to grow food as well as starting the Royal Farm at Windsor. Robert Bakewell of Dishley Farm in Leicestershire studied animal breeding and found that by putting the best male to the best female something better was produced, thus founding the recording of pedigree and the establishment of the animal breed societies we see today. He improved cattle and sheep by hiring out rams and bulls in exchange for records of fertility and growth rates to further his research and improve his business. Through his attention to detail and by using records as the basis of educational courses to train other farmers, he brought about huge improvements in livestock production. Much of this missed the remote moorland and dales where farming populations were continuing to migrate to a better life, or so they imagined. However, there were families in the Dales who saw opportunities in the underexploited land, in the water powered mills and the mineral wealth that lay beneath the surface.

The industrial and agricultural revolutions of the 18th century started the development of modern Britain. Small towns became cities bringing together commerce, legal, religious and professional interests. Towns developed where industry was already established around natural

---

3    Known as Turnip Townshend.

resources. In Yorkshire, the power of water flowing from the Pennines attracted wool processors with their associated trades of top makers, dyers, spinners and weavers. Inventive engineers designed machinery for these mills that increased efficiency to satisfy growing markets, thus creating ever larger profits. Wool came to Yorkshire from all over the country and increasingly from the colonies, in the ships that returned from the new lands having taken out the essentials to the growing Empire; tools, seeds, livestock and human beings. The Cutty Sark now moored at Greenwich was at one time a wool clipper.

The dales, moors and mountains remained very much as they had been in the days of the monastic communities. Villages supported trades such as bakers, blacksmiths, tailors, shoe makers, butchers, joiners and carriers. Cow keepers, the lowest rank of farmers, produced milk and calves which were sold to farmers who grew crops and bred oxen to plough and sow. Crops were still grown on medieval strip systems giving each farmer a variety of plots. Much of the land was 'open' and used as common grazing for animals.

As urbanisation increased, the demand for food could not be sustained by farming systems based on this feudal regime. New agricultural techniques, ideas and opportunities were starting to develop especially around new towns. The practice of enclosures slowly developed allowing land owners and yeoman farmers to stake out land. This they then drained or fertilised to increase crop yields. King George III encouraged the legal processes of enclosure, removing ancient land laws going back to William the Conqueror thus establishing new titles to land. These new owners of enclosed land arranged systems of tenure creating the tenanted system we know today.

The demand for minerals increased and local groups, often professional people, obtained extraction licences from land owners. The mineral rich territories were often rough and exposed. Heavy materials had to be moved both in and out using pack horses. Streams were diverted to flush out and to clean extracted ores. Mine work was difficult and hard with men, women and children working long hours, sometimes having to walk considerable distances to the mines. Many mineworkers died or were damaged for life, in rock falls, under laden trollies or through sheer overwork.

The landscape was slowly changing as men toiled to 'modernise' food production and extract minerals and timber. Oxen and horses could pull and carry, but the erection of boundary walls to enclose land in the dales called for hundreds of men to lift, carry and build stone walls. The sparse timber cover was cleared so that land could be better used for grazing or growing crops. Over centuries drove roads had been worn across remote countryside, connecting towns and cities to the land which yielded the essentials for urban communities to flourish. Beef and mutton 'on the hoof' used these exposed rough drove roads, while the main trade routes were crowded with the horse drawn carts of the carriers full of goods such as boots, knitwear and forged hand tools. Others moved rough timber heading for the large water powered saw mills adjacent to growing industrial communities. A steady flow of rural migrants headed away from the poverty of country hamlets and villages, hoping to find more prosperous times in the growing towns and cities. Water was used as much as possible to move volume and weight. The estuaries became distribution centres and smaller rivers, with smaller craft, took goods inland. The development of canals allowed goods to move around the country more cheaply.

Despite this furious activity and movement of products and people, much of the countryside remained wild and rugged. To cross from Scotland into England over the Carter Bar on the Cheviot Hills, travellers required a token of safekeeping from bandits, an activity controlled on both sides of the Border by gipsies. Any movement of gold or other valuables had to be accompanied by armed men. Three men lead the improvement of the transport infrastructure around the country building canals, roads and turnpikes: Metcalf (Blind Jack), Telford and McAdam. They surveyed the routes, negotiated the necessary wayleaves with land owners and dealt with the problems of bog, marsh and incline. They supervised the building of tunnels and bridges and organised turnpike tolls. Thousands of navvies were employed, many from Ireland.

In Wensleydale, Askrigg, Hawes, Middleham and Leyburn gradually developed. In country parishes, the vicar, usually the younger son of a local aristocratic or upper class family, was effectively the administrator over education, the poor and the faith of the community with primary regard for the interests of the landlords by ensuring workers were behaving obediently in their frugal feudal communities. Non-conformist chapels, many served by travelling middle class ministers, took up the cause of underprivileged farmers and their labourers. A national survey in the late 18th century showed that 50% of worshippers on Sundays were attending chapel not church.

Many of the characters in this book arrived in Wensleydale in the 18th century as professional, or business men, seeking commercial opportunities. Leisure time was scarce for the working class, but on village festival days, usually with landowners absent, the community came together. Hunting, a rural pastime and tradition since ancient times, was a classless sport for much of the year. In the hills and mountains it was not the preserve of the landowners as it was in the shires. For anyone, in the right place at the right time, it was there to enjoy. In Wensleydale, hounds were kept to hunt the hare, fox, deer and otter. In summer, the river was fished with the most productive stretches strictly controlled by estate water bailiffs.

# Chapter 2

## The Other beginnings

Jane Ritchie and Margery Freeman were second cousins twice removed with their genetic link going back to the 17th century to a family called Other. There is mention of a Dominus Otherus at the time of Edward the Confessor and Magna Carta refers to a Fitz-Other with Lordships in Surrey, Hampshire, Middlesex and Buckinghamshire. Family tradition is that the family was descended from a walrus hunter called Othere in the time of King Alfred. However, the family tree starts with John Other who farmed in the village of Pickhill, beside the River Swale, lying to the east of the Great North Road, the link between London and Edinburgh since Roman times. There was a thriving trade not least in livestock heading south to fatten on better land for the expanding industrial populations. To farm near this main commercial artery was to be in a position to diversify into such enterprises as the provision of horses to travellers either as hirelings, or to be purchased in part exchange. Horse feed, accommodation for travellers, blacksmithing, carriage repairs, harness making and general trading were all possibilities.

John married Mary Wiseman in 1570 and their only child John married Margaret Grayson receiving land at Kirklington in a marriage settlement, thus becoming a yeoman and not a tenant farmer. John and Margaret had two sons. The eldest, Thomas (1604-1658), married Elizabeth, her surname is not recorded, but we know they had four children. Their eldest son, another John, married Allison who died shortly afterwards in 1660. He married secondly Anne and they had a son Thomas and a daughter Ann.

By the time Thomas was born in 1667, the family had moved to farm in West Tanfield, a village to the west of Kirklington. Thomas Other of

West Tanfield married, we know not who, but in 1701 his son and heir Christopher was born. In 1752 Christopher registered his name in the North Riding of Yorkshire County records as a property owning yeoman number 677. He married Alice Metcalf in 1729 in the village of Thornton Watlass a few miles away. One of the family trees suggests she comes from Preston.[4] Their daughter Isabella married a Ralph Robinson from Redmire.[5] Their son, another Christopher, married Elizabeth Heselden in 1757. Elizabeth came from a land owning family in Horton in Ribblesdale to the west of the Pennines. She and Christopher had six children: Alice (born 1758),[6] Christopher (born 1762), Margaret (born 1764), Bryan (born 1767), Thomas (born 1769), and Elizabeth (born 1771). Bryan died aged two, and neither Christopher nor Elizabeth ever married. Thomas therefore became his father's heir inheriting his yeoman's vote as well as his land. Christopher's life style had changed from the days when his forebears were tenants on their small farm on the banks of the River Swale nearly 200 years before. As a registered landowner, he was well off compared to the majority of farmers who were stuck in the restrictive and precarious tenancy system based on mediaeval land law.

As the Industrial Revolution gathered pace, the gossip and news flowing up and down the country from cities and industrial towns in the south made it clear that although commerce was developing fast, so too was crime. Every load that came and went up and down the Great North Road, or through West Tanfield heading east and west, had been bought and would be sold for coinage, much of which was gold. Merchants, landowners and the rich middle class were lending money in exchange for security on property, or shares in a business. Paper promissory notes were being talked of as a way of safely moving money instead of the heavy bulk of gold bullion. Banking was becoming an essential business within a growing industrial society bringing with it new found prosperity for the bankers.

---

4    Presumably Preston-under-Scar, a village on the north side of Wensleydale.

5    This suggests they moved to Redmire in the early to mid-1700s.

6    Alice married James Foster from Stainforth in Ribblesdale and her grandson Bryan Foster married Isabella Robinson of The Cliff, Leyburn. It will have been through this connection that Christopher Other met his first wife Anne Stackhouse.

Daniel Defoe, the politician and writer, toured the North determined to go as far as the Scottish border. He left London heading eastward round the coast then turned west inland to the Roman road, drifting from side to side along its length visiting expanding towns and cities. His aim was to report back to London, and hence to government, on the state of the nation's commerce at the start of the Industrial Revolution. From his political perspective, the speculation in London about new found riches in foreign lands clearly meant there was a need for change. Industry would have to fuel the necessary growth. As this would often risk conflict with the natives of these foreign shores, it was necessary to build ships capable of travelling uncertain distances across the oceans, and the sending out of armed men. Defoe noted the state of the countryside as he travelled, but gave little information about the farming and rural life as his concerns were primarily about raw materials, industry, manufacturing, ports and ship building. What we know is that as he saw the Pennines looming to his west he recounted how difficult and, in many cases, how dangerous it would be to stray too far into them.

Defoe visited the expanding industries around Leeds and travelled thence to the castle towns of Knaresborough and Ripley. He progressed to the spa at Harrogate, then to the cathedral city of Ripon before joining the Leeming Lane section of the Roman road at Boroughbridge. He then visited Bedale, or Bedall as he spelt it, where he concluded, "I found nothing that comes within the compass of my enquiries." He did remark however that the town was a centre for breeding horses, as well as racing. During his stay he heard that the Arabian stallions, foundation of the racing thoroughbred, had been much used in the area, creating a lucrative market for locally bred horses. The blood lines of all today's thoroughbred horses can be traced back to one of three imported stallions. Two were Arabian: the Godolphin and Darley – both names still used in the 21st century by Sheikh Mohammed as the titles of his racing and breeding operations. The third sire was Turkish, named the Byerley Turk,[7] who had been captured after the siege of Budapest in 1686 and brought back to England.

---

7    The Byerley Turk by Jeremy James tells his story.

The heavy horses of northern Europe had been bred over generations for hauling loads and carrying heavy men in armour. Further south, across Europe and around the Mediterranean, horses were bred to travel long distances across hot arid lands carrying lighter people. Goods were carried on camels, donkeys, mules and heavy horses. It was King Henry VIII who first initiated the introduction of these fast light animals to cross with the large, tough and cumbersome British horse. Horse breeding for sport and racing led to a demand for small men to ride them. Defoe mentioned the number of little men he encountered on his visit to Bedale, also admiring the noble breed of oxen sold at the fairs in North Allerton. These were used locally for draft purposes before being sold to go south to be 'fatted' for the London market.

He progressed to Richmond[8] and was impressed by the thriving manufacture of knitwear with stockings of all sizes selling for eighteen pence per dozen or three half pence per pair. This was the sort of commerce and industry he had come to find. He regarded the River Swale, flowing beneath the castle walls, as a tumult from a rough and dangerous country which he had no intention of visiting as it was of no commercial account. What he failed to realise was that people in the Dales, and across into Westmoreland, were washing and spinning wool for others. They lived on farms and in villages, knitting while walking and shepherding, as well as in the evening by the fire, supplementing their small incomes with a craft developed in monastic times and handed down through the generations.

There is no record as to why Christopher and Alice moved west to the village of Redmire in mid Wensleydale in the 1700s. It is thought he must have inherited Old Elm House and land from a relative. It was almost certain that the move was before daughter Alice was born in 1758. The house was simple, but with accommodation for servants. The stone lintel over the entrance door is engraved "C&A O 1694" which presumably is the date his relative, probably a Christopher and his wife with a name beginning with A, built the house. This inheritance presented him with new opportunities in the emerging business of wool processing which was developing in mills powered by the Rivers Yore and Swale. In the

8    Defoe's only venture into the Yorkshire Dales.

surrounding hills and valleys people were mining low quality coal from drift seams. More importantly, under those Pennine hills there were reserves of valuable lead and copper, essential elements of industry, that were largely unexploited. The local farmers, all tenants, were breeding sheep and cattle to be sold at seasonal fairs. The economy was founded on small businesses trading products and raw materials to merchants who bulked up goods to transport and sell to larger merchants and traders, sometimes providing credit to the buyer. The giving of credit carried with it risks in a trade based on gold coinage which endorsed the idea that properly organised short term lending, based on paper credit notes, was clearly the first step to establishing a banking system requiring a secure guaranteed capital base beyond the reach of most people.

The Other line is the common thread of this story which stretches back to the start of the sixteenth century. Christopher's wife Elizabeth Hesledon came from Ribblesdale across the Pennine moors to the west on one of the main turnpikes running from east to west connecting the industry and ports bordering the North Sea with those on the Atlantic coast. This formed a bridgehead from mainland Europe over the North Sea and across Britain to new lands in the Americas. The trans-Pennine routes carried thousands of European migrants escaping social inequality and unrest in their homelands heading for the land of new opportunities.

Christopher and Elizabeth's eldest son Christopher only lived until he was 31, dying a bachelor in 1794 leaving Thomas to inherit the Elm House Estate. It was Thomas who built the present Elm House on the site of the original grange.[9] He was great, great, great grandfather to Jane Ritchie and the great grandfather of Margery Freeman, the two principals of this book. Thomas Other, the new squire of Redmire, married Margaret Stapleton in the neighbouring village of Wensley in 1800. This was a tragic union for Margaret died during the first year of marriage. In 1803, Thomas married the 23 year old Jane Lister of Coverham Abbey in the Abbey church and they had seven children: Elizabeth Alice (born 1805), Jane (born 1807), Christopher (born 1809), Thomas (born 1811), Isabella (born 1813), Margaret (born 1815) and Edward (born 1819).

---

9    A grange was a monastic farm or collection of agricultural buildings often used as a centre for collecting and storing tithe produce.

Jane Other died in 1829 aged 49, and is buried in Redmire churchyard. Three of her children, Christopher, Elizabeth and Margaret feature in the genes of our two principals. Christopher is the great, great paternal grandfather of Jane Ritchie and Margaret is her maternal great, great grandmother. Elizabeth Other is the paternal grandmother of Margery Freeman. Jane Ritchie commissioned this story of her remarkable family, which brings in thirteen different genetic lines, to place a seal on a family that has had such an influence on the economy and community of Wensleydale over a period of four hundred years.

As the 17th century turned into the 18th the foundations of modern Britain were falling into place. The House of Lords represented the interests of large land owners with the less powerful House of Commons representing the common people: the yeomen farmers, professionals and retired military men. Suffrage was about the ownership of property and the voting power bestowed by it, which meant that the vast majority of the rural population had no democratic power. In the House of Lords the main concerns were land laws, land tax and high rental values of ownership. Both Houses approved taxes for commodities such as malt and wheat to raise money for land reform. Neither House had any great interest in farming the land as long as it yielded rents; nor did they know, or understand, the people who worked in rural industries. The quality of life did not improve in expanding industrial communities, and freedom from the restrictions of rural rule came at a price as new workshop barons continued to pay the least for doing the most. There were however, crude houses to be had in return for hard labour by all members of the family, young and old, as long as there were no challenges to the hardship and injustices they suffered for their pitiful reward.

Thomas Other (1769-1834) was ambitious and became a banker. Money was there to be made in the Dales' communities. Through his early financial dealings he co-founded the local bank of Hutton and Other & Co and he introduced his son Christopher to the firm when he was only 17. The bank developed into the Swaledale and Wensleydale Banking Company (initially the Richmond & Swaledale Bank) establishing banking houses in Hawes, Leyburn, Masham, Bedale & Richmond. Richmond was the head and most eastern office, nearest to Darlington and within easy reach of the Great North Road which was still the nation's main arterial connection from the south to Scotland. He was understandably very proud when the family bank notes became the main currency in the area, but gold remained the basis of trade. Banks received gold coinage from farmers on fair days, and from miners, small manufacturers, merchants and shop keepers on a weekly basis. Some of this money was placed in branch vaults and the rest, the base capital, was moved to the main vault in Richmond, eventually to be deposited with a larger bank in London. Horse drawn vehicles transporting bullion were always accompanied by armed outriders. In the peaceful Dales, which remained the Bank's main business area, there was never serious trouble. However, movements of bullion anywhere near main highways and turnpikes carried considerable risks. The Backhouse Bank in Darlington, with which the Swaledale & Wensleydale Bank eventually merged, always took great care with bullion transfers due to their proximity to the turnpike system.

Christopher became Chairman of the Bank just prior to his father's death in 1834, when he was only 25. Two years later, he advised the board to become a joint stock bank and later witnessed the Bank's merger with the Backhouse Bank prior to his own demise in 1896.[10] This last merger was in preparation for the 'new' Backhouse Banking Company to become one of the regional family banks which formed Barclays Bank. The Barclay (Hertfordshire), Backhouse (Darlington) and Gurney (Norfolk) families were Quakers and much trusted as honourable, honest and strict financiers. Christopher was a wealthy young man and when his unmarried Aunt Annie Lister, his mother's sister, inherited the larger part of Coverham Abbey in Coverdale, he knew it would eventually become his house, as indeed it did in part on her death in 1887. The property was however bequeathed to both him and his heirs as a joint inheritance, a fact which would come to haunt him in later life.

The abbey estates dispersed during the Reformation covered vast areas. Coverham was a Premonstratensian Abbey founded in 1120 by an order of regular cannons from Premontre in France with patronage from Middleham Castle. Jervaulx Abbey, to the east, belonged to the

---

10    Most of the negotiations were done between his son-in-law James Winn and Jonathan Backhouse.

Cistercian Order. In 1535, Coverham came under a Dissolution Order. Thomas Wray, described in various 16<sup>th</sup> century accounts as a member of a 'numerous clan' living in and around the parishes of Coverham and West Witton, was appointed Seneschal, or steward, with the right to claim salvage value of what remained after the valuable fabric, lead and any precious metals had been removed to London. Thomas had a son Christopher Wray who became Lord Chief Justice. He gained a Baronetcy and was known as the progenitor of the Wrays of Coverdale.

Under Wray's stewardship, the Coverham estate passed to Charles Lascelles in 1536 who sold it a year later to Herbert Orme, who in turn sold it to Richard Croft in 1563. In 1657, a George Wray bought Hestholme[11] in Wensleydale and in 1665 he bought the Lordship of Thoralby from the Corporation of London. In 1674, he bought Coverham Abbey. He died a rich man describing himself in his will as "Middleham Gent". His son, also George, lived at Coverham Abbey by then partly converted into a house. He married Dorothy Topham, the daughter of a yeoman who bought with her a marriage settlement of land at Caldbergh, a hamlet two miles east of the abbey grounds. They only had one child, a daughter called Dorothy who inherited Coverham and Caldbergh which was conveyed to her husband known as Wray Atkinson. The property remained in the Atkinson family until a daughter married a Lister. Edward Lister (1751-1808) married Jane Hodshon (1758-1829) and they had twelve children. Their eldest son Edward Atkinson Lister (1780-1856) inherited the house which he left to his youngest unmarried brother[12] who in turn left it to his youngest unmarried sister Annie, Christopher Other's Aunt. Edward Lister left the rest of his estate to be divided between his surviving children in order that their education should be provided for.[13]

Land changed hands in many different ways in those days, rarely being sold publicly. Most went down the family line entailed to sons thus preserving the links to wealth and the privileges of ownership: to vote, hunt and mine. Marriage settlement by a bride's family to the husband's was standard practice.

---

11    A house near the confluence of the Ure and the Bishopdale Beck.

12    He died in 1870.

13    Christopher inherited his late wife Jane's sixth share. She was Edward Lister's eldest daughter.

# Chapter 3

# Cousin Margery

To explain further the genetic links between these two women we start with Margery Freeman who was born at Elm House, Redmire in 1903. Her paternal grandmother Elizabeth Burrill was a daughter of Thomas (1769-1834) and Jane Other of Elm House. Margery's father was Charles James Burrill (called Charlie) of Cotescue Park, a house across the fields from Coverham Abbey in Coverdale, whose first wife Annie Robinson died having had two children William Robinson Burrill and a daughter Elizabeth known as Bessie. Annie was a co-heiress of Henry Thomas Robinson of the Cliff,[14] a house to the east of Leyburn. HT (as the family call him) Robinson had no sons thus his four daughters jointly inherited his considerable wealth when he died.

After an appropriate period of mourning for his popular wife, Charlie married Ada Cockcroft, daughter of Doctor John Cockcroft of Middleham. It is this union that plays such an important role in the genetics of the old lady who died in the council run old people's home in Leyburn, in 2004 aged nearly 101, for she was Ada's only child, Margery. Ada's mother, Ellen, was the daughter of Thomas Kirk,[15] a tenant of Gale Bank Farm on Lord Bolton's estate, which surrounded the villages of Redmire and Wensley. Thomas' first wife, Elizabeth Bell probably died when they were living in Morton Palms, part of the ecclesiastical parish of Haughton-le-Skerne near Darlington, as that is where their three children were born (Richard, Charles and Jane). Each summer he visited the annual Brough

---

14    Inherited from his elder brother Ralph Robinson.

15    Thomas Kirk was born in Raskelf, a village 13 miles north of York in 1782. There is a record of 1855 referring to Mr Thomas Kirk of Gale Bank's Abstract to title to an estate called Byers Green in Co. Durham.

Hill Fair which preceded the Appleby Horse Fair which still thrives in the 21st century and attracts thousands of people. At Brough, Thomas met a gipsy girl, Elizabeth Nagley, who was probably from the Scottish Border town of Yetholm, the centre of the Scottish gipsy community. He was attracted to her and became friendly with her family staying on in the evenings listening to the gipsy talk and music around the fire. On their third annual meeting she agreed to return with him to Gale Bank as his wife when he succeeded to the tenancy from the father of his first wife in 1830. Three children were born at Gale Bank; Elizabeth, Henry and Ellen born 30th April 1837.

We know little more about the Kirks. Thomas died aged 94 and was buried in Wensley on 2nd December 1876. His second wife died aged 74 on 6th May 1881 and is also buried in Wensley. The 1851 Census records her birth place as Gathale,[16] Yorkshire and the 1871 Census records Easby although it is more likely that neither is correct. By 1881 there were no Kirks in Wensley. The scant family history that Margery was told by her mother was recorded in a small notebook held together with rusty staples and written with a thick pencil. The note is undated. Margery incorrectly recorded her great grandmother's name as Ellen, and thought her great, great grandfather was called John or William. No proof has been found to validate the gipsy ancestry, or to explain where the name Nagley came from. Nagley is not a recognised gipsy name, but it may have been used to describe a nag's man,[17] an expert at showing horses to prospective buyers at the horse fairs. No record has so far been traced of John Kirk's second marriage, but his second wife did sign the marriage certificate when her daughter Ellen married John Cockcroft, the doctor in Middleham.

All that is known about Ellen's life prior to her marrying was that she attended a small private school at Cotescue Park, variously the home of some of the families featured in this book. According to the census her fellow pupils were: Elizabeth Ann Winn aged 8, Anne Agnes Other aged 10, Christopher Other aged 9 and she herself approaching 15. At the time

---

16    Near Settle in Ribblesdale.

17    Margery notes her great grandmother as being a "horse coper's daughter". A coper is a dealer.

she could never have imagined that her fellow pupils would become part of her larger family in the years to come.

Margery's father, Charlie Burrill, was a solicitor who died in 1910 aged 64, when she was only seven. He was a wealthy man. His father had been manager of the Swaledale & Wensleydale Bank in Masham who had married Elizabeth Alice Other, one of Christopher Other's sisters. Charlie married Ann Robinson, the eldest daughter of the wealthy H. T. Robinson, and through her acquired Cotescue, a house on the hillside above Coverham Abbey. He had met her socially over the years and they became better acquainted when he was articled to her father's Leyburn law practice Chapman and Robinson. When he qualified he was invited to become a partner with Thomas Topham. On Topham's death he joined solicitor and land agent Hugh Maughan in his Middleham office. Such was his wealth that he was able to retire when aged 44.

Charlie Burrill bought Elm House from Christopher Other's daughter-in-law, Frances North, using his wife's inheritance and moved there from Cotescue. He then lent Cotescue to his Uncle Christopher Other who had found himself homeless with financial cramp due to a protracted and very costly legal battle with Frances, who had remarried after her husband's early death.[18] She had contested the ownership of Elm House as well as Christopher's interest in Coverham Abbey. On Charlie's death Elm House passed to his second wife Ada for her life, and then to Margery's half-brother, William Robinson Burrill-Robinson. Will had been given the second name Robinson to recognize his mother's family. In order to inherit the Robinson Trust lands and arms he had to take his grandfather's surname becoming William Robinson Burrill-Robinson. His first cousin once removed similarly became Robert Chapman-Robinson when he inherited the Robinson Trust which was dissolved at the end of the 1960s when the male entail was broken.[19] When Ada died in 1931, Margery managed Elm House for Will until he married Henrietta Mabel Lister in 1935. Margery then moved out of Elm House and rented Northgate in Redmire.

---

18    Thomas William Other died in 1882.

19    Hyphenated names today reflect sex equality and unmarried partnerships rather than inheritance of arms & property.

William Robinson Burrill-Robinson died in 1962 outliving Mabel by two years. Much of his life had been spent shooting, fishing and attending to his garden, but he had also undertaken a wide range of civic and public duties. He was a long standing member of the Leyburn Magistrates Bench, a County Councillor, Chairman of the Board of School Governors and the Rural District Council as well as holding senior positions over the years in the Conservative Club, and the Leyburn Market Club – a dining club for the main landowners in the Lower Ure Valley. He was President of the Leyburn Agricultural Society and the Wensleydale Longwool Sheep Society. In fact, he had an influential finger in many pies and not much happened in the area that he didn't know about.

Ada Cockcroft would have realised her good fortune when she married into such a respected and wealthy Wensleydale family. The Cockcrofts personified the high standards of most doctors in general practice in that they saw no difference twixt the upper and working class. They charged for their services with their methods carefully graduated from no charge to workers' families on a steadily increasing scale upwards for the upper classes and landowners. Ada's paternal grandfather, William Cockcroft, was born in 1810, the fifth son of a shoe making family from Hebden Bridge in the West Riding of Yorkshire. Aged 16, he travelled to Middleham to live with his uncle, a curate in the parish. His was a lowly clerical position as it was the practice of Rectors and Vicars to retain the tithes and 'livings' paid by farmers and the well-off, leaving subordinate curates to live a frugal life on the pittance they were given or to rely on family support. Curate Cockcroft arranged for William, a very clever lad, to become apprenticed to the town's physician Dr Edmondson whose father and grandfather had followed a similar calling.

This was before the days of formal medical qualifications and William had to learn the art, craft and skills of diagnosing, prescribing and mixing medicines as well as essential and basic surgery on the job. Conveniently he married the Edmondson's daughter, Mary, and eventually inherited the practice. Mary bore him seven children before dying at the age of 35. Their eldest boy, John, born in 1838, followed the family tradition becoming the fourth generation to care for the health and welfare of the small, widespread dales community of Middleham and Coverdale. He was the first in the family to have formal professional training. At 22 he took his M.R.C.S. and L.S.A. in Manchester before going to St Andrew's in Scotland to take his M.D. At 24, he returned home to work alongside his father. He had accumulated in two years a string of qualifications which today would take six or eight years demonstrating just how medical science has moved from art and craft to science and sophistication over 175 years.

Medicine in the second half of the 19th century went through a period of enormous change. The apothecary of old became both a chemist and a doctor, practicing as a general practitioner and a surgeon performing savage amputations and operations which relied solely on the pain killing influence of morphine. Gradually surgeons began to specialise in specific disciplines of medicine as research moved forward at a considerable pace.

In 1866 John Cockcroft, aged 28, married Ellen Kirk, the gipsy's daughter from Gale Bank, who gave birth to Ada in 1868. In 1872 Ellen died while giving birth to her second daughter who sadly succumbed to a severe epidemic of whooping cough that swept through Wensleydale. Margery's father had died when she was only seven and she turned to Grandfather John who was still practising as a doctor for a male role model. She accompanied him on his journeys to the homes of patients around his moorland practice and came to know the network of tracks, the farmers, gamekeepers and the people who lived in the big houses, some of whom were race horse trainers.

Dr John always had five fit horses available either in the paddock, or stable, enabling him to reach any part of his far flung practice in the minimum time, day or night. One stood at night, partly saddled, ready to carry him to any emergency. He removed tonsils, amputated limbs, pulled teeth and withdrew pleural fluid from bronchial patients on kitchen tables scrubbed clean. Then with strong men to hold the patient down as the anaesthetic wore off, the operation commenced. His instruments were boiled on the kitchen range and for days after he made regular calls to ensure the diet and healing wounds of the afflicted were going according to plan. He rarely took holidays, but shot and fished in season. He knew and understood the moors and coverts around Lower Wensleydale as well as the owners and game keepers themselves; all of whom were his patients. When he travelled in his dog cart, with his retriever following, his rod or gun could oft be seen protruding from under the canvas cover.

He retired after WW1 when he was over 80. His nephew, returning from the Royal Army Medical Corps, took over the Middleham practice. No longer was there a need for horses as he had a car. Pharmaceutical products were improving year by year and country doctors worked with hospitals on more serious operations. For the twelve years of his retirement, John could be seen on fine days sitting in his garden overlooking the road through the town wearing his frock coat and top hat from which his side whiskers protruded out round his face. He raised his hat to all who passed and they returned his acknowledgement. He had become an institution. In the spring of 1930 there was a General Election and despite having lost much of his speech and movement and being largely bedridden due to a stroke he insisted that his nurse push him through the town to vote. He rode proudly in his bath chair wearing grey flannel pyjamas under an Inverness coat and top hat. Word quickly went around the community that "t'owd Doc" was going to cast his vote. Having made his mark he went home, the entire population seemed to have turned out cheering and waving to the old man who had played such an important part in all their lives at birth, sickness and in death. He doffed his hat all the way and when he arrived he tottered in on his sticks, across to his favourite chair, lowered himself down into it and cried. The next time he journeyed through the town the crowd was there again,[20] but this time in silence as he was in his coffin.

---

20    Dr John Cockcroft died aged 92 on September 7th 1930.

# Chapter 4

## The Gipsy's great granddaughter grows up

Margery always regretted she hadn't been sent away to school as it would have given her more female friends in later life. There were no suitable day schools in the Dale so an alternative was found. The Reverend G. T. Whitehead, Vicar of Thornton Watlass near Bedale, had a daughter of similar age to Margery called Sylvia and the two families agreed to share a governess for their daughters. Sylvia would stay at Elm House during the week, travelling back and forth by train between Bedale and Redmire stations. She was a strong willed young lady with a rebellious nature, caring little for the strict rules of the vicarage. Margery was totally the opposite, being quiet and naturally conforming to her mother's wishes which made her reserved amongst people. The girls however made a good pair each counterbalancing the other's character. They received a comprehensive education which started with the three R's and further developed with literature, geography, history and languages.

By the age of seventeen Margery was well read, fluent in German and with a good knowledge of the world, its history and emerging possibilities. As her schooling came to an end, she undoubtedly dreamt of an adventurous life, but this was not to be as her mother had already decided she should go to the Royal Academy of Music in London. With mild protestation she agreed and lived as a paying guest with friends of her grandfather while attending the Academy. She arrived with only a basic skill on the piano.

Sylvia was 16 when the Elm House period came to an end. Her elder sister had met the son of a brewer from Sheffield who had invited her to go to a ball in Bath, naturally accompanied by a chaperone. Mrs Whitehead sent the teenage Sylvia to act in this capacity. Trevor Thornton-Berry, the brewer's son, fell head over heels in love not with the intended, but with the younger Whitehead daughter. Trevor had served in World War One and gathered life's experiences in plenty. He was potentially rich, but with the handicap of a totally dominant mother who controlled his every move. During his military training on Salisbury Plain and at other barracks she followed his regiment in a caravan she had had made especially for the purpose. He was continually trying to be like other men, but it was made impossible for all the time there was the presence of the lady in the caravan. However, his status improved considerably amongst his fellow cadets when word went round that the 'camp follower' was having an affair with the commanding officer, one Col. Arundel Begbie.[21]

Trevor told his mother about Sylvia and received her approval to approach the by now retired Reverend G. T. Whitehead to ask for Sylvia's hand in marriage. He made the necessary arrangements to go to Flanders Hall in West Burton.[22] Sylvia accepted his proposal and Trevor picked his moment to seek her father's approval to be accepted as the potential son-in-law. Then, with considerable cheek, Trevor placed a condition on the marriage which was that his mother had also been consulted and insisted that Sylvia should first become a competent bridge player. The retired vicar set to work on a series of bridge lessons and Trevor's mother approved the purchase of a small estate in Herefordshire where the couple could settle down and have children. There were two by 1926 when Rev. G. T. Whitehead sent word that the Swinithwaite[23] Estate was to be sold and he would help them buy it. Once settled in, Trevor persuaded his already twice divorced mother to marry Col. Begbie as "it was so inconvenient for the staff at Swinithwaite Hall to have to make up two bedrooms when they came to stay."

Even though Trevor was at last well away from his controlling mother, he still had to maintain his daily routine of writing to her. She replied with the same regularity often vehemently disagreeing with this or that

---

21    Col. Begbie's sister Margaret was the wife of Rev. G. T. Whitehead.

22    The Whiteheads rented Flanders Hall from Henry Robinson Chapman-Purchas.

23    Swinithwaite had been the second home of Sir George Pilkington, Mayor of Stockport. He sold James C Winn his Walden farms and both men planted sycamore trees alongside roads that ran through their estates.

decision, which they had come to concerning house decorations, furniture or staffing. By the time WW2 started there were five children and Sylvia was still not 30. During the period leading up to hostilities Trevor entertained fellow officers from the large garrison at Catterick, but when the war started he had to put up with Swinithwaite Hall becoming an auxiliary mess as Sylvia continued the hospitality. Trevor, who served in the Observer Corp, found it necessary to make various domestic changes such as turning all house phones over to coin boxes when he found that airmen from the U.S. base at Leeming were regularly calling home on his phone line which infuriated him. His hospitality was intended for army colleagues not the slick, well off and highly informal and untidy air crew. They were 'Yanks' who had been slow to answer the call to arms and now they were "overpaid and over here."

After the war, the Thornton-Berry marriage was in tatters and Sylvia went to America, but she returned disillusioned. Trevor arranged for her to live in the Old Vicarage at West Witton, with her mother, only a mile or so from him. Once when asked by her daughter-in-law if her son Humphrey had ever had any of the usual children's diseases Sylvia had replied, "How on earth would I know?" Another of her classics, which describes the woman within, was again to her daughter-in-law during a shopping trip, "Darling you don't buy clothes to please men, you buy them to annoy their women."

At an early age Margery followed Sylvia's example by falling in love. In her case with her first cousin Frank Burrill, a dashing pilot in the Royal Flying Corps, who lived dangerously flying over the battlefields of France on reconnaissance and bombing missions hurling explosives down on the enemy trenches. Like many of his fellow flyers, he was eventually shot down during a foray behind the line. He was soon captured and imprisoned in the Holzminden prison in Brunswick near the river Weser. He was an enterprising fellow, brave and athletic, well suited to become an enthusiastic digger of escape tunnels. A number were dug and usually found, but he took part in one attempt and was the last to be re-captured when the guards discovered the exit beyond the perimeter wire.

After the war, Frank returned to a large 18th century house in Middleham called The Grove.[24] He had no training fitted to peacetime, no job to go to, but was anxious to farm like so many war weary men seeking peace in their rural homeland they had saved from the Hun. As he had no land in Yorkshire he decided to take a farm in Dorset from where he returned north occasionally to hunt. He was one of hundreds of war heroes who were country sportsmen with a love for hunting, shooting and fishing and it was cruel fate when he lost an eye from a stray shotgun pellet while out rabbiting with friends, having fought for four years unscathed. Afterwards he wore an eye patch which probably, to an admiring teenager, was added attraction to this brave warrior returning home with tales of chivalry, accompanied with ribald good humour.

Margery was upset when her mother deemed her relationship with a cousin to be far too close for her even to consider furthering their growing friendship and it was utterly impossible that they would ever be allowed to marry. However, Ada need not have worried for Frank was killed on 31st December 1925 during a visit to Yorkshire to hunt with the Bedale Hounds when they met at Gatenby, near the original home of the Other family at Pickhill. Their second fox of the day took the pack across the River Swale, swollen with rain from the upper dale. The riders were "flying", their blood was up and no river would stop them. Some kicked their horses on to jump the torrent plunging and leaping again, hopefully, to reach the far bank. The less courageous pondered, some gradually descending into the muddy torrent where the river bottom was fairly firm, but the water rose above their stirrups. Some horses managed to swim diagonally with the flow to hit the opposite bank, while others, including Frank, felt the legs of their horses washed away, rolling them over into the full force of the water, submerging them with feet trapped in the stirrups. Frank was not one of the survivors. His horse was unharmed and taken home by Margery's half nephew, Kit.

---

24     Thomas Other, Christopher Senior's brother, had lived at The Grove and had thought of setting up a silk worm business as the garden had a mulberry tree in it. His only daughter died as a child and her ghost is sometimes still seen.

Margery went to the Royal College of Music in London in 1920 aged 18, a country girl unused to the clamour of metropolitan life. Having grown up with a love of racing, hunting, fishing and shooting she had to adjust to the chaotic humdrum of city life. The streets were a disorganised entanglement of motor cars, horse drawn carriages and carts. The pavements were a continuous flow of humanity, and away from the main areas, there was a lot of obvious poverty. Her friends back home were sportsmen, game keepers, river men and huntsmen who she had mixed with in her spare moments. London, however, had its compensations as she found the pleasures of the theatre and musicals of the day. There were still hordes of young men, returned from the horrors of France, seeking excitement as compensation for the hell of war with little thought for their futures, just living for the morrow. In old age, Margery admitted that the classical music of the Royal College of Music had not been to her liking, preferring that of the 1920's musicals and the songs of Gilbert & Sullivan. While there she played piano and violin as well as studying to become a conductor and accompanist. She excelled with the violin and her teacher, the renowned violinist Maurice Jones, accompanied her to Bohr's Music Studio, in Wardour Street, to select an instrument, making sure the bow she would use in her future career was of the very best quality. When she returned home, she became involved with the Wensleydale Tournament of Music and Song, composing a symphony and songs which were almost certainly never played in her lifetime. She also founded the Aysgarth Choral Society.

Ada intended for her daughter to become a piano accompanist, and on leaving the Royal College of Music, Margery applied for a job accompanying a singer who, much to her surprise, turned out to be a black lady. At the interview she was told that part of the job entailed preparing "fish suppers" for the singer's son. Margery felt insulted by the notion that she would be expected to carry out domestic duties for she was an accomplished musician and promptly turned the job down. However, the need for further job hunting became unnecessary when she was summoned home to look after her mother who had become ill. Ada died on 10th June 1931, aged 61. Her obituary in the Parish Magazine referred to her love of children.

Margery returned to Elm House as an adult, having left as a shy and innocent girl. As her mother's health deteriorated, Margery assumed Ada's role, routines and responsibilities, the most important of which was to ensure her half-brother's life ran smoothly. Will was a man of means with property and investment interests who spent much of his time shooting during the autumn and winter then taking his rod and flies to fish during the warmer months. In autumn and winter, Margery watched and worked with the game keepers burning heather on the moors. She learnt how it had to be dry enough to produce a good fast burn to remove the old and make way for the new while not damaging the peat surface and the flora and fauna beneath it. In spring she joined the keepers trapping vermin, protecting nesting grouse and maintaining the shooting butts and moorland paths. When the grouse season started on August 12th, she went beating, flanking, loading and, occasionally shooting. At the end of the day she could be found packing grouse in baskets in the game room at Elm House and then taking them to Redmire station in the game cart, pulled by a smart cob, for the train journey to restaurants and hotels in London. She followed hounds hunting otters, the predators of fish stocks in the river, a sport she had learnt the art and skills of as a child from her grandfather, the doctor. She was a lifelong supporter of the Wensleydale Harriers, often following them on their regular forays over the higher pastures and moorland to keep the fox population in balance to protect new born lambs in spring time as well as nesting game birds on the moors and in the woods. This was the life and home she had to step away from when her half-brother married Henrietta Mabel Lister[25] in 1935. Margery very sadly left Elm House.

Henrietta was the daughter of Doctor Charles Edward Lister (1862-1907) who had departed Britain after qualifying in the midst of a family disagreement. His great grandfather was Edward Lister (1751-1808) of Coverham Abbey so his father, also Edward, was Jane Other's nephew. This was Henrietta's link with Coverham Abbey. Charles went to Australia where he married Florence Smith who had worked in a tobacconist's kiosk. They travelled to Tasmania to set up a medical practice in a land

---

25    Will's best man was Robbie King of West Witton who had played Rugby for Hartlepool and was an excellent shot.

with a climate similar to Yorkshire where there was fishing and shooting in abundance. Henrietta Mabel was born in 1895 in West Ham, Essex. Poor Charles died and was buried at sea when he was taking Mabel, as she was called, back to stay with relatives in London so that she would have an English education. Florence, now a widow, saw that she could regain her freedom back in the lively atmosphere of the Australian mainland by forsaking the hard sporting and medical life she had found herself in in Tasmania. Nothing more is known of her. Charles' brother Alex died in 1895, so Mabel presumably inherited any family money.

The relatives who adopted Mabel lived in Ealing organising her education at the local Girls High School from where she progressed to the Slade School of Art and Drawing, a new avant-garde establishment where Mabel met young people wanting to shake off their inherited shackles of Victorianism. She proved to be a gifted, and eventually became a well-known, watercolourist. From the Slade she falsified her age and joined the Scottish Women's Hospitals[26] London Unit as a chauffeur. She went with them to Serbia where she drove an ambulance, for which she was decorated with a Serbian campaign medal. Adventure was now in her blood. In 1918 she marched through London in the victory parade, but the record of these events is scant and merits further research. What we do know is that she had a rebellious nature with a strong desire for social equality which was the mood of many young people at the start of the 20th century. The Slade had a reputation for free thinking that fostered a belief that the old social order was a thing of the past.

Mabel started to paint at the end of 1918, very soon creating a following for her watercolours. Her social life continued amongst a group of politically radical friends, most of whom were modestly well off. By 1924 she was spending time with new friends who were enthusiasts on the new automobile racing circuit at Brooklands where women were adding race driving to the growing list of female conventions to be broken such as riding astride when hunting or out hacking on Rotten Row. They were going to parties without chaperones and proving they could do anything the men could.

---

26    The Scottish Women's Hospitals were founded by suffragist Dr Elsie Maud Inglis.

Mabel saw the mile long banked circuit as a personal challenge as she stood cheering and watching racing cars driven by glamorous young men reaching high speeds on the steep curves. She determined to take up the sport and bought a Bamford-type Aston Martin. She was not though a mechanic and needed one to keep it running efficiently and to fit one, or other, of the two bodies that came with it. One had a single seat for racing and the other two seats for touring. Mabel had been at school with Florence Elsie Waters who had an older brother Jack. Their parents were in the theatre business but Jack had broken away from the family tradition on the stage to train as a car mechanic. During WW1 he was a driver in the Royal Flying Corp in France. Mabel retained him to maintain the Aston and allowed him to drive at some of the more competitive race meetings. However, Jack couldn't leave the stage behind, eventually changing his surname to Warner, becoming an actor and hitting the big time when he was successful in getting the role of P. C. George Dixon in BBC's long running series Dixon of Dock Green. He also appeared in films such as The Blue Lamp in the hey-day of black and white movies filmed in Pinewood and Shepperton Studios. His sisters, Elsie and Doris grabbed fame as a popular music hall act 'Gert and Daisy' during WW2, when they kept the nation in happy mood by their humorous banter on the BBC's Home Service.

The one and a half litre side valve engine of the Aston, known as 'Bulgie' due to the shape of its racing body, was too slow as more efficient bodies and engine designs were introduced. The only time Margery went to see Mabel race was at Brooklands in June 1924. Her race was cancelled owing to the death of her friend, Capt. Troop, so Margery never saw her cousin compete. Troop was a determined dare devil and carefree driver with a fine reputation, but on this occasion he went too high on the banking, lost control, and went over the top killing himself. Mabel stopped racing in 1928 after four seasons, but kept the car. She turned her attention to the ballet, using the stage name of Henrietta Listacova. Why she chose to put "cova" on the end of her name is a mystery, but probably it refers back to her life in the Balkans.

At dancing Mabel excelled, but what type of ballet troupe she was in is not known. However, based on her previous lifestyle, it can be assumed that it was more downmarket than up. In the mid 1920's, Mabel visited

Wensleydale and met her Burrill and Wright cousins. In January 1935, she[27] became engaged to Will Burrill-Robinson. The Aston went with her when she got married, and although it was still licenced in 1936, it proved unsuitable for an artist who was travelling the narrow, often unmade-up roads of the Dales. When war started it was stored in the Elm House garage. During the war a soldier from Catterick Camp whose army lorry had broken down at the end of the Elm House drive, found Mabel and he asked her whether she could help him store some cans of petrol for him. Mabel was not bothered about the appropriate behaviour of a magistrate's wife, and the two of them hid the jerry cans in the garage where the soldier noticed the Aston Martin, covered in dust, but nevertheless obviously a rare example. He made her an offer for the car. Mabel had no use for bargaining; she had a rich husband and deep down she probably knew she would never race the car again. Some weeks later the soldier collected his 'bargain' which to his surprise took no starting. He parted with his £35 very happily. What happened to the jerry cans of petrol we know not. The car is now fully recorded on the World Aston Martin Owners' Register.

Will was a fairly staid individual with traditional local interests and responsibilities. He had been educated at Charterhouse and Clare College, Cambridge. He was a man of means; a magistrate, an alderman and chairman of a variety of business and community committees and boards, including being Chairman of the North Yorkshire County Council. His life revolved around his official, social and sporting affairs. It would have been surprising if Mabel had not became rather bored, and was probably bemused by her new lifestyle. She could paint, dance, race cars, drive trucks, and had an unconventional attitude to life, but her married routine limited her to formal dinners, unexciting parties and luncheons, all attended with Will.

This all changed for the better for her when she met artist Fred Lawson, an exhibitor at the Royal Academy, with a studio in Castle Bolton village. Bolton Castle attracted her. Gaunt and stark with ramparts towering up from the northern edge of Wensleydale where Mary Queen of

---

27    She was living at Bathurst Mews, Hyde Park.

Scots had spent a brief sojourn between her capture and being moved to Fotheringhay to lose her head. Around Lawson[28] there were other artists and friends who liked impromptu parties with drinks and the occasional charge of opium. Mabel painted amongst her new found circle, specialising in winter landscapes, and must many a time have smiled, wondering what on earth her mother back in Australia would think if she could see the daughter she had long ago deserted.

When her half-brother married, Margery resigned from her responsibilities and interests in Redmire and Elm House to give Mabel a fair start as the new mistress of the house. It was something she had not wanted, nor expected. To recover, she decided to travel to Tasmania to visit her Burrill cousins before returning to Redmire where she rented Northgate House. During Margery's absence, Mabel, in an effort to make her mark, cleared out the untidy sheds and stables in the yard behind the house and threw out the horse blanket, brushes and bucket of Margery's race horse before it met its premature death. These were sacred symbols of an important part of Margery's past, and she held this act of vandalism by Mabel against her for the rest of her life. On her return from Tasmania, Margery was relieved to find her much cherished flying gloves had survived Mabel's clear out and much later in her life she presented them to Jane's youngest brother.

During the Second World War, Mabel ran keep fit classes for Redmire women in the Elm House dining room and had evacuees to stay who attended the village school. On one occasion, when Mabel had been staying at Elm House when Margery's mother was still alive, Margery had been asked to 'do the flowers'. There were none in the garden or the greenhouse, so Margery, ever resourceful, picked some yellow cabbage flowers and set them in various vases in appropriate places around the house. Mabel was much impressed and asked the variety of the attractive decorations for future use to be told they were yellow delphiniums. She believed Margery and sent some of the flowers to a seeds house for them to identify the variety which she thought were possibly a new mutation hoping to get the breeding rights. The seeds man pointed out that her

---

28    Lawson and his artist wife Muriel Metcalfe rarely drank and never took drugs.

seeds were in fact from the cabbage variety Fletchers Best. Margery never revealed what Mabel said to her on receiving this news which put paid to the large sums Mabel had imagined she might get for this new variety.

Henrietta died two years before Will.[29] In her later years she settled down to a more conventional life. She was highly regarded by many local people who fondly remembered the middle aged bride who arrived at Elm House to join Will, widely thought of as a man of the old guard.

---

29    She is buried in a Harrogate crematorium.

# Chapter 5

## Margery's poetry

There was another life for Miss Margery Burrill about which little is known, even by relatives and close friends. For on her death, a small red leatherette note book came to light which describes her life between the wars. It is simply inscribed in ink: Margery Freeman (her married name) of Redmire. It contains forty one poems written over a decade. There is a second inscription in grey ink on the first page: "the uncut gems in a beggar's hands" and beneath, written in pencil, "by Marion. J. Yorke". This small red book is, I believe, an autobiography covering an important period of the life of a young woman who was unsure about her future. She had lived and learnt in London and lost the man she loved, as well as her mother and family home. Were the uncut gems in the beggar's hands in some way her? Her gipsy genes were strong. She possessed the natural resilience and basic instincts of an ancient nomadic race. Of the forty one poems "Dusk Dreams" probably gives the best lead to her life in the inter war years:

> Through evening dusk comes stealing
> As the sun sets on the sea,
> A sort of peaceful feeling
> That you are still with me.
>
> I feel the touch of your gentle hand
> And hear your laughing call
> And round me the calm of your presence abiding over all.
> This twilight dream enfolds me,
> (I forget you're a long time dead!)
> I should see you stand beside me
> If I did but turn my head.

Oh I know it can't be true, my dear
Just the fault of the dusk and sea
Yet the hour of dusk holds magic
When the senses wander free.

Her heroic cousin, Frank Burrill, was never to be her man as the family had stopped the flowering of this romance. For a decade, Margery slipped away travelling the world. She loved the sea, and when she was at home she spent her time in the woods, on the moors and by rivers. The little red book holds secrets unexplained. Margery was often unhappy during this period and frequently reflected on the "what might have been". There was always an unrealised love lurking in her thoughts as in "A Fragment", but was it Frank?

I had not seen you for long years, and yet,
You came again, and now I can't forget.
Through night and day I'm haunted by a smile
Once madly scorned, that now makes life worthwhile.
Strangers almost since our childhood days
Our paths have wandered in far distant ways,
To cross at last, to please Fate's whimful plan,
And so we meet---- a woman and a man.......

To imagine oneself to be walking beside Margery and her poetic thoughts is perhaps the most certain way to understand her life in the period between her musical life in London and the start of WW2. "Evening" is the first step you take which explains the romance for her homeland.

Coppery sky above me,
Coppery sky beyond,
A coppery gleam on the mountain stream
And the golden bracken frond.

Silent the wheeling curlew,
The cotton grasses nod,
And I'm sitting still on the top of the hill—
Alone with my thoughts and God.

Then "Pavement of Life" sets the pattern of her attitude to people and life, again undated, but written in about 1925 when she was 22 and living back in the Dales. London and its memories remained fresh in her mind.

This life is like a busy street
With all the folks you chance to meet;
Some push, some loiter,--all go by,
Some cast a laugh, and some a sigh.

Sometimes a friend's path will divide
And take them sorrowing from your side,
But still you hope in later days,
To find a junction of the ways.
Some folks go staggering 'neath their load
While others pass across the Road
On to the unknown Other Side,
Across the Road of Death so wide.

Some seem to pass right down the street
And never find a friend to greet,
While others having found a friend—
Follow their victim to the end;
But best of all street friends are they
Who never push or block the way,
But join you till your pathways fork
And never tire you with their talk,
Or make you know the friends they know,
Whom you don't, or bore you so.

Each makes his friends, so let it rest—
You always choose your own friends best.
Just take your way as best you can,
Be courteous to your fellow man;
Don't push and strive to lead the way,
But just be happy, just be gay;
Don't hurry on, nor yet be slow,
And spread a smile where e're you go
That some tired heart may take fresh grace
For having seen a smiling face

In June 1927, a total eclipse of the sun occurred in Yorkshire. The newspapers created a sense of great anticipation and occasion. Margery thought about this great natural moment during her daily walks. She saw another side to the possible consequences of this much heralded natural phenomenon expressing her growing frustration at the ever increasing numbers of tourists who were disturbing the peace of her Dales countryside.

### The Ballad of Night (or Day) in June 1927

They say the great eclipse is due
The twenty-ninth of June,
And everyone's agog to see
The sun behind the moon.

So buy some patent spectacles
To shade your eyes from glare,
In the hope of seeing sun spots;
Or if "Baileys Beads"[30] are there

To see this rare phenomenon
You rise at half past three,
The mornings cold and dewy
And you miss your cup of tea.

You sleepily put on your clothes
And hope the sun will shine,
The morning looks depressing—
Someone says "it's fairly fine!"

And those that can't get up in time
Will dance all night instead
Then hurry home to see the sights—
And spend two days in bed.

---

30  During an eclipse the thin edges of the sun break into spots as it disappears and then reappears. These are called Bailey's Beads.

There'll be thronging crowds of people
On each hill top, crag and scar,
Who'll arrive by train and motor bus,
By cycle, foot and car.

There'll be sheaves of broken bottles
Scattered o'er field and lane,
While the tourists' paper trade mark
On the district will remain.

There'll be scientists from Greenwich
With professors old and wise,
Who when that day's work is over—
Will have telescopic eyes.

And house wives all are busy
Boiling stones of beef and ham,
And baking tins of tartlets
To be filled with curd and jam.
While their husbands working also
With some cardboard, paint and tin,
Display a sign for "Parking Cars",
And "Breakfast served within."

By the time Margery died, the peaceful life in the Dales she had known so well had changed. The bus services were little used, the trains from Northallerton to Hawes Junction had stopped, and there were cars and motor bikes filling the lanes and roads with tourists in every village and town. On the farms, 'Bed and Breakfast' was subsidising incomes and a group of enthusiasts had reopened a section of the old Wensleydale railway from Leeming Bar to Redmire. In her youth Margery left Redmire Station occasionally and went to London. Who she met and where she went will never be known although she talked of shows she'd seen, particularly light opera, which usually meant The Doyle Carte Company's Gilbert and Sullivan performances at the Savoy Theatre. Later she went to the Savoy for an entirely different reason which is not mentioned in her poetry. What is clear though is that she loved the sea, harbours and travel, going to Tasmania three times during the inter war years to see her cousins. She describes this part of her life vividly.

## From the Bows

Wild seas, evil seas
Rolling vast and high
Black troughs and far flung spray
Under a leaden sky.

Eerie seas. Mysterious
Black beneath the night.
The sob of churning water
As a wave slides out of sight.
Smooth seas, blue seas
Opal in the dawn.
Ripples rosy-tipped that fade
As the day is born.

Rough seas, smooth seas,
All the seas that be,
Make an ever changing path
That lulls the heart in me.

She'd left England and was heading 'down under' through the Suez Canal.
The first stop was Marseilles where she went to the church of Notre Dame.

Dim the light on aisle and chain
Models of ships hang shadowed there
Over the faithful bowed in prayer-
To Mary, Notre Dame de la Garde.

The flickering candle flakes and drips
Heart felt prayers on muted lips
For those who go down to the sea in ships
Mary. Notre Dame de la Garde.

You with your child held high on your arm
Know the terror of love's alarm,
Grant that the seas be fair and calm
Mary. Notre Dame de la Garde.

Mary, Mary be not stern
(Behold how low the candles burn!)
Hear our prayers, in mercy turn-
Mary. Notre Dame de la Garde.

The next port of call was Aden as the ship left the Red Sea and entered the Gulf of Aden heading for the Indian Ocean, where she would cross the Equator. Australia was the next stop.

### Aden

At Aden, at Aden
Beneath a blazing sun
I've watched the brilliant waters
Like molten metals run
And by the bay, the scattered town
Crouches below the mountains brown
The sun baked hills no green can crown
At Aden in the sun.

White buildings with green jalousies
Along the burning street
Fierce smells, a twist of burning dust,
The patter of bare feet;
And on the road with idle ease
Pass Arabs, Bedouins, Sudanese
Swahilis, Turks--- a gaudy frieze
Of colour down the street.

A camel lies and chews its cud
Cattle and asses straw,
The dusty roadway is his bed
His driver squats before
Motionless, save when the flies
Cluster the corners of his eyes.
Gay vendors call their merchandise
At Aden in the sun.

There is a page torn out just before Aden. I wonder why? This was in 1934. As she left Freemantle for her return journey she wrote "Envoy".

Slowly her bows are turning and the long wharf slides astern,
And I, on the deck am wondering if ever I shall return?
I will never come here feeling as I did when I came before
A stranger unknown and unknowing, a waif on a foreign shore.
If ever the fates are kindly and my wandering path shall end
I'll come again to Australia, as a friend shall come to a friend.

The last word 'friend' is smudged, with a tear perhaps? She did return, twice. She loved the fishing, the wildlife, gum trees and the loneliness, but she found the regular bush fires hard to understand.

### Grey Gums

Grey gums standing bare and high
Sweeping fires have long gone by
Gaunt arms plead with a summer sky
Wondering why?
Soul and beauty have perished in pain
Life that has gone cannot spring again
Only the stark grey ghosts remain
Waiting in vain.

She went again.

### Repair

I passed through where the fierce bush fires had blazed
And through the miles giant trees were razed
To blackened hulks upon a bare black ground,
And desolation cast grim shadows round.
Through all that once was smiling bush land scene,
Gone were the sassafras, tree fern and myrtles green,
No more would wattles plume in spring,
Nor scented shrubs their wealth of perfume fling
No tall gums whisper and no wild birds call
The hush as of deep death is over all.

It chanced that after bare five weeks had passed,
I rode along the track where I had last
Seen devastation, and in mute surprise
As fabled Phoenix from the ashes rise
I saw first shoots of fern and bracken furled
Bravely and greenly from a blackened world.
So nature ever sleepless had begun
To heal again the harm that man had done.

I think it must have been her final visit that inspired the piece on "Joe".
Had she ridden with him on the trail? We can only guess.

They found him dead on the stock route
As the Heelagong sheep passed through.
So they told at the nearest station
He'd been dead for a day or two.

He was only a cattle drover
A -wandering come-by-chance,
Riding back to cash his trip
With a saddle branded Vance.
He was known as Joe to the stations
No home, no friends, no kin.
He'd trail the cattle a thousand miles
No creed or hope-save gin.

The station hands said "blast him"
(He had no kith or kin)
So they made him a box of peppermint wood
And lifted him carefully in.

In the graveyard above Toodygay
The grave digger gave the hole
And a few came from the homestead
In respect for a stranger's soul.

And from some cottage garden
(In England a hot house show)
A cluster of red magnolias
Was laid in the grave of Joe.

Back home in Wensleydale, having docked in Southampton, and having travelled through London in the midst of the Great Depression, and through similarly depressed Midland and Northern towns and cities, she walked in the garden.

### Sun Wearied

Under the elm, past the nut bush hedge,
On the sun dappled grass to the brown streams edge
Where water whispers from ledge to ledge.
That's home.
The lingering dusk and the evening breeze,
Two owls that call from neighbouring trees,
As you search the world over, you can only find these
At home.

The sun baked sands are not for me,
The palm fringed coast, or a limpid sea
There's only one place I want to be
That's home.

And so to bed.

When I lie at night awake
Such wondrous journeys I can take
To places that I used to know
Where eucalyptus and wattles grow,
And maidens' hair grows wild on banks.
Where palm trees stand in serried ranks
And willows weep around a lake.

And down the creek, beyond the ford
Where silence is the overlord
A kookaburra laughs to see
A yellow wattle shower on me
When breaking through the noon day hush
A little breeze comes through the bush
And scatters yellow foam abroad.
I stand again upon a cliff
Remembering how I wondered if
The sea below would ever reach
That yellow pebble on the beach?
The sea gulls dip with wailing shrieks
So close they come that on their beaks
I see the scarlet stain on each.

Margery was reflecting in this last piece about what might have been.
Her return home and once more living within the rigid conventions of a
conservative society and an impending war combined to put a stop to the
spirit that had 'broken away'.

# Chapter 6

## Married life and widowhood

Margery settled uneasily back into the life of the Dales, occupied with her interests in the Wensleydale Tournament of Song, the Aysgarth Choral Society, exhibiting flowers and produce at local shows and, of course, fishing, shooting and hunting. She was though becoming more of a loner preferring the river bank to the hunting field or grouse moor. Talk of war was to be heard again in the late '30's, which most people chose to put to the back of their minds. The last conflict was to have been "the war to end all wars."[31] Surely the four years of absolute horror the people of Europe had experienced could never be repeated.

As soon as war became a reality Margery joined the auxiliary services. Since the age of 18 she had lived in many different guises. There was the student of music who enjoyed the night life of London, the dutiful family girl who returned home to nurse her dying mother, the sporting 'tom boy' who was equally happy as a guest on a shooting day or to be with the beaters and flankers on the moor. Then there was the young lady seen boarding a train at Redmire Station heading to London where she vanished into a life that can only be understood through some of the references in her letters, poetry or from conversations remembered. Her travels have been recounted through her verse, all of which she put aside in 1939 when Hitler's policy to rule and change northern Europe became a reality. At home, government was trying to revive an agriculture that had fallen into deep recession with cheap imported food flooding in to British ports from around world. The ships carrying these supplies would now be haunted by enemy shipping both on the surface and below the waves. The Nation's larder suddenly became insecure, desperate action

---

31   H. G. Wells in 1914.

was called for. 'Dig for victory' became the clarion call. Margery stepped forward.

Home produced jams, soup, vegetables and fruit were taken from her kitchen and the garden to old folk in the village. Her collection of horticultural catalogues was used to decorate fire screens which were then sold to friends and neighbours with the money going to the war effort. In 1939, aged 36, she was invited to join the Hang West Division of the North Riding of Yorkshire as a magistrate at Leyburn Court House. She became one of the first lady magistrates in the County. This gave her a recognised place in local society and a new confidence, status and, not least, a chance to be seen to be useful in times of trouble. She sat on the Bench until 1973 when she reached the compulsory retirement age of 70 when she received a formal letter of thanks from the Lord Chancellor, Lord Hailsham, but either she forgot receipt of it, or ignored it, for she complained right up to her 100th birthday that her 34 years of service had never been properly recognised. Few people sitting with her, or coming before her in court, would have known of her gipsy genes.

Margery was married on the 10th of June 1941. She was 37. She must have regretted not being able to get married in Redmire, but London no doubt suited her husband. Reginald Gwyn Freeman, aged 42, was a mariner who she had first met through the family with whom she had been a 'paying guest' over twenty years before, during her musical training. The marriage certificate describes Reg as a bachelor, Chief Officer in the Merchant Navy, residing at Savoy House, Savoy Row W.C.2, and recorded that his late father had been a man of independent means. Margery was a spinster with neither profession nor occupation, giving her address as Northgate House,[32] Redmire, Wensleydale. Her father, the late Charles Burrill, was also recorded as a man of independent means. The wedding took place in the Savoy Chapel, conducted by an honorary Canon of St Paul's Cathedral. She was unusually stylish on her wedding day, but sadly she had had no one with her to share the fun of buying her wedding outfit.

---

32    Margery was renting Northgate at this point.

The ceremony was attended by very few people including for Margery a mystery guest: Lady Wexford was probably an Irish relative of Reg's but Margery wasn't sure who she was. The Yorkshire Post's correspondent reported that she was given away by her half-brother, Alderman William Robinson Burrill-Robinson of Elm House Redmire, wearing an ice blue crêpe frock, a brown hat, a silver fox fur and carrying ice blue flowers. The small wedding party adjourned to the Piccadilly Hotel for luncheon followed by a short honeymoon at a venue unknown. The groom then resumed his service on a freighter, loaded with cargoes of food and war materials, sailing to the port of Arkhangelsk (Archangel) in Russia, which took the ship north of the Arctic Circle, round the tip of Norway and into Beloye More, a sea loch off the Barents Sea, a dangerous trip with sub-zero temperatures for much of the year. Frost bite was almost unavoidable and crew members frequently lost fingers, toes and sometimes even ears.

A teenager from Sussex, Cadet Freeman started his marine training at the Merchant Navy College in Hull. In 1915 he became a midshipman in the Royal Navy on a cruiser of the fleet, HMS Hyacinth; he was then promoted to sub-lieutenant on torpedo boats stalking German U boats in the English Channel. He had a reputation as a brave and skilful sailor never fearing danger. In peacetime he returned to merchant ships joining the P&O[33] line as fourth officer on a captured German liner, renamed Mantua, returning U.S. troops home. This was the start of a notable career at sea. He was promoted to second officer on Mantua, and in 1937 he was promoted to second in command on his first luxury passenger liner, the 24,000 ton Strathmore travelling the Australia, China and Japan route. When the second war broke out his ship was requisitioned as a troop carrier, transporting Australian troops to North Africa, sailing the dangerous route through the Mediterranean where enemy ships and submarines constantly lurked. The Strathmore established a reputation amongst the military as a 'lucky ship' avoiding many of the hazards of the oceans for the entire war. Or was Captain Freeman simply an exceptional captain? Reg didn't remain with the ship for the duration of the war as he was promoted to command the freighter on the Russian trip through icy and treacherous waters just prior to his wedding.

---

33    Pacific & Orient.

Margery presented Reg with a silver St. Christopher which he always kept hanging on the bridge head rail of his ship. When he died Margery hung it on the dashboard of her car. It wasn't real silver, but was one of the few possessions she cherished, having accompanied Freeman over hundreds of thousands of nautical miles. Whether it had kept him safe through four years of constant danger only St. Christopher knows. Today St. Christopher hangs behind the sun visor of Jane Ritchie's car.

After the war Reg took command of another captured German liner, renamed Empire Raja, which he regarded as an excessive statement about a British Empire that was obviously on the wane. In 1948 he travelled to the Vickers Armstrong Ship Yard at Walker on the Tyne to take command of a new cargo ship, the 9,000 ton Surat. The ship was commissioned to improve food supplies to Britain from around the world supplementing the home grown rations of a hungry population. For the last eight years of his career he commanded various P&O liners sailing the Far East and Pacific Service. His last ship was the Himalaya, a large modern liner, carrying 1,200 passengers with a crew of 630, a crewing ratio rarely met in these times of cruising for all.

He retired in 1959, having been married for eighteen years, during which time he travelled the world meeting thousands of passengers, taking shore leaves, occasionally at home, but frequently in Australia where nothing was known of his life ashore. Margery was never invited to join him when he opted to take his breaks in Australia. However, there was an occasion when, knowing he was to take a long leave in Oz, she thought she would give him a pleasant surprise. When he left his ship to start his leave, there was Margery on the quayside. He greeted her, they talked a while and then, without apology, he left and she holidayed alone before returning to Redmire. There was talk amongst P&O colleagues of his 'friend' in the office in Melbourne, perhaps simply rumour, but certainly a small sturdy leather suitcase, always locked, was with him wherever he went. When on home leave he never explained why he visited the village Post Office daily. The contents of the case remain a mystery that, if ever found, could explain a lot more about the life of Reg.

Between getting married and her half brother's death Margery bought a house half a mile out of Leyburn at Harmby. When Will died she returned to Elm House, with Reg in tow, to set about putting the garden back as her mother had had it before Mabel arrived on the scene altering everything. In 1959 Captain (Retired) and Mrs Freeman assumed a 'normal married life' for the first time. Margery was busy as a magistrate and on the committees of the W.I., the Tournament of Song and the Middleham Moor Gait Owners Association. She was a regular church goer, and a competitor at local agricultural and produce shows. Village life brought her into contact with old and needy people who she regularly visited and helped. She was a Governor of Wensleydale School and a member of the Wensleydale Society with a keen interest in archaeology, often invited to go on University of Leeds digs as a volunteer excavator. On top of all this she took responsibility for the remaining family properties with an occasional treat, fishing.

From 1948 she wrote articles and short stories, under various noms de plume, ranging from Marcus Freeman to Margery Burrill and Janet Freeman-Burrill. Her first published piece was on fishing in Tasmania, published in 1949 in a small country sports magazine which eventually became the official organ of the newly formed British Field Sports Society, promoting and protecting the interests of the hunting, shooting and fishing community. Her last piece was written in 1958, just prior to moving back to Elm House, when she wrote a short story 'Old Tosh' intending it to be read on the BBC's North Countryman programme on the Home Service. However it was turned down, probably because it was far too short at 790 words for the fifteen minute slot of the daily short story programme.

Her post-war writing never compared with her pre-war poetry and explained little more than is already known. However, it did illustrate her comprehensive understanding of hunting, fishing and shooting. She understood field sports both from a participant's point of view during the seasons as well as the intricacies of year round management of stream and moorland. She reminisced occasionally to friends about her travels and recounted her annoyance at bad manners in the sporting field, often by young men either poorly educated or simply plain rude. She was a prolific writer for nine years with only half her writing published, for which she received modest fees, but she stopped writing when Reg died.

Their married life was far from normal and she decided it was better not to know too much about his 'other side'. Those who remember Reg as part of Wensleydale society, do so with great affection, usually referring to him as "poor Reg".

Margery's life revolved around her many interests, but out of a strange loyalty to her husband, she developed a genuine interest in shipping. Although affection towards him did not come easily, she was proud of his long service career, especially of his naval record through two world wars, when he faced danger in harsh climates for long periods without complaint. It was probably a disappointment that his undoubted bravery and skill at sea was not acknowledged with a decoration. His retirement coincided with the busiest point in Margery's life which was the turning of the next page. She was in her late fifties, the restoration of the gardens at Elm House were to dominate her life, leaving little time for fishing or shooting. She did though derive huge pleasure from teaching a young fisherman, Ian, the ways of the water, the habits of the quarry and the art of casting a fly. Her Magistrates Court work, the Tournament of Song, contributing to the management of Middleham Moor and her various societies and social work meant there was little time for Reg. He maintained the lawns, equipped with a lawn mower which "spewed out grass like spinach". When he wanted peace and quiet, Reg would resort to climbing a long ladder to decorate the house, or to inspect the roof while feigning total deafness. He had been invited by his brother in law, Will, to become a trustee of the long established and complex Robinson Family Trust which must have come as a welcome opportunity to have a local involvement away from Margery's influence and control.

Entertaining at Elm House was a rare event. Jane Ritchie remembers rather formal teas with the Freemans and the occasional nectarine from the peach house, but there was little other socialising. She always liked Reg, as a child preferring his company to that of her Cousin Margery. Later at Northgate House, after the sale of Elm House, the Ritchie family occasionally went to lunch after church on Sunday. The fare was the same every time: over roasted chicken and potatoes, over cooked yellowed sprouts followed by a bought sponge case filled with tinned pears and lime jelly. Margery was not a good cook. Jane's Aunt remembered once going to a wartime tea party hosted by Margery, when all the food was either naturally green, or had been dyed green. Jane sometimes wonders if that was why, in later life, Margery didn't like the colour green.

Margery had a lifetime interest in racing which may well have started when, as a small girl having to entertain a visiting child she would sit upon the Elm House pig, whose role it was to consume kitchen and garden waste and provide meat in return, and make it gallop down the drive and back demonstrating her accomplished riding ability. However the pig would only perform the ritual once. Having shown off, Margery would then invite the other child to take up the challenge, but the pig stood still. Adults, not least the servants, unaware of this party trick were always puzzled by the resulting grubby knickers. The trick in her performance was never revealed until much later in life. At one point she bought a race horse on the advice of one of her many friends in Middleham, but it died prematurely. She kept its saddle and grooming kit in its memory until it was disposed of by her sister in law when she became the chatelaine of Elm House. However Margery's deep interest in racing continued unabated remaining with her into old age, satisfied by the small silver screen.

When Will died in 1962, Margery took over his position as Chairman of the Middleham Moor Gait Owners Association. She also inherited his gaits on this common land, the freehold of which is held by Middleham Town Council in perpetuity. The ancient gaits are held by surrounding land owners with each representing the number of sheep, or cattle, the holder may graze over the gait season of the six summer months. Those unused by their owners were sold by auction, but today the racehorse trainers exercising race horses on the moor buy the surplus gaits. Unlike her brother, she refused to combine the role of Secretary with that of Chairman so a solicitor was appointed to the role. Jane Ritchie is currently the Hon. Secretary and inherited 1½ gaits from her cousin.

Middleham has been renowned for breeding and training of thoroughbred horses back to monastic times. The original Arabian stallions, introduced by Henry VIII to improve the quality of the traditional heavy English war and draft horses, were used extensively in the area. During WW2 racing slipped into decline, farming and food took greater importance and parts of the hallowed moorland turf were ploughed to grow cereals. As the Chairman, Margery's role was to preserve peace and harmony between trainers, graziers, landowners and the citizens of the town who increasingly sought to control the recreational facilities offered by their common land. However, her priority was to support the ancient rights of gaits and consequently the graziers and she refused to be bullied by incomers who aspired to control land owned by the town. Margery knew the trainers, amongst whom were Dick Peacock, Sam Hall, Captains Neville Crump and Wilfred Lyde, all great characters in a racing business which was using new techniques and becoming increasingly more professional and international. During morning exercise on the gallops, there was constant talk of races entered, owners' quirks, 'good things' and after races had been run, occasionally the elation of a winner, or sad stories of the more frequent losers. Margery allowed herself seventeen shillings and sixpence a week to bet on the horses before WW1, an amount that changed little, but she rarely went racing after WW2 and once the telly arrived she was able to watch without facing travel and crowds.

Her empathy with all things natural was her birthright. Her love and aptitude for field sports, her love of music, especially the Tournament of Song and the Aysgarth Choral Society, and the popular music of the mid war years were with her from an early age. Frugality and her tough attitude towards people, particularly those who ran against the tide of acceptable behaviour, made her a formidable character. She is known to have occasionally conducted meetings at home with strangers with a loaded shotgun on the table, and a pitchfork always lay beneath her bed. When she decided to sell Elm House her age was showing, she was a lone widow who was becoming increasingly reclusive and clinging to the ways of the 'old days'. She moved back into Northgate House[34] in Redmire then when shingles deprived her of much of her sight she had to go to a care home in Leyburn. To anyone going round the house after she'd gone it was an unforgettable experience. The place was run down with curtains in tatters, carpets threadbare, furniture inadequate with the junk of ages spread around.

---

34   This time she bought the house.

Margery took trouble throughout her life to keep in touch with selected relatives amongst them some of the Cockcroft family. She was particularly pleased to meet a relative of Reg's, Amanda Yeoman, who had come with her husband from Cornwall to live in Laverton near Ripon. A valued friend in her widowhood was Jane's mother Margaret Ritchie, her second cousin once removed who lived in West Burton across the River Ure from Redmire. They met regularly and corresponded, putting together their combined family archives which form the basis of this book. In 1970 Margery wrote to Margaret about a relative who inherited the Coverhead Estate, with a number of tenanted upland farms and a grouse moor at the head of Coverdale, in which she said: "He has no pride of possession, nor any feeling for his ancestral inheritance. He is the life and soul at parties, but all he is really interested in is hard cash in his hand. I am appalled."

Margery lived at the Council run Brentwood Lodge Care Home in Leyburn for fourteen years in her own small bedroom from where she kept in touch with letters to friends and family, enjoying minibus outings in summer, but, 'not the obligatory ice cream from Brymor[35] thank you very much'. She watched and rarely missed racing on the TV, but her failing sight meant that sound was really more important than the scene. A stray cat she called Gold befriended her and kept her company on the garden seat on sunny days, but gradually her eyesight failed and the isolation of extreme age took over. She lost her niece Betty Wright and her great friend from Buckden, Nancy Cutliffe-Hyne, both very sad occasions as inevitably she had the feeling she was the last of her generation. She became increasingly frugal insisting on wearing clothes until they were sometimes more hole than garment with the cheapest gym shoes from 'Woolies' as Woolworths was affectionately known to her. Any new clothes, given as presents, were left unworn to save them from 'the bash', as she called the Brentwood laundry. Margaret Ritchie visited her on Wednesdays until she died, and her daughter Jane every Saturday morning.

Her gift for poetry is intriguing. Most was written during the time she roamed abroad returning from time to time, frequently feeling low and not fitting comfortably into her home community. She lost her first and,

---

35   The chill of ice cream set her teeth on edge.

possibly, her only real love and constantly sought a purpose which she eventually found when she was appointed as a magistrate. During those travelling years and settling into Wensleydale, she wrote one last piece at the back of the small red book, in pencil, which was read at her memorial service.

The service for the celebration and thanksgiving for the life of Margery Freeman was held at St Mary's Church, Redmire on October 19th 2004. Jane did not have to keep her promise that she would not allow relatives to be rude about her, and that the service would be conducted according to her wishes: Margery had in fact outlived all the relatives she had worried about.

20th November 1903-10th October 2004.

The hymns to be sung were: Praise, my soul, the King of Heaven and The day Thou gavest Lord is ended.

And then the Nunc Dimittis: "Lord, now lettest thou Thy servant depart in peace". Margery left instructions that this was a triumphant song and must not therefore be sung slowly. Sue Whitehouse, the vicar, made certain the congregation followed her request.

And finally from the back of the little red book: Prie-Dieu[36] Margery's own prayer that Jane asked the vicar to read.

> Oh God, if thou wouldst grant me one gift yet,
> Give me, I pray, the power to forget
> The mem'ries that bring sorrow and regret.
>
> Of all the scenes indelibly impressed
> Upon my mind, let me remember best
> The sunny days when I was happiest.

---

36    Prie-Dieu is a stool, normally knelt on with a low seat and a high back.

Grant in thy mercy quiet content to me,
That I, in all, may understanding be,
Learning to value what I hear and see.
Keep me I pray, from bitterness and strife
From foul suspicions of evils rife;
Teach me to value little things in life.
So give me strength to help my fellow men
That, when I die, Saint Peter with his pen,
May write against my name "She Tried."

Amen.

When Jane reflected on the funeral that evening she was happy that everyone had celebrated Margery's life in the way she had wished and that there had been no rancour from any of those present. Jane had asked a friend of Margery's to read the story of the Creation after which he gave a eulogy befitting the occasion with his reminiscences of being taught to fish on the lawn of Elm House. Margery was laid to rest between Reg and her mother. The whole production would have been approved of by the day's central figure.

Often when people die more comes to be known about their lives from friends, acquaintances and those who kept secrets only to be told after death. Reginald Gwynn Freeman died aged 71 on the 13th June 1970. He lived with Margery for 11 years after his retirement and, from all accounts, their lives were not particularly happy. They rarely went out or entertained. Occasionally they holidayed in Scotland with all expenses paid by Margery. Children coming to their house usually preferred him to her. In fact, she confessed to Jane's mother, she had never expected Reg to return to England when he retired and when he died she made no fuss, burying him quietly in Redmire church yard. Jane's father wasn't told of his death until several months later and was very upset not to have been able to attend his funeral.

The locked case that always accompanied Reg held neither mystery nor interest for her and she got rid of it by taking it, locked and unopened, to her solicitor to deal with as he saw fit. When Reg retired from P&O there had been a ceremony and presentation in the head office which she did not attend. The parting gifts from his fellow officers were a lamp and a bale of towels. Margery believed the lamp, which she would have liked, was sent to an unnamed person[37] in Australia! She commented wryly that she had plenty of towels. In February 1958, Captain Freeman had become the first P&O captain to sail across the Pacific from Sydney, via Hawaii, to New York. In the island capital, Honolulu, he was presented with an engraved wooden model of the island carved in relief, which one would have thought he would have cherished, but what did he do with that? Margery never saw it, but had heard of it, so perhaps there is a house, or a family, in Australia with a lamp engraved in Reg's name alongside which is Hawaii in wood.

Margery died as the 21st century started. Technology was advancing on a monthly basis. Only twenty years before, the mobile phone had developed from a cumbersome piece of communication equipment into a hand held miracle package capable of connecting to anywhere on earth and containing as much of the collective knowledge of the world as a library full of books. Journeys to Tasmania and Australia that had taken Margery weeks now took only hours and the global population had more than trebled in her life time. When Thomas Other married Jane Lister in 1803, farming, mining and manufacturing were developing using new skills and limited scientific knowledge. In the early 19th century, machinery was being powered by water, coal, wind and steam replacing animal and man power. The new looms, presses, mills, air pumps, winding gear and furnaces caused social chaos as the working class moved from rural to industrial occupations seeking a new way of life. The nation was governed by the 'landed class' with scarcely anyone in either of the Houses of Parliament coming from outside an exclusive circle apart from well-bred professionals such as lawyers, doctors and gallant soldiers with a few working class individuals who, through good luck or connections, had managed to find an education and opportunity. The decisions and actions of the Government were feared around the world, but it was one that knew little of the lives, minds and circumstances of British working men, farmers, tradesmen, shop keepers let alone their women. Lord Dudley, at a Farmers' Club dinner in London in the early part of the 19th

---

37    Jane thinks she was called Gladys.

century referring to the men of Westminster, said "They know less of your art than this orange in my hand." He squeezed it to make his point.

The countryside was largely farmed by tenants with rents to pay, but without the right to vote despite the fact that the profitability of the food they produced had been dictated by legislation from Westminster. The Malt Tax, Corn Laws, Poor Laws, Settlement Acts and Enclosures each placed either restrictions on, or costs to, production. One sixth of England was owned by less than one hundred people and as working families started to move away from the large estates the land agents could see that the dwindling manpower, which provided comfort and wealth to their employers, would cause problems as it soon did. In the early years of the 19th century there were sporadic labourers' revolts around the country that were savagely put down by the militia and police. Men were killed and others found guilty of crimes of affray, looting and theft to be transported to the New World which, for some, would have been far preferable to remaining in the enforced poverty of their village community. In their departure they were separated from their family and rarely able to return, or to send home their modest savings.

The Settlement Acts of Tudor and Stuart times had tied the working class to the land of their birth and if there was neither work, nor wage, they were supported locally through Poor Law Commissioners who collected dues from across the class framework. However, the farmers who originally employed them had to pay the majority of the tax. Mechanisation on the land continued, more men were dismissed with their dwellings pulled down and destroyed. William Cobbett was on his Rural Rides in the 1820's and wrote of his anger when he saw the scale of poverty amongst the rural population, the dereliction, the vacant parsonages beside large churches, reflecting the populations of former times, but by now used only by the few old workers who remained awaiting their turn for the churchyard. The curates attending to these skeleton congregations were impoverished, being denied the tithes of their living which were collected by their controlling superior clerics and they were thus forced to collect meagre sustenance from sympathetic farmers and landowners of which there were not that many. They in their turn could no longer distribute money to the poor and needy of the parish as their predecessors had done in better times. The senior clerics, generally from wealthy families usually had private money. They ruled the humble curates and it was they who were therefore held responsible "for the wasting parishioners and crumbling churches." They took 'livings' from the squire, tithes from the farmers and paid their curates a pittance on their infrequent tours of inspection when they stayed to wine and dine in fine houses with the fine people.

This was a dark chapter in rural history as families were forced from villages by sheer economic impossibility into towns, cities and industrial areas where poverty ruled and groups of undesirables thieved to survive. Alcohol was sold cheaply and indiscriminately to urban and rural communities alike. The non-conformist religions took action against the devil 'booze' and temperance societies encouraging pledges against drink became commonplace. Housing was scarce in the new centres of population and new arrivals could usually only find rough shelter for their dependants, and they frequently walked miles to their place of work. Those who were lucky might earn a pound a day before repeating the journey in the evening. The Game Laws were so severe that poachers could be transported out of the country simply for netting rabbits or coursing hares. The tenant farmer had no rights to control rabbits, hares or grazing deer amongst his crops and an army of agents, stewards and game keepers kept watch over them. The larder of the wild was firmly shut to all but the landed classes, their personal friends and favourite servants.

Magistrates, mostly landowners, parsons and other professionals ensured the law of the land was strictly applied and suggestions that education should be introduced to the working classes to accompany the growing complexities of industry and trade were often summarily dismissed. This was the background to life in the 19th century when the families written of in this book came together. Margery was born into a family very much committed to the Victorian way of life with her adherence to good manners, frugal living, honesty and religious commitment remaining with her throughout her long life.

# Chapter 7

## A Bank is born

Jane is the eldest of four children. Their mother, born Margaret Radegund[38] King, and their father, Christopher Julian Ritchie, share the line of Thomas and Jane Other through their eldest son Christopher born in 1809. He was Christopher Julian Ritchie's maternal great grandfather. Their sixth child was Margaret born in 1815 who married William Robinson King Senior. Thus Christopher Other is Jane's great, great grandfather and Margaret Other her great, great grandmother. Jane's genetic line from Thomas and Jane Other on her paternal side includes the families of Stackhouse, Winn and Ritchie, and on her maternal side, King and Robinson.

In 1804 Thomas Other and John Hutton, a landowner from Marske in Swaledale, founded a small banking partnership called Hutton and Other & Co. along with Mr Wood of West Burton and opened their first customer counter in Leyburn. In those days banking was commonplace in large cities and industrial towns but virtually unheard of in more remote market towns. The venture was an immediate success which was further endorsed when they were appointed Deputy Receivers of Taxes for the North Riding of Yorkshire by which time there were additional branches in Bedale, Masham, Richmond and Hawes. In 1825 disaster nearly struck when their London guarantor agents, Sir Peter Pole and Company who held their bullion reserves and property securities, were forced into liquidation. However Hutton, Other and Wood were prudent managers who controlled the circulation of their notes at well below the value of

---

38    The name Radegund comes from the name of the Cambridge nunnery dedicated to St. Radegund which became Jesus College after the Dissolution of the Monasteries.

their reserves which at that time were primarily in gold. As they were a respected local bank and known to everyone in the Dales' communities there was never a run on cash based on rumours of impending collapse as happened frequently in metropolitan areas. Investment policy was based on loans to sound local businesses such as wool processing, mining, trading companies and merchants who moved the produce of the dales out and essential supplies in. Farmers rarely borrowed in those days as the majority were tenants without the security of land and theirs was a way of life. Many professionals, in particular speculating solicitors, were frequently asking for loans to back, or buy, their clients' ventures or other 'good things' they heard of over dinner, after church or at meetings of various local organisations. By 1836 the bank was soundly established, although it was a minor player in an expanding international business. The Industrial Revolution was gathering pace and the British Empire continued to turn the atlas pink. When Thomas died in 1834, his son Christopher was already Chairman, and in 1836 the Board of Directors unanimously agreed that the bank should become a Joint Stock Company in the name of The Swaledale & Wensleydale Banking Company. The Directors were John Hutton of Marske Hall near Richmond, Christopher Other of Elm House, William Ware of Leyburn and Isaac Fisher of Richmond. The Bank issued its own bank notes for the next sixty years.

As the 19th century came to an end, the Swaledale & Wensleydale Bank became part of the new Barclays banking group. Barclays Bank was established by the amalgamation of twenty small regional banking companies in 1896. During the merger discussions they worked closely with Jonathan Backhouse and Co., a Quaker bank based in Darlington, which had a powerful industrial lending base and strong connections in Teesdale and Weardale. Quaker bankers had a reputation for strict and honest adherence to lending agreements and as a result were regarded as totally trustworthy and soundly capitalised. In the rough conditions of the Dales, dealing with mining companies, farmers, dealers and merchants, these high principles were often scorned.

Bankers travelled to meet rural customers and Quakers were easily identified by their traditional large brimmed bonnet, formal black jacket and white breeches with black stockings. Many a man despised their apparent pomposity, unmovable honesty and strict regard for their God. On one occasion, in the King's Head Hotel in Barnard Castle, a traveller in brooms and brushes was drinking his fill by the fire in the snug. On seeing Jonathan Backhouse enter he immediately challenged him to show his money. He had had two good deals that day and flashed a large wad of grimy notes. Could Backhouse beat it?

"I don't bet my man, but I'll show you what I will do once I've purchased my glass of lemonade."

The man watched with a sinister mocking grin fanning his cash in his hand awaiting the return of this teetotal Christian.

Jonathan returned glass in hand. He placed it on the table opposite the broom man and took a crisp new £5 note from his vest pocket, moved forward and threw it on the blazing fire.

"Your turn sir," he said.

From the grubby wad a five pound note was drawn and thrown into the flames. The man grinned, raised his eyebrows, settled back in his chair, gulped his ale, fanned his cash again, but said nothing.

Another newly printed Backhouse note, this time for £10, was taken from the vest pocket and duly placed upon the ashes of the traveller's note. This was no small amount to commit to the flames

"Your turn again sir."

"You must be mad," retorted the man of trade to the banker.

"Sir you have burnt one of my notes. Thank you for your five pounds for it's now in my bank. I have simply burnt two pieces of paper."

In 1819 Jonathan Backhouse was taken to task by the Earl of Darlington of Raby Castle for blocking him from an industrial investment opportunity in the new railway from Darlington to Stockton. His Lordship took great exception to this, and instructed his senior agent to inform all his tenants that in future all rents, paid twice yearly, should be in Backhouse notes, not gold as was the farmers' usual form of currency especially in the more remote communities. The Raby Estate rent roll was enormous coming from many thousands of acres of land, mines, farms and numerous small businesses in water mills, forests, cottages, shops and hostelries in hamlets, villages and towns across his vast domain. Backhouse heard of the aristocratic plan and instinctively knew he was trying to break the bank as a lesson in future never to challenge his assumed privileges as his rent roll would far exceed the normal gold reserves in the vaults. The banker urgently required to increase his reserves and that meant a journey to London which had to be kept a secret as villains lurked in the town pubs just to pick up such news to sell on to more sophisticated and violent men.

Scared that this would come to the ears of one of the many gangs of felons who frequented turnpikes at night, especially the Great North Road, Jonathan decided to make the trip alone. He drove a post chaise, hired from a coaching yard near Scotch Corner, to London and back in four days. Horse changes were every twenty miles and his non-stop time was faster than Dick Turpin's ride over a lesser distance some years earlier. Tired and battered by the weather, he thought he'd failed as he crossed the Tees Bridge at Croft early in the morning. He was well behind schedule; rent day had been the previous day and the agent would be coming to Darlington, High Row Bank to pay in the rents at bank opening time. It was a shock when the off side front wheel spun off. The vehicle lurched down onto the rough road, it was still dark and there seemed to be no one about to help.

An old man suddenly appeared from a cottage. Jonathan handed him a sovereign and he held the tired, sweating horses as some of the bullion was moved from the front offside to the rear near side of the carriage, as he did so the hub slowly rose from the ground and he proceeded into Darlington on three wheels. When the Earl's agent appeared, accompanied by a man carrying a large bag packed with Backhouse notes, he went straight to the counter and said the Earl wanted to cash the notes into gold. The scene was set. The clerk went to Mr Backhouse's office. The senior partner returned, followed by the clerk, to oversee such an important transaction which he did deliberately and most slowly.

He instructed the counter clerks to check the final amount twice having previously told them to do so slowly. The agent waited. When the task was completed the senior clerk reported to Jonathan Backhouse who then ordered that the gold be brought up from the vaults. In a quiet voice he then said to the agent, "Now, tell thy Master if he will sell me his castle and lands I will pay him with even more metal." It was said that the two men never spoke again, but in one of the rooms in Raby Castle there is an old photograph of one of the Backhouse family and Lord Barnard with a group of Masons at a meeting in Staindrop. On that memorable day Jonathan Backhouse 'Balanced the Cash', an expression still used today at the end of the banking day, but is now done by a computer in the blink of an eye.

Thomas Other was born in Redmire in 1769. He married his first wife, Margaret Stapleton in 1800. She died in 1801, aged 26, having had no issue. In 1803 he married Jane Lister, born in 1780, who had eight children before she died in 1829 at the age of 49. Thomas was a registered yeoman giving him the all-important vote and setting him apart from the majority of local farmers and tradesmen in the area who were mostly tenants. He was a co-founder of the Swaledale & Wensleydale Bank who worked hard to improve his family's finances and social position at a time when the nation was becoming the most powerful and influential economy in the world. In those early days banking was mainly about lending to commercial business and relied on integrity, honesty and a shake of the hand, after which the lender's knowledge of local affairs kept him in touch with success or failure. It is also worth remembering that women were never considered as worthy borrowers.[39]

As his financial position improved, he built a new mansion on the site of the old grange at Redmire, renaming it Elm House. The family owned tenanted farms in the area and he had come a long way from when old Joseph lived in Pickhill 200 years previously. The family had progressed from tenant farmers into banking; he was rightly a proud man determined to build on his success. Thomas and Jane's children were:

---

39  Women were not usually allowed to take out bank loans until 1895-1905. This followed the Women's Property Act 1885.

Elizabeth Alice born 1805 who married William Burrill of Masham; Jane born 1807 who married Thomas Topham of Middleham; Christopher born 1809; Thomas born 1811 who married Ann Atkinson of Patrick Brompton; Isabella born 1813 who married Robert Wiley of Winterfield near Catterick; Margaret born 1815 who married William Robinson King (Jane Ritchie's great, great grandfather); Edward born 1819 who married Elizabeth Clark of Basford; and finally, in 1821 Alice Elizabeth was born and married Richard Jameson of Cottingham near Hull.

# Chapter 8

## Christopher Other of Elm House and Coverham Abbey

It was their eldest son, Christopher, the fourth of that name, who took the family to a new level in the social and business community of Wensleydale and neighbouring dales. He married Anne Stackhouse of Lawkland Green on the Lancashire/Yorkshire border and they had four children. Anne was a kind, considerate and educated woman[40] whose early unexpected death on 8th October 1853 giving birth to her fifth child was a great loss to her tough and resolute husband. Four years later in 1857 in London, Christopher married Eliza Anna Lamb, a doctor's daughter from Middleham, who was the sister of the wife of his great friend and partner Mr Hutton. Eliza was a plain lady, but Christopher probably wanted someone to manage his domestic household. It was a decision he lived to regret.

The family had become staunch members of the powerful middle class which formed a conduit between aristocratic, industrial and upper middle class wealth with the capital essential to maintain and expand small businesses such as farms, mines, shops, merchant businesses and processing. Close links to the professional classes were integral to the success of this economic structure. The working class farm labourers, miners and domestic servants were at the mercy of a class system under which they had no option but to live and work. Many people were dismayed to read in the local paper on 15th October 1896 that Captain Christopher Other, Major Scrope and Sir Frederick Milbank had announced their

---

40    She was a boarder at Mrs Watkinson's seminary, New Road, Halifax. There is a collection of letters written to and from her parents during her school days.

support for the Liberal Party. This heralded the start of a period of radical change as the balance of power shifted. Politics were always to the fore in the Dales, not least in the Richmond division. At an election in the late 19th century, John Hutton, the Conservative and Unionist Member was unseated by the Liberal, Mr F. D. Ackland, whose tenure was to only last one term after which the new Conservative candidate, the Hon. W. G. A. Orde-Powlett was returned, restoring the right wing politics which have remained in place ever since.[41] When Ackland took the seat there were riotous celebrations, which the Tories reported had turned into riots against noted members of their Party. Mr James Winn's house at West Burton had been one target as the village was seen as a Tory stronghold. The paper reported that the "Liberal rabble arrived in the village raising their political retribution on the residents." Little damage was done and some of those involved said they had not intended to demonstrate any ill-will towards Mrs Winn who was very ill at the time.

Christopher had been born into the privileged and wealthy lifestyle his father had worked so hard to establish. The majority of farmers were struggling to compete against the pressures of cheap imported food with local traders struggling as a result. A few progressive farmers and landowners had seen the need to increase food production and were developing new seed varieties and improve livestock and implements but the majority remained wedded to their old traditions with impoverished labourers slaving by hand in order to keep themselves and their family off the poor list. Should they be dismissed and replaced by mechanical devices, they were then listed as paupers and effectively became a tax on the meagre profits of farming. William Cobbett found a dangerous undercurrent of social revolution running through rural communities as he rode through the countryside. Many estate owners and larger farmers were knocking down cottages previously lived in by workers, forcing them to move away from the area thus reducing the local Poor Tax largely paid by farmers. Activists on behalf of the 'new poor' were mindful of revolutions in France and across Europe. Cobbett became a powerful national voice on their behalf and was eventually, rather late in life, elected to the House of Commons.

---

41    The Richmond seat is currently held by the Right Honourable William Hague MP.

Christopher Other was a big man weighing over 18 stone and standing at six feet three. He had a dominant personality from an early age and as soon as his education was complete he entered the family firm. He joined the local militia battalion, a private movement which was gathering strength in many rural areas as small outbreaks of civil unrest caused concern amongst the rich. The majority of people strongly objected to high rents, cheap food imports and unfair taxation. Christopher became a Class A, senior commissioned, volunteer of the 12th Company North Yorkshire Rifles and, as an acknowledgement of his Class he provided his own rifle, uniform and the rest of his essential military accoutrements. Class B Volunteers, the non-commissioned officers, supplied their own uniforms and accoutrements while the Class C Volunteers, the equivalent of lance corporals, only had to buy their uniforms. The lowest rank, Class D, had everything necessary provided from Company funds. The Company was raised by Lord Bolton, a descendant of the Scrope family of Bolton Castle, meeting on the first occasion at the Bolton Arms Hotel in the centre of Leyburn. Christopher was Captain of the Company rifle squad which regularly travelled south to the shooting grounds of Wimbledon and Bisley for national and international small bore shooting competitions. During the Crimean war Christopher built the Town Hall in Redmire as a Drill Hall.

He was a Deputy Lord Lieutenant of the North Riding of Yorkshire, a Justice of the Peace and Chairman of the Leyburn Board of Governors, the organisation that looked after the school. Through this list of appointments he knew all that was happening locally. On July 4th 1864 he was admitted to the Lennox Lodge of Freemasonry, putting the final influential brick in place for life as an ambitious banker. A combination of primogeniture, marriage settlements, whereby families passed property to sons-in-law on the marriage of daughters, and the importance of the preservation of family names, made land ownership a complex business. Arrangements and transactions were conducted by local solicitors many of whom also acted as managing agents of land with additional roles similar to accountants today, advising their clients on investment taxation and other financial matters. Land held its value during this period and, importantly, acted as the primary form of security against debts and borrowing.

The Stackhouse properties on the Lancashire/Yorkshire border were settled on the marriage of Christopher and Ann and he inherited his mother's sixth share of the Lister Coverdale properties. His personal wealth and collateral became handsome. In 1840, there were six servants at Elm House including a nursery nurse caring for their first born, Ann Agnes. There followed three more children: Christopher Junior, Thomas William and Jane. Christopher and H. T. Robinson together invested in Yore Mills[42] on the Ure below Aysgarth Church and Christopher supervised its rebuilding after a fire. Its most famous order was the material for Garibaldi's[43] loose red blouse uniforms for his army.

Ann Agnes, named after her mother and her mother's sister who had died as a child, married Dr George Wright on 28th November 1861. Christopher Junior joined the Bank and was Mayor of Richmond the year his younger sister Jane got married to James Clarkson Winn of Askrigg in 1873. The wedding photo is taken in the stable yard of The Grove, Richmond described as the Mayor's residence. It is not known why her brother gave her away instead of her father, but judging from one of his wills which refers to the fact that she hadn't been given a marriage settlement and leaves her a sum in lieu, it looks as though he didn't approve of the match. There may also have been an argument involving the second Mrs Other as a letter from one of the Robinson bridesmaids refers to the interfering 'Mrs O' and the stress of the bride. Her veil was still down for the photo after the wedding which was most unusual. Christopher Senior's youngest sister, Aunt Jameson, had helped to hide the presents from "Mrs Other's prying eyes" and to cut up the cake.

Christopher Other Junior went to Nice to try and recover from tuberculosis. He wrote several letters to his sister telling her how ill he felt. When his brother and father realised how seriously ill he was they travelled to Nice where they found a grim situation. It took them three days to get there accompanied by an English nurse, Mrs Dawson. On 21st

---

42  On May 6th 1887, Christopher paid £800 for the late H. T. Robinson's share of the Yore Mills Company, then a corn mill.

43  Garibaldi was an Italian mercenary commander born in Nice in 1807 who caused discord in the Mediterranean and even ventured to America during their Civil War.

February 1875 Christopher Senior wrote to his younger daughter Janey informing her that her brother had died at 9pm the previous night and that he would straight away return with the body, to be buried next to his mother in Redmire Churchyard. He asked her, with the help of her sister, to organise a family lunch and the mourners' attire: 8 immediate relatives to wear hoods, black scarves and silk gloves; 16 lesser relatives to wear silk hat bands and gloves; 9 bearers to be provided with silk hatbands and common gloves. He wrote to her husband James Winn from London informing him that he would arrive with his son's body at Leyburn station at 11.30 am on the Saturday and would expect to go straight to Elm House for the lunch he had asked Jane to organise. Of the second Mrs Other there is no mention.

In 1867 Jane Other's diary makes references to Mrs Other going to Middleham where she had a house. A letter to his solicitor marked 'private' refers to Christopher Senior's intention to divorce his second wife. This may have been his real reason for gifting Elm House to his son Thomas on his marriage to Frances Ballard in 1876. The second Mrs Other is listed in the 1881 census as living in Middleham not at Coverham. Divorce was virtually unheard of in those days, and Christopher was concerned about the financial implications. Their judicial separation was referred to during the Wright v Other court case. She was given an allowance for her life and she did attend his funeral.

Following the death of Annie Lister in 1872, Christopher moved to Coverham Abbey. He had inherited a sixth share of the Coverham estate from his mother and now assumed ownership of the house, although Annie had in fact left it to him and his heirs jointly. It isn't clear whether his younger son Thomas and his wife Frances actually lived in Elm House. They are recorded in the 1881 census as being in Cambridge with Frances' parents, and when Thomas becomes ill in 1882 they moved to Exmouth in Devon where Thomas died aged 38, predeceasing his only child, Thomas Archer Windsor Other[44]. Little Tom, as he was referred to by his family, was totally ignored by his grandfather. Christopher Senior and his son Thomas had gone to court over compensation of compulsory

---

44    His birth place is recorded as Redmire and his baptism was at Redmire Church.

purchase of land at Redmire bought by the North East Railway Company so that could have been where the bad feeling started. However, it doesn't explain a grandfather's attitude to his grandson and heir. Frances needed money to help her father whose drapery business in Cambridge had failed, so she mortgaged Elm House to her late husband's very efficient Leeds solicitor, one Walter North. Any sort of goodwill towards his daughter-in-law was from then onwards totally impossible as far as Christopher was concerned.

Christopher was highly regarded in the area both as a banker and an influential member of the community, all of which he was proud of. There is little doubt that whilst loyal to his siblings, Christopher thrived on his power and influence. He totally underestimated his widowed daughter-in-law, Frances, and her concern for her son who, it was reasonable to assume, was his hereditary heir. He seems to have ignored his grandson from birth, even before his feud with Frances went to court. He was Chairman of the Bank, with assets in excess of £1 million. He owned a considerable property portfolio over a wide area and his financial affairs started to unravel when he decided to sell Elm House over Frances' head to his son-in-law George Wright[45] in order "to keep it in the family". Whether that referred to Christopher not wanting his wife to have it, and why he did not consider his son's widow as family is not explained in the court papers. Frances was still young and attractive. She needed to support her parents and she was certainly not going to give up her inheritance from her husband let alone having it sold beneath her feet by her father-in-law. She admitted during court proceedings that her main reason for marrying Thomas in the first place was to become the mistress of Elm House. Mr North moved swiftly to establish his client's claim on both Elm House and Coverham Abbey on behalf of Little Tom, and a long and tedious legal wrangle started with neither side prepared to give ground.

Christopher was incandescent as the costs of litigation rose like an autumn tide threatening to swallow up a large part of his wealth.

---

45    James Winn had been initially offered Elm House, but he said he was
      happy with the house he already had and didn't want or need another.

Counsel's opinions were sought and refuted by either side; there were appearances in the High Court in London with affidavits and subpoenas flying between the two parties. Christopher reacted angrily, but North, a thorough and energetic attorney, promptly issued a plea against him. The response was to hotly deny that any such arrangement had been made in favour of Frances with regard to family properties. The deed of gift to Thomas included a sentence stating that Elm House was not to be a dower house. On the occasion of the marriage, according to Christopher's statement, Thomas had an income from two properties, namely Longber on the Yorkshire Lancashire Border and the Scar House Estate at the head of Nidderdale, where large reservoirs for Bradford's water supplies were being planned. However, it was not proved whether Thomas held title to these despite receiving the rents.[46] Additionally, he had shares in the family bank, a holding in Russian Bonds, but strangely he paid four per cent interest on a mortgage on Scar House to his father which left him with an annual income of around £1,000.

Prior to Thomas's marriage, Christopher had realised the couple would be short of income and as his heir could not be seen to fall behind either in appearance or socially, he proposed to Samuel Ballard, father of the bride, that they each make a Deed of Covenant of £200 annually to be paid during their respective lives. Ballard initially declined, but immediately before the marriage service he felt Christopher's full force cajoling him to approve the proposal. Very reluctantly, he agreed. Christopher gave Thomas a further £1,000 as a wedding gift. Although the Deeds of Covenant were accordingly drawn up, they were never transferred.

When Christopher moved to Coverham, the legal papers relating to the Elm House estate had remained in a box in the house safe. Shortly after his son's death he returned to collect the title deeds with a view to selling the family home to one or other of his sons-in-law in order to 'keep it in the family'. However, the safe had been opened, as had the deed box, and the Elm House estate documents removed.[47] He was furious,

---

46    Ann Agnes and Jane went to court to get increased compensation from Bradford Water Co. when the Scar House estate was compulsorily purchased.

47    The deeds had been needed for the house to be mortgaged by Frances to her late husband's solicitor Walter North.

but took no action completely overlooking the possibility that the deeds would be used against him in the future. Initially, he offered the house to James Clarkson Winn,[48] Jane's husband, for £5,000 knowing it to be worth far more. The offer was declined, leaving him with only one option which was to turn to his other son-in-law George Wright,[49] his daughter Anne Agnes's husband, a doctor who the Court thought unlikely to be a man of appropriate means. George happened to be grouse shooting in Wensleydale at the time so Christopher sought George out, finally running him to ground in the waiting room at Leyburn station. With no polite introduction to his sudden need to talk, he outlined his plan. He had little time, but he managed to persuade George to accept his offer. George almost certainly thought that the deal would be of great benefit to his family, and wouldn't have expected the subsequent court case of Wright v. Other.

Next morning Christopher instructed Winns, the Askrigg solicitors, to draw up a conveyance transferring Elm House to Doctor George Wright. In court documents, sometime later in the lengthy legal posturing, it was stated that Mr William Winn "was well acquainted with all family titles of the Other family" possibly implying some coercion apart from a normal client relationship. A cheque for £5,000 had been drawn on Dr Wright's Swaledale & Wensleydale Banking Company account in favour of Christopher Other who denied in court that there was any agreement for him to buy the house back at a later date, claiming that the advantageous sale price simply represented capital he intended to make over to his daughter on his death. Neither was there any agreement on the treatment of rental income from the surrounding tenanted land, and there was still a question over the sum of money from the land transferred to the North Eastern Railway Company on a compulsory purchase order for the new railway line. This ran up the Dale from the Great Eastern Line at Northallerton across to Ribblehead, passing immediately behind Elm House before reaching Redmire station. The old ways of handling legal

---

48    James did not own The Grange at West Burton until he bought it in 1903 after his father died. It had been his mother's dowry. This may have influenced his decision or he may have liked living in West Burton. His wife may not have wanted to live in the house where her mother had died.

49    The Wrights were living at Knap House, Hornby at the time.

matters, particularly in relation to land, were being exposed. No longer was the shake of a hand enough and certainly the domination of men with money over lesser men was also over.

On the 28th December 1882, just eight months after Thomas William's death, North was planning to marry his client Frances Other. He responded to the big man's rebuttal about all that had been said and implied in a thoroughly effective way. Two vellum documents, written in copper plate, arrived at Coverham Abbey for Christopher in the joint names of Mrs Frances Taylor Other and Mr Walter North. He can never have imagined that such a blatant attack on his personal wealth could ever happen, especially in the name of a member of his family. The first document dealt with land, farms and dwellings in Feizor, Austwick and Lawkland in the County of York, which had been placed on the market by Christopher without prior warning to any of his children, to whom it had been left in trust by Christopher's first wife. The sale, however, failed as it was a time of rural depression, rents were low, if indeed paid, and land values were falling like a stone. He had already sold his late in-laws' house in Lawkland Green privately, without consulting his heirs. The second document pointed out firstly that Elm House had been sold illegally, in contravention of a Land Settlement Agreement, and that secondly Mrs Frances Taylor Other had made her interest in Coverham Abbey over to Mr Walter North, the property having been left in part jointly to her husband Thomas through a codicil to the will of Annie Lister in 1872. Legal processes relentlessly moved to London, barristers were appointed, and more subpoenas issued. George Wright went into court against Frances Taylor Other regarding her ownership of Elm House. So a strange court room battle ensued with Christopher's daughter-in-law fighting his son-in-law.

The outcome of the property puzzle, woven by Christopher, was eventually finalised, after considerable expense to Christopher, as Frances was awarded costs. It left him homeless with two properties, once his, in the ownership of a man with no blood link. His Counsel had relied on some obscure law dating from Queen Elizabeth I whereby a voluntary gift was treated differently from a sale. Because Walter North had swiftly registered the mortgage of Elm House, that seems to have had precedence, and is the reason that George Wright and Christopher Other lost the case although the judge made it clear he didn't think much of their claim. As Mr Ballard had reneged on his agreement to pay a marriage portion for his daughter, which at the time was a normal practice, and Christopher Other had specifically excluded the use of Elm House as a dower house, Christopher's reaction was perhaps more understandable than it seems today.

On 6th February 1884, Walter North married Frances Taylor Other[50] and they sold Elm House to Charles Burrill, nephew of Christopher Other. For Christopher, this must have been both disastrous and socially embarrassing. He had nowhere to go and was separated from his second wife. He, probably wisely, never sought another wife. Charles Burrill took pity on his uncle and rented him his former home Cotescue, standing to the north above Coverham Abbey. Eventually, Christopher bought Frances' share of Coverham Abbey and he left it in trust for his daughter Ann Agnes Wright's second son Christopher. The Wrights had seven children (two daughters were drowned when the family first moved to Heysham),[51] and eight grandchildren, who carried the name of either Other or Stackhouse as middle names, in recognition of their various inheritances. Anne Agnes lived until she was 88 and her third child, Christopher Other Wright, known as Christo, married his second cousin Elizabeth Burrill (Bessie), daughter of Charles and Annie Burrill of Elm House, Redmire. They were to have four children. When their financial situation became difficult, Christo sold Coverham and they moved to Ireland for the hunting.

On the 20th of June 1888, Christopher, 'the Guv'nor' as his sons referred to him, raised his pen to write a codicil to his will of 1884. Much had happened in the four years that had elapsed since the original version

---

50   When Walter North died, Frances moved to Bournemouth and called her house there Coverham Abbey. James C. Winn went to the wedding of Thomas Archer Windsor Other on 3rd July 1909 and the Wrights and Jamesons sent presents. He and his wife Nellie had two daughters.

51   In June 1895 shortly after the family had moved to Heysham Lodge, Mabel and Harriet went swimming in Morecambe Bay and although the family dog their mother sent into the water to try and rescue them reached one of them, the tide swept both girls away.

appointing Charles Burrill as his executor. Charlie was replaced by William Walker, Manager of the Swaledale & Wensleydale Bank's head office in Richmond. In writing his revised last will and testament he dealt first with minor bequests, cancelling small amounts to his housekeeper and wine merchant, replacing them with acknowledgements of the help and professional services from William Walker and his long time solicitor John Teale of Leyburn. To each of his servants, at the time of his death, he left twenty pounds and an assurance that their wages would be settled up to date. He then dealt with the Yore Mills Company[52] property purchased from the Trustees of the H. T. Robinson Trust which included houses, land, machinery, debts and stock in trade representing the business which he bequeathed to his son-in-law, James Winn and his heirs, along with a sum of £3,000. He left silver plate, including a presentation piece from the Bank on his retirement, to his daughter Anne Agnes Wright. He then instructed his trustees to attempt to purchase Walter North's interest in Coverham Abbey for the benefit of his grandson Christopher Other Wright. However, after only a year, he wrote another codicil leaving land, houses and buildings adjacent to Coverham, purchased from the Trustees of the late Thomas Edmundson, to his daughters as tenants in common. A month later, in March 1889, he drafted another codicil adding a bequest of £200 to his gamekeeper at West Scrafton, a moorland property adjacent to, but not previously defined as part of his ownership. It is therefore assumed that Christopher had leased or bought the grouse shooting on the moor.

There then followed four further versions of his death wishes dated 1889, 1890, 1892[53] and 1894. The last written two years before he passed away. In the 1889 version, he appointed James Clarkson Winn as an additional Trustee with William Walker and defined previous agreements and bequests involving his second wife Elizabeth in Middleham, from whom he was divorced. He also introduced his leasehold property interests in Nidderdale on the Scar House Estate.

---

52    On 6th May 1887 Christopher paid £800 for the late H. T. Robinson's share in the Yore Mills Company.

53    Christopher bought himself a bath chair in 1892.

In August 1892, he wrote what he intended to be his last will and testament in his own hand, signed by Messrs Heaton and King. The trustees remained the same. He dealt with freehold and leasehold properties in Coverdale far exceeding anything previously mentioned, along with his share and interest in the Coverham Abbey Estate and his grazing rights (gaits) on Middleham Moor. Then he introduced more land, houses and rights in Nidderdale, Kirkby Malzeard, Redmire, Ribblesdale, Aysgarth, Yore Mills and Wensley. In all, thirteen properties were listed, and a total of 4,083 acres, both leasehold and freehold. The beneficiaries, his daughters and grandchildren, remained the same. That, it appeared, was that, except that in 1894 when ailing and staying in Heysham with his daughter and son-in-law George and Ann Agnes Wright, he bought them a house in Morecambe[54] which was itemised in the last will.

The final outcome was an estate divided between a number of beneficiaries, heirs and others.

What this possibly reveals is that Christopher hoped to invest in a branch railway line running up Coverdale to Kettlewell in Wharfedale. This project came to nothing as the long tunnel from Horsehouse under Coverhead would have cut into an uneven geological fault in the limestone strata putting the tunnel at high risk of flash flooding and collapse. The Wensleydale branch line across the Pennines, linking the Carlisle to West Yorkshire line at Garsdale Junction to the east coast line from London to Edinburgh, no doubt sparked the idea. This was a main artery from east coast industry to the ports on the west that were a bridge to Ireland and across the Atlantic to the Americas. Christopher would have recognised the commercial logic of the value of the railways which could be passed on for the benefit of his partners and shareholders. Quarries would be able to move large tonnages of material, the farming industry would transport wool and wool products more easily to the mills and Dales milk, cheese and butter would be only a day away from consumers in the large towns and cities. Trains would bring in heavy new equipment, livestock and tourists.

---

54    As Heysham Lodge was a Wright property he probably bought the Morecambe house for Anne Agnes to move to should she outlive her husband.

In Nidderdale and Colsterdale a large complex of reservoirs was also being planned to take water to Bradford, the world wool centre, and Leeds. Christopher's Coverdale railway dream, if it indeed was his dream, was speculative, ambitious and dependent on holding strategic freehold or leasehold agreements. The Nidderdale line was narrow gauge for dam building to be removed on completion. However, the Masham line was standard gauge from Ripon, but narrow gauge onward to Leighton Reservoir, again only a temporary line which remained open during WW1 to service the army training camp at Breary Banks, home of the illustrious Leeds Pals regiment which had few survivors. How much Christopher invested in this vision is not known and he was not alone. A lot of money was lost around the developing world as the flexibility of motor transport became more fully understood and railways lost much of their original attraction.

The character of Jane Ritchie's great, great grandfather Christopher Other is difficult to summarise. Undoubtedly, he was a young man born in the early years of the 19th century to a lifestyle previously the preserve of the landed aristocracy. The wealth passed down by his father, Thomas, came as the result of three hundred years of family progression as his forebears moved successfully away from their simple agrarian lives. Improved farming methods developed to service demographic change, as the indigenous rural labour force moved away to where industry was expanding, using the powerful combination of water and mineral resources. The Other family had moved westward across the great Roman Road to farm in West Tanfield on the River Ure where it flowed out of Wensleydale towards Ripon. The first Christopher Other, registered as a free yeoman, number 677, thus qualifying for the democratic vote, took his family up the dale to the small estate in Redmire which he probably inherited from a distant relative. He was in fact moving against the economic tide, but it paid off.

There is little detail of Christopher's private life. He was a very hard worker with an excellent brain, well suited to his opportunist character. His letter to Janey shows total trust in his daughter's ability to organise a funeral and his draft letter to Thomas, when they are arguing over the compulsory purchase, shows crossings out as he takes care to find the right words. Once his mind was made up, he stuck to his guns to the point of complete unreasonableness. His faithful solicitor John Teale from Leyburn gave up acting for him over the court case with Frances, probably because of his intransigence. He was a loyal friend, as his speech demonstrated when he was presented with a silver cup[55] by the Directors of the Bank in 1887, using the occasion to speak highly of his partner Mr Hutton. Hutton's wife was Eliza Lamb's sister which perhaps explains why Christopher married her. He had a happy first marriage, and was so upset when Anne died that he ordered a private funeral, but one gets the impression that his sons disappointed him. He may well have found Elm House had too many memories or that Coverdale was a better place to expand his land ownership. It was there that he had a herd of pedigree shorthorn cows.[56] He went to Nice when his eldest son Christopher was dying; he attended Thomas's wedding but not that of Janey. Whatever he thought of James Winn when James married his daughter, he left him Yore Mills in one of his wills so he must have thought better of him as time went on. In the end Yore Mills was left to Jane Winn who leased it to her husband. His mother-in-law left Christopher her portrait.

His high profile in the lower Dale made him a notable figure. He was active in local politics[57] and bought land specifically to get his sons' voting rights. His intransigence over his attitude to his daughter-in-law cost him dear. Whether he got wind that she was going to mortgage Elm House, or whether it was that he was convinced that he had drawn up the deed of gift so it could not be a dower house, is simply not clear. It is very probable that he was speculating on the proposed railway line up Coverdale when he bought land but that came to nought. He died at Coverham[58] following a stroke, almost certainly a disappointed and unhappy man.

---

55    The cup was valued at 150 guineas. The presentation marked Christopher's 50 years as Chairman during which time he never missed an AGM. In 1834 the Bank's capital was £42,000 and in 1887 it was £63,000 with reserves of £50,000. The shareholders had received gross dividends of £500,000 over 50 years.

56    The Leeds Mercury of September 28th 1886 records their sale.

57    He was a staunch Liberal.

58    His funeral cortege left Coverham Abbey at 1.00 pm and proceeded through Middleham and Wensley, escorted by a guard of honour of non-commissioned officers of the Wensleydale Rifle Volunteers under the command of Colour Sergeant Instructor E. Smith.

# Chapter 9

## The Winns of Askrigg and West Burton

James Clarkson Winn was a banker with the Swaledale & Wensleydale Bank who inherited the Grange, West Burton through his mother, Elizabeth Clarkson of Capel Bank, West Witton. The Winn family built Winnville in Askrigg, now the White Rose Hotel, and before that they had rented Nappa Hall, an ancient 16th century property belonging to the Metcalfe family to whom they were related.

The Askrigg Winns used the same crest as the Winns of Nostell Priory so it is assumed that they were a junior branch of that family. In the time of Elizabeth I the Winns were Welsh textile merchants who were in London dealing in the finest fabrics. Such was their reputation they were appointed drapers to the Queen and were therefore prominent in the City of London and staunch liverymen, amassing a fortune in a very short time. When they heard a fellow liveryman was bankrupt, they investigated his assets and negotiated to buy his land holdings in Yorkshire, almost certainly 'on the quiet', the normal practice of land dealing. This gave them a new found status as owners in 1654 of what is now the Nostell Priory Estate. Their loyalty to the Crown during the Civil War was recognised with a baronetcy when George Winn became the First Baronet in 1660.

In 1665 bubonic plague again ravaged the country, having been introduced by black rats escaping from ships entering the Port of London from around the world. The rats left by the ships' ropes which eventually resulted in the introduction of compulsory stops[59] being placed on all ships arriving in ports in future. The plague gripped the nation in fear as word spread

---

59    Stops were funnel shaped baffles on the ropes connecting ships to land which prevented rats leaving ships.

up and down turnpikes, lanes and water ways as the disease tightened its horrific grip. Rural communities closed their approach roads allowing neither visitors nor traders to enter. Despite these precautions, a huge percentage of the population met with an early death. Graveyards, even in small country parishes, grew larger. In 1666, the Great Fire of London destroyed the disease taking with it infected dwellings, workshops, offices and warehouses. In most villages and market towns the disease had also run its course.[60]

A young journalist of the day, one Daniel Defoe, was just starting out on his career. Daniel was the son of a tallow chandler whose family survived the Great Fire. As a Puritan, he had been brought up as a Dissenter. By 1668 the Winns had amassed more wealth and built a mansion to endorse their success and status at Nostell near the site of the old Priory. Sir George kept good company on his visits to London and, like Daniel Defoe, heard the talk of new inventions and the growing demand for exports of British goods and people to service the growing empire. This excited Winn and Defoe and many others, especially in the City. George returned to Yorkshire where coal mining was expanding to fuel the industrial revolution and young Defoe set off on his travels around Britain to assess the true economic state of the nation so that he could publicise the details, good or bad. He rode around the coast, starting by heading along the north shore of the Thames estuary. He then visited the coastal and river ports and harbours where boats were built and goods collected from inland communities for transport to London. Goods were then distributed around the nation and to the expanding world beyond. Defoe found that the nation was living in ignorance of the facts.

New machines were being installed close to reserves of coal, wood and iron ore. Rural people were flocking to rapidly growing industrial centres to escape rural poverty which was largely imposed by the landed class. The resulting social problems were being ignored. A new urban poverty was putting considerable stresses on the growing number of industrial

---

60    Bodies of tall men covered in pitch found under the lawn of the Grange, West Burton were thought to be those of marauding Scots who died from the Black Death whilst on a cattle raid. The village of Eshington was wiped out by the plague and West Burton was settled in its place.

communities. Rural families, often travelling on foot with children and a few sticks of furniture packed on a cart, arrived in strange places to find neither a social structure nor adequate supplies of food and drink. Back in their villages and hamlets food production fell as they left, and farmers started to invest in new implements to replace them. Gradually, through the leadership of the growing non-conformist churches, solutions were found, but not before thousands of people had suffered, starved or died.

Defoe and Winn, unknown to each other, adopted very different roles for the rest of their lives. Although a poor man, Defoe was a flamboyant risk taker who never shrank from speaking out regardless of the consequences. He had a good brain, political ability and a sharp pen with which he wrote books as well as articles of great controversy. He even spied against Scotland for the Crown, but he was no business man. Sir George Winn Bt., meanwhile, found he had coal beneath his feet at home. Having appointed agents to deal with the agreements and terms with mining company owners, he moved further afield to find deposits of iron ore to build foundries that could benefit from using the heat from his coal.

There is no doubt that James Clarkson Winn carried many of these Winn characteristics. His forebears and descendants were professionals often in a world of hardship, yet an integral part of the landed class system. Sir George, the first baronet, had become a landowner, but as time went by the extended family became lawyers, bankers, army officers and vicars, effectively serving the ruling class and ensuring their control over capital, the law of the land, faith in the established church and obedience of the populace. Successful marriages were those which brought with them capital or land settlements, which in turn could improve business opportunities, social connections and influence.

The Metcalfe clan are probably the oldest family in Wensleydale and are today spread around the globe. Every few years they hold a family gathering, with folk travelling back to Yorkshire from every corner of the world. The Metcalfe stronghold was originally Nappa Hall, built in the 16th century, standing on the north bank of the River Ure four miles east of Askrigg. Over the years the Metcalfes extended their land holdings north over the moors to Swaledale. The Hon. Philip P. Carey, the York

Herald at the College of Arms, Queen Victoria Street, E.C.4, examined the pedigrees of both the Metcalfe and Winn families in 1929 and found that a Betty Metcalfe, daughter of Richard Metcalfe of Calvert Houses in Swaledale, had married a George Winn. Both were born in 1774. They had three sons: John became Vicar of Aysgarth, Richard Metcalfe Winn (1800-1876) married Isabel Fothergill and moved to Bower Bank, Pooley and George Winn (1808-1880) became a solicitor in Askrigg. Richard's daughter Mary (born 1848) married Robert Thompson of Inglewood near Penrith, a noted farmer and owner of the Inglewood Shorthorn herd, thought to be the best herd of shorthorns in the country at the time. Mary's daughter Ella married a Rev. Richard Wordsworth and their son Richard, a great grandson of the poet, became an actor and, with his sister, promoted William Wordsworth's legacy in the Lake District.

The Winn family rented Nappa Hall from 1756 to 1851. The first to do so was George Winn born at Thornton Steward, a village fifteen miles down the River Ure to the east. The last Winn at Nappa was George (1808-1876). He lived there until he built Winnville in the Askrigg main street. Betty Metcalfe's mother Elizabeth was a Hutchinson. Her sister Martha married William I'Anson,[61] an attorney who practiced in London. It was their beautiful daughter, Frances, who became renowned as the 'Lass of Richmond Hill' celebrated in the song written by her husband Leonard McNally, first sung at Vauxhall Gardens, the popular spring and summer venue for the gay young things of London. The McNallys lived in Dublin and are buried in Dannybrooke Church.

Parson John Winn was born at Nappa Hall in 1799 and became the last vicar of the 'Great Parish' which stretched from Lunds in the west to below Aysgarth in the east. He lived at Nappa Mill. In 1821, William Cobbett made his renowned ride around England looking at what was happening out in the countryside where the remaining peasants dwelt under the control of the landed class, a situation the government chose to ignore. It was the likes of Parson Winn who had done little to prevent the

---

61    John I'Anson came over from France and fought for Henry VII at the Battle of Bosworth in 1485. He probably settled in Hauxwell. The I'Ansons had left England as Jansens after a House of Lancaster defeat during the Wars of the Roses.

run down churches that Cobbett found. Cobbett gathered much useful information from the poor curate clergy who were trying to serve their small flocks. He returned to London, the 'Great Wen' as he disparagingly called it, to report the facts that were being kept both from the public and parliament. In many ways he was a man of similar concerns and ambitions to Defoe, but his province was rural rather than industrial. Farming and food production were the responsibility of tenants who had no right to vote, no power to control the imports of cheap food from abroad, or to resist unfair rent rises. Industry however, had successfully established its importance in servicing the growth of the home economy, as well as across the expanding Empire, furthering Parliament's ambitions to increase international power and influence. Successful industrial families increased their wealth at an amazing rate, many gambling on the rush of new technology that kept coming to the patent offices of London. Some won, others lost. Following the lucrative farming period during the Napoleonic Wars rents rose, but with victory food production returned to its previous gloom. Farmers continued paying rent at the same level as well as the Poor Law Tax against their steadily falling profits. Cobbett was furious to find rural churches largely neglected, apart from those serving large estates. Parsonages[62] stood empty with services conducted irregularly by the poorly paid curates. The senior cleric collected tithes from farmers and the livings paid to the parishes by lords of the manor. They dealt out meagre livings to curates while living the life of lords themselves.

It was against this background that the Reverend John Winn lay contentedly asleep in his bed at 3 a.m. on New Year's morning 1860 when he heard his servant boy cry out that there were men in the house. He leapt from his warm feather mattress, fumbled for a match and lit his candle. Indeed there were intruders downstairs. He could hear their shouts. Scared and having no thought for the boy, he returned to his room frightened. It was dark, very dark. He heard heavy boots striding up the old stone staircase with gruff voices shouting, "Where are you parson? We want your money." He dived from his room across the passage into

---

62   Wensleydale livings had not been endowed with parsonages and clergy lived in their own houses until Victorian vicarages were built. Churches were modernised at the same time.

a lumber room and stood silently. He heard the boots and gruff voices fired by drink, doors opened and slammed shut. Suddenly his door flew open. He nearly collapsed with fear for his life and whimpered, "For the love of God". It fell on deaf ears. A lantern, his lantern from the stables, illuminated two Irish labourers. He recognised them as coming from the family who came over from Kerry regularly to make hay in summer and to dig drains and make roads in winter.

One man carried a hay spade,[63] a large, heavy, sharp steel knife two feet long, with which he struck John, severely gashing his face. The pain gave Parson Winn courage and he grabbed the weapon, whereupon he was picked up and hurled down the stairs. He could take no more. He relented, telling the men to come to his bedroom where they held him roughly and glowered over him in the yellow light as he gave them £25 from beneath his mattress. The servant boy, Thomas Dolfin, had taken cover with the housekeeper and when the criminals had gone they bathed the vicar's head and put him back to bed.

A week later, at the magistrate's court in Leyburn, the leader of the thieving pair, Michael O'Brien, was committed to the Assizes at York where the Chairman of the Court took little time to hear the evidence, await the jury's return and to receive their verdict of guilty. He instructed the Clerk to record a recommended sentence of death by hanging. However under the circumstances of the crime[64] O'Brien, later tried in York Crown Court, received instead penal servitude for life which, in those days, meant what it said. He never saw Kerry again. Many years later, the labourer who had escaped returned to ask for work. Not surprisingly he was not hired.

The Dales hills held valuable deposits of lead. The mineral rights were owned by traditional landowners such as long established aristocrats, city merchants, institutions and speculative investors. Mining companies negotiated rights to extract from the veins deep down in the hills. These

---

63  Parson Winn installed a stained glass window in the vestry at Aysgarth Church depicting the story of the man who fell amongst thieves in thanksgiving for his survival. The thieves depicted in the glass carry hay making implements.

64  O'Brien was the only one of the two who was caught and as no one had been killed this is presumably why the sentence was reduced by the higher court.

*Wedding of Annie Robinson & Charlie Burrill, The Cliffe, Leyburn. 1873*

*Annie & Charlie Burrill with Will on the pony.*

*Mabel Lister as Henrietta Listacova – "Green Javanese Idol".*

*Elm House Halloween Party Race Meeting 31.10.1936.*

ELM HOUSE

Hallowe'en
Race Meeting

Saturday, October 31st, 1936
at 11 p.m.

Hon. Stewards :
MESSRS. PULLEM and BUMPEM

Judge :
MR. JUSTICE BLIND

Starter :
HERR KICKOFF

Hon. Vet. Surgeon :
DR. TUBAHAUS

### 1. NORTH RIDING HANDICAP.

1. Mrs. Hield's — Sparkling Eyes
   by Excitement out of New House.
2. Mrs. Young's — Good Spirits
   by Happiness out of New Arrival.
3. Mrs. Parker-Jervis' — Hunter
   by Gift out of Grotian.
4. Miss Burrill's — Northgate
   by Assignment out of Hield.
5. Mrs. Schofield's — Pretty Frock
   by Model out of Molyneux.
6. Mrs. Stringer's — Sleek Head
   by No Hair out of Place.

### 2. GAME SHOOTERS STAKES.

1. Mr. T. R. King's — Turnover
   by Cannot Get out of Ditch.
2. Col. Chaytor's — Strong Runner
   by Bounce out of Covert.
3. Mr. O. Cooke-Yarborough's — Dusty Road
   by Comment out of Queen Mary.
4. Mr. J. H. Farmer's — Taken In
   by Gaekwar out of Alne.
5. Mr. T. Thornton-Berry's — Sherriff
   by Gum out of Pocket.
6. Mr. C. O. Wright's — Hot and Bothered
   by Leg Pull out of Farmer.

### 3. LADIES PLATE.

1. Mrs. Cooke-Yarborough's — Harrassed
   by Family out of Hand.
2. Mrs. King's — One Short
   by Beth out of Witton.
3. Mrs Wright's — President
   by Chosen out of Women's Institute.
4. Mrs. Farmer's — Popularity
   by Never out of Spirits.
5. Mrs. Thornton-Berry's — Family Group
   by Picture out of Tatler.
6. Mrs. Chapman-Purchas' — Trophies
   by Peter out of Kenya.

### 4. REDMIRE HANDICAP.

1. Mr. A. Hield's — Two Brace
   by Shot out of Gun.
2. Mr. F. Chapman's — Popular Hunt
   by Good Sport out of Harriers.
3. Mr. R. Parker Jervis' — Hearts Content
   by Blushing Bride out of Masham.
4. Mr. R. Young's — Home Again
   by Transfer out of India.
5. Mr. N. Cooke-Yarborough's — Latest Model
   by Glovers out of Ripon.
6. Mr. R. Chapman's — Holiday
   by Uncle out of Bachelordom.

### 5. MAIDEN STAKES.

1. Miss M. Willoughby's — Good Company
   by Flying Visit out of London.
2. Miss K. Young's — On Her Own
   by Brother out of Middleham.
3. Miss P. Cooke-Yarborough's — Camisole
   by Sewing out of Crepe de Chine.
4. Miss A. Brown's — Slim Figure
   by Exercise out or Doors.
5. Miss R. Cooke-Yarborough's — Youngest Member
   by Not Long out of School.
6. Miss K. King's — New Car
   by Generosity out of Uncle.

### 6. ELM HOUSE STAKES.

1. Mr. H. R. Chapman-Purchas' — Fortune
   by Double out of Tote.
2. Mr. R. Whitehead's — Magazine
   by Type out of Printing Press.
3. Dr. Wood's — Groggy Knee
   by Chill out of Gardening.
4. Rev. Trotter's — Vicar
   by Presentation out of Wensley.
5. Mr. W. Schofield's — Tummyache
   by Inside out of Order.
6. Dr. Cockroft's — Certain Cure
   by Liquid out of Bottle.

*Middles pages of above.*

*Mabel Burrill-Robinson at a shoot.*

*Margery Burrill on board ship going to Tasmania.*

*AA sign in Richmond North Yorkshire commemorating solar eclipse.*

*The Leyburn Bench.*
*Back row extreme left Lady Jane Scrope, fourth from left*
*Lord Bolton. Extreme right Col. Philip Straubenzee. Seated second from left*
*Will Burrill-Robinson, Richard Scrope, Margery Freeman.*

*Margery Freeman visiting neighbours with home produce*
*– not necessarily very edible!*

*Ellen Stackhouse née Crumbleholme*

## In Affectionate Remembrance

OF

# CHRISTOPHER OTHER, JUNR.,

Who died at Nice,

*February the 23rd, 1875,*

**Aged 32 years,**

And was this day Interred in Redmire Churchyard,

*Elm House, March 6, 1875.*

*Christopher Other Jnr's funeral card*

NOT LOST
BUT GONE
BEFORE

*Reverse of above*

*The Yorkshire Shooting Team at Bisley: Christopher Other standing on right, Frank Chapman seated far left, Sgt. Cockburn second from right*

*Thomas and Frances Other.*

In Loving Remembrance of

# THOMAS WILLIAM OTHER,

WHO DIED AT EXMOUTH,

ON THE 3RD DAY OF APRIL, 1882,

IN HIS THIRTY-NINTH YEAR,

And was interred in Redmire Churchyard on April 10th.

———

"His trust was in God."

"But the Lord doth nought amiss,
And since He hath ordered this,
We have nought to do but still
Rest in silence on His will."

*Thomas William Other's funeral card.*

In affectionate Remembrance

OF

# ANNIE LISTER,

## Of Coverham Abbey,

Who Died August 9th, 1872,

Aged 75 years.

———

Interred at Coverham, on
Tuesday, 13th August.

*Annie Lister's funeral card.*

*James Clarkson Winn at Askrigg.*

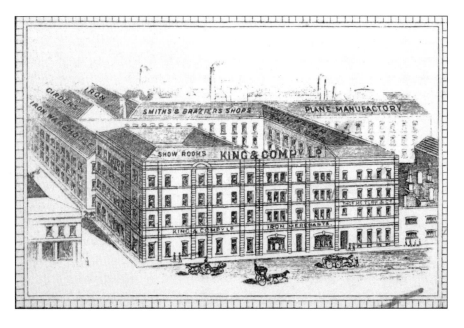

*King & Co visiting card.*

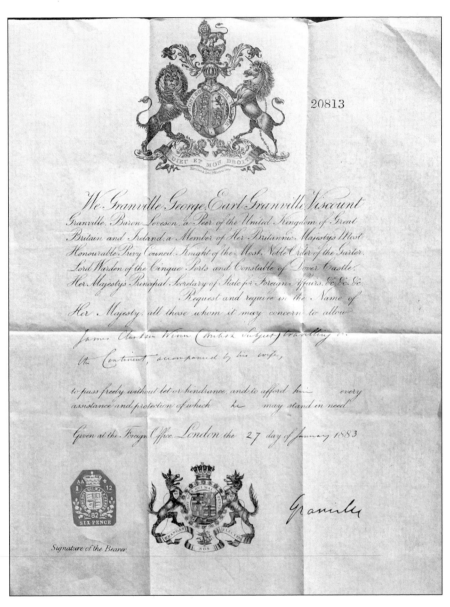

*James Winn's passport*

# THREE GENERATIONS OF THE KING FAMILY.

*WILLIAM ROBINSON KING, J.P.*
*1819 - 1893.*
*The First Chairman.*

*WILLIAM ROBINSON KING.*
*1854 - 1921.*
*The Second Chairman.*

*WILLIAM BERNARD ROBINSON KING.*
*1889 - 1963 O.B.E., M.C.*
*Director.*

*3 generations of the King family from the "House of Kings".*

# FACSIMILE SIGNATURES OF SOME OF
## THE KING FAMILY.

*Henry : King*

HENRY KING — 1713-1789.

*Henry King*

HENRY KING — 1779-1848.

*W Robinson King*

WILLIAM ROBINSON KING, J.P. — 1819-1893.

*W. R. King*

WILLIAM ROBINSON KING — 1854-1921.

*W B R King*

WILLIAM BERNARD ROBINSON KING.
1889- —

*King signatures from the "House of Kings".*

*Collection box in aid of the Navvy Mission Society owned by*
*Mrs King of Hull.*

*The King family at The Mount, West Burton.*

*H. T. Robinson founder of the Robinson Memorial C of E School, West Burton.*

*Bill King with his mother Florence Muriel King, née Theed.*

As ye have therefore received Christ Jesus the
Lord, so walk ye in Him: rooted and built up in Him,
and stablished in the faith, as ye have been taught.
COL. ii. 6, 7.

*1906.* German Measles

Had slight attack of German Measles.
Jan. 14th  whooper O.T.C. L had photographs taken.
Tough.   Shot at Hythe. Return'd, New City range.
26.  Went back to School  Middle 4. B Holroe.
Started Greek
Feb. 27th  My Brother Bob had an accident at Rugby
Dealt with Sanglini & dard frame Shock & hlangle.

March 2nd  I went to Cambridge for the Funeral on Mar. 8.
5th  Went back to Fotheston for 10 days.
15  Return'd to School.

April 11th  Came back for Easter.
27 & 6  had Influenza for some week.

May 10th  Went to London. Played Netball York. Zoo
Westminster House of Parliament & Westminster Abbey.
Went 15th to the St Lions Wembley.
12. Went back to School.

June

O Jesus, I have promised
To serve Thee to the end,
O give me grace to follow
My Master and my Friend!

July 9th  Went up to Rugby to shoot for Cadet.
"  Back to Fotheston.
30 Came home to Fotheston.  3 days early owing to
slight attack of Influenza, also pink-eye.

Aug.  Got drawing prize.
Constance Brenda came for the holidays
Bathed in sea for 1st time.

Sept.  Swe got the Inkland table.

Oct.

Nov.  Played for home at football (tie)
Dec.  Got Influenza & pink-eye.
Stayed at Langtleam Hotel. Saw "Raffles."

*Bill King's diary 1906.*

companies were often financed by middle class families who employed local men to slave away firstly to identify deposits and then to mine as fast, and for as long, as they could endure. Lead prices determined the rental and royalty values on each deposit. Families such as the Others, Metcalfes, Winns, Westgarths and Harkers were mine owners, financiers and managers who bought mineral rights, effectively gambling on the abundance of the deposit. The exchange of agreements between distant agents in cities and their clients, the actual landowners, were sometimes so slow as to allow mining operations on a good deposit to remove large quantities of lead before revised royalties kicked in.

The Winn brothers, Parson John and solicitor George, first ventured into lead speculation in 1844. They took a prospecting licence for the notorious Stags Fell vein, belonging to Lord Wharncliffe, on the basis that they had a two year period to assess the vein and then, if sufficient yield was there, a 21 year lease would be negotiated. The prospects were good, a mining gang was assembled, the smelter built and production started with excellent yields of high quality product. However, in February 1850, cattle on the surrounding fells were dying and men deep in the mine were refusing to work in acrid fumes coming from the rock and also percolating up to the surface. The managers advised that a long deep flue was essential if the vein was to be further exploited. The Winns backed out, unprepared to take the risk. They had drawn good profits and it was time to move on. The flue was subsequently financed by their competitors and the mine restarted in early 1860 and by December a year's production, 63 tons, was loaded at Richmond Station, representing a small fortune. On hearing this the Winns were very put out, and decided to return to lead prospecting in 1861, taking a lease on the Sargill Mine near Askrigg and trading as The Sargill Mining Company. The lease was with Lowther Estates who, on instructions from Lord Lonsdale, had progressively acquired one of the largest mineral portfolios in the country.

Reverend John was regarded by the locals as a "close and tight fisted owd bugger". Production in Sargill was known to have fallen, but the quality had been good. A railway line was being laid from Northallerton through Wensleydale, stopping at Hawes and Redmire, connecting to the line between Carlisle and industrial Yorkshire and Lancashire which promised lower transport costs. Long term prospects were good. However, things didn't turn out that way as the railway's progress was slower than they anticipated and the ore had to be smelted. The nearest available smelter was over the hill near Kettlewell, at the top of Wharfedale. The Winns realised they had failed to think their investment through. The costs associated with the long hilly journey to the smelter, using pack ponies, would be prohibitive and, once there, the smelting charges would be non-negotiable. They couldn't walk away and lose their capital invested so they took courage, built a smelter and employed extra labour. Very soon their yield fell and word got round that at last the Winn brothers had come to grief.

Early one morning the brothers were at the now silent Sargill mine discussing their problem when an old miner, David Harker, came over the hill from Swaledale. Ignoring them, he strode past, took a candle from his coat, lit it and went to enter the mine. The Winn brothers watched, expecting some acknowledgement, annoyed by the intrusion, but they got no apology. They waited for him to emerge and when he did so he ignored them again. John Winn shouted at him to explain himself.

"I've come to look for lead." said Harker. "It's rare scarce by look't and ah needs to look more."

"Well get on and work now man for tis still in the forenoon and send us word," said the Parson.

"Nah I mun 'ave a bargain on paper fust, I don't mistrust ye mind, but that's the way of me business."

Reluctantly they agreed on the spot, that whatever lead was produced in the first six months, they would receive only a token levy per bing, the volume of measurement of the day. This would help establish Harker and would get the mine back into operation to benefit the Winns. No lead, no pay, for either party. The necessary paper was hastily drawn up by legal brother George who told Harker he must go to the office in Askrigg to sign and to have the document properly witnessed. For Harker this was a considerable extra distance to travel, but he did so without question and made his mark, witnessed by the clerk.

After five months the Winns returned to the mine to review progress and estimate their royalties. What they found made them furious. Harker, with the help of a few friends, had built a dam at the back of the shaft, blocking the small stream that flowed along the floor. This accumulated a head of water. Having completely sealed the tunnel they allowed time for the tunnel, beyond the wall, to fill and then they burst the dam, at some great risk to themselves. The water flushed out the passage floor to expose a rich seam of quality lead lying beneath. Bursting and flushing was a technique used only by expert miners and to avoid being drowned, as the dam burst, they built a high shelf onto which they jumped as the water rushed out and where they remained until the flood subsided.

Mean old Parson Winn was having none of this and accused Harker of hiding the truth from them when he first surveyed the mine assuring them there was little ore to be got. Harker, having made his mark, had sent word back to Swaledale saying he needed some loyal supporters to come and work night and day. Within two weeks they completed their damming. They flushed and then mined as fast as they could intending to work right through to the end of the six month agreement, paying no royalties and then to return home all the richer. There was no way that the Winns could prove anything untoward, the miner had speculated just as they had on an unknown situation. They had no practical experience of lead extraction, but Harker had. The agreement stood, Harker and his friends decided to carry on, the mine prospered and was eventually sold to Henry Pease of the Darlington banking family in 1867.

The railway eventually reached Hawes in 1877, by which time lead extraction from Wensleydale was becoming uneconomic as veins were exhausted. The railway company had no regrets as lead was replaced by large flag stones, mined from above the town of Hawes, to pave city streets around Britain. Miners became quarrymen sending away 15,000 tons each month from the station. Steam lifts were used to raise the hewn stone onto the wagons thus speeding the process, reducing labour costs and making a considerable profit for the railway as tonnages increased.

Lead mining had been an important investment for banks, in particular the Swaledale & Wensleydale branch in Hawes. The Other family had appointed Oswald Routh Whalley as their manager when the branch opened in 1842 and he remained in that position until his death in 1888. The Whalley family had lived in the dale since the reign of Richard III when royal bishops had appointed Sir James Whalley, priest, to sing daily services at Hawes chapel for a year, paying him seven marks for his duties. There are still members of the Whalley family living in and around Hawes.

Not long after the failure of their lead mine investment, Solicitor Winn's eldest son George Junior came "to an untimely end." It was a Saturday. He instructed the groom to harness their best and fittest cob into the gig for him to travel to Richmond where he had arranged to lunch with friends. Having eaten well he set off on the road to Leyburn, over bleak moorland with the cold wind sinking under his cloak, serge suit and shirt. He was going for an early dinner with H. T. Robinson of The Cliff, to the east of Leyburn, after which he intended to call at the Chantry in West Witton, five miles further west, to visit his fiancée, Miss Emma Clarkson, for a late night drink. Henry and George enjoyed their repast discussing the various happenings up and down the Dale accompanied by the usual excellent wine from the Robinson cellar. George then asked the butler to instruct their groom to set the cob back in the shafts and he headed off up the Dale to his beloved's home which he reached soon after eight. The following Tuesday James Clarkson Winn wrote from Askrigg to his wife Jane who was staying at The Osborne in Bournemouth. The envelope has two post marks one for Bournemouth and the second is Bedale April 25 1876.

*"My Dearest Jinnie,*

*I have just rec'd your nice kind letter and I am thankful to be able to say that we all seem to bear our sad affliction with greater strength than one would have thought – tho' of course we are fully aware that our loss is great indeed, and one that can never be repaired. My poor old father and mother do feel this trial most keenly. My poor dear brother had been at dinner at The Cliff to meet the directors[65] who have retired and left Leyburn about a quarter to eight and came to Chantry stayed there*

---

65    Directors of the Swaledale & Wensleydale Bank.

*till about 11 when he started for Askrigg he had lighted lamps. The night was unusually dark and he appears to have missed his way in going into the ford and got into that ill-fated pool just below the ordinary course.*

*I am thankful to be able to say that I was up here on Wednesday night and we were talking about his going to Leyburn and I asked him to come and stay the night with me on his way back as I had Dr Routh with me and I thought it would be another inducement for him to come to me. Oh if he had but done so. He however said he would come down on Sunday. I was just starting to walk to church[66] when the policeman passed me on a horse. I asked what was the matter and he said there is a gentleman drowned. It at once occurred to me that poor Geo was coming from Leyburn and it might be him. I turned back got my horse and galloped to the sad spot.*

*I found that my fears were too well founded. The body was removed to Carperby Inquest. Today the corpse comes here this afternoon funeral tomorrow at 2. Only the Clarksons, Baker, Routh, Whaly and Baldeston are asked.*

*I do feel I have lost the only one I had to look to for advice in any thing. You know how very highly I prized his opinions.*

*All send their kindest love and may God bless you my darling and help you to bear this terrible loss your ever loving husband J. C. Winn.*

*I am thankful that Routh is here. He is with me now. Remains till after Wednesday he is very kind and very useful. J. Chapman and R. Hutchinson were all night last night they both do deeply mourn one's and their loss. We will some of us come to you as soon as possible. I will come the first hour I can leave but I feel a great duty devolving on me now, which believe me shall be carried out to the best of my ability to you all. I dare say I shall not be able to write to you tomorrow.*

*Oh Jinnie, I <u>dread tomorrow</u> but I will send you a telegram in the evening to say how we are I know you will be anxious to hear.*

---

66    St Andrew's Church Aysgarth.

*Good bye my darling.*

*Half past one Lizzie*[67] *has just arrived says Mr Stephenson was uncommonly kind and she met with great kindness all the way. She got to York at 10.30 last night.*

Normally George and the pony would easily have seen their way home, but it was black and his eyes would not adjust, nor probably could the pony's. It took two hours in the cold damp air to reach Aysgarth, some five miles further up the dale. On the way he met just one person travelling on foot, heading to Leyburn, who shouted good night adding, "good luck". Just half a mile on, they heard the roar of the river as they approached the ford at Harper Wath. The track down to the river was narrow and one wheel mounted the bank of the track and unbalanced the gig forcing the pony straight across the river into deep water and off the line of the ford which went diagonally upstream.

George never arrived back in Askrigg. The groom, who had waited up, woke only once from his dozing thinking he had heard wheels approaching. He went out, nobody there. He looked at the stable yard clock, it was ten minutes to one and the guv'nor's son had not returned, so he must have decided to stay away the night. Next morning, at dawn, a labourer crossing the river on the narrow foot bridge by the ford, noticed the gig with its wheels wedged against a rock in the stream with the dead pony still in the shafts. George's body had been washed downstream towards Aysgarth Falls and when it was recovered later, to be laid out at the inquest in Carperby, it was reported that George's watch had stopped at ten to one, the same time as the groom had heard the sound of carriage wheels in the stable yard in Askrigg – or so the story goes. George was much missed by his friends who placed a memorial window and plaque in Askrigg Church. Emma Clarkson later committed suicide by putting a pistol to her heart as she lay in bed.[68]

When she was about twelve Jane Ritchie rescued a large portrait photo of George from a family furniture store as she thought he was good looking

---

67    J. C. Winn's sister Elizabeth Ann Winn had probably travelled from Scarborough.

68    October 12th 1884 aged 32.

but her father persuaded her to let him burn it as he didn't think he was a very suitable 'pin-up'! All photos of George, and the family have several, show his left profile: obviously a very deliberate pose on his part!

The final quarter of the 19th century was one of great change. Road metalling was gradually providing a smoother surface in readiness for steam and internal combustion to replace horse power. Railways were being pushed out into the British countryside connecting towns to cities, ports to industry, mines and quarries to factories, and along every route there were village communities suddenly being pulled into a new era. The Industrial Revolution was still going apace and the British Empire was expanding. Exports of every imaginable kind were being shipped thousands of sea miles and the holds of returning ships were filled with food cheaper than that produced in Britain. Farming suffered while other industries thrived and the workers in these places, fortunate to have jobs, were experiencing living standards their forebears had only dreamt of when they left the villages of their birth blindly heading for industrial prosperity. However, mechanisation was putting more and more people out of work and industrial poverty was once more increasing with social unrest simmering as the rich got richer and many of the poor slipped back into abject poverty. In Wensleydale, as in most farming areas, life stood relatively still and the status quo existed.

James Clarkson Winn was George and Elizabeth's second son and he was brought up in the family home, Winnville, now The White Rose Hotel, in Askrigg with his brothers George and William and his three sisters. He married Jane Other, daughter of Christopher Other and his first wife Anne Stackhouse. He was Justice of the Peace, County Councillor, Trustee of the Robinson Memorial School in West Burton, and Chairman of the Board & Union, which controlled the poor house and Board school. He was a director of the Swaledale & Wensleydale Bank and it was he who worked with Jonathan Backhouse to merge their banks with Barclays. Not a lot happened in the two Dales that he didn't know about. He joined the 12th North Yorkshire Rifle Volunteers (the Upper Wensleydale Company) on March 6th 1860 as ensign at a meeting at Palmer Flatt along with Capt. Frank Chapman of Gun, Rod & Rifle fame. He was promoted to lieutenant on 17th May 1869 and resigned in 1872.

James and Jane were great benefactors. They donated a font in memory of their 'three little ones' that died, and the church clock to St. Andrew's at Aysgarth. Unfortunately, the former has become a target of the 21st century fixation with Health & Safety as the chain suspending the lid is now deemed potentially dangerous to babies about to be christened. He also installed the water supply for West Burton.[69] To celebrate the completion of the project James Winn gave a dinner for the workers along with one male member from each household in the village. After dinner he introduced a series of recitations and songs from the company, asking his nephew Jack Winn to start by reciting his poem Cluck, Cluck, Cluck. Twenty further contributions followed and the evening ended with two verses of the National Anthem.

They had only one daughter who survived infancy, but they had eight nieces and nephews some of whom regarded him as a constant source of advice, often linked to a request for financial support. James' sister-in-law, Anne Agnes Other married Dr George Wright when he was practising in Middleham. Dr Wright was the grandson of a Steward of Hornby Castle, near Lancaster, who carried the same surname as the current resident of the Castle, another George Wright, who left the bulk of his estate to his namesake. However, the will was contested on the grounds that the estate was entailed to a distant claimant, one Admiral Tatham. After three costly court actions the Admiral won and Dr Wright was all the poorer.

James had a good relationship with George Wright's eldest son John, called Jack. He practised as a solicitor in Lancaster and married Sarah Charlotte (Lottie), daughter of Mrs Henry Illingworth Bowring[70] of Allerton Hall, Gledhow, Leeds. They bought Halton Park,[71] near the Crook of Lune. They had no children and appear, from letters, to have been generous people. For instance, in May 1907, he sent James 50 Cuban cigars, apologising that 150 from the box had already been given away. Jack added that he felt these were very much superior to those he had bought when last in London at the Army & Navy Stores in Victoria

---

69   Since replaced by a mains supply.

70   The Bowrings were a shipping family.

71   Probably bought with Lottie's money.

Street and he was awaiting a further consignment from Manila. On their arrival, he would send samples to West Burton.

Jack used James as his adviser for the property portfolio he inherited from his mother in Coverdale, which she had inherited from her father, Christopher Other Senior. In November 1900, he asked for references for a Thomas Dawson of High Field Farm, Carlton in Coverdale who was applying for the tenancy of a farm at Arkleside. Dawson assured his prospective landlord that he had sufficient cattle and that he would buy 200 ewes without having to borrow, and that all in the Dale spoke well of him. James advised Jack to get a character reference from the local doctor, Dr John Cockcroft – grandfather of Margery Freeman. A favourable reply was duly received from Dr Cockcroft and the tenancy was granted. Sadly Jack died when he was only 53. He had acted for Frances North over the sale of Longber and Feizor farms showing there was no animosity with his mother's sister-in-law.

Jack's brother Christopher, called Christo by the family, married Bessie Burrill, Margery's older half-sister and they were often short of money. Both Jack and James were called upon to pay for their daughters' school fees. On leaving school Anne Agnes' son Hugh Stackhouse Wright became articled to a solicitor in Malton supported by an allowance from his father drawn through the Swaledale & Wensleydale Bank in Richmond. On February 15th 1900 James received a letter from the Richmond bank manager, Mr Walker, about a meeting with Hugh who had informed him that he was "going to join the colours in the struggle in South Africa with the damned Boers". As one of Hugh's trustees he was passing the information on, remarking, "the boy is obviously a high flyer, but unless he sticks to one line, goodness knows where he will come down." Winn duly arranged to meet Hugh at his York Club.

Two days later a letter arrived from Hugh apologising for the fact that he had been unable to meet his Uncle in York as he had a cold and the doctor had informed him it was due to far too much hard work preparing for his legal examinations. James again invited him to the Club for lunch in order to discuss his notion of entering the militia. He had noted that "hard work" was underlined in the letter. Another letter duly arrived from Hugh explaining he already had "Pater's" consent and therefore, he assumed his Uncle's and that, underlined once more, "the other man", namely Walker, must consequently give his consent and allow him the necessary cash to buy his military uniform and tropical travelling equipment. Hugh stressed he had not time to meet his Uncle for lunch, adding he would delay his exams and hard work, "to proceed straight way to Chelsea Barracks" where, Colonel Hay of the 8th West Yorkshires, advised him he should go to learn drill for a month before actually applying for his commission. In closing, he added he thought it very wise of his father to agree as had he not, there would have been a row as his Country desperately needed him.

Later in the week Hugh sent James another letter confirming that Colonel Hay wanted him to be ready for Chelsea in March, so could Uncle James please proceed and organise the necessary funds, as his going to Africa was surely better than his father continuing to finance his legal career. Time passed before another letter arrived, this time from Blackdown Barracks in Hampshire, on regimental stationary embossed with a leaping lion crest and underneath "The King's Own Rifles". There was an enclosure for his Aunt Jane thanking her for the chair she had paid for. It was "a ripper, very comfortable and makes my quarters look most palatial". He explained that the barracks were awful, miles from civilisation. There were neither tennis courts nor a cricket pitch, so he had asked his brother Jack if he could have his motor bike. He tells his Uncle that Pater has stopped his allowance of £100 per annum, on the grounds of being unable to afford it any longer so he now had only £50 yearly from his Trust. This in his view, was entirely insufficient, as he had to keep up with the other chaps in the regiment, in fact "it's an awful bother and I would be most awfully obliged for your advice." He points out that all will be well in five years when he has his own regimental company and, finally can the anticipated cash go into his new bank account at Cox & Co, 16 Charing Cross. Had the family bank moved him on or had he left them, possibly with an overdraft?

The last communication in the archive to Uncle James was posted on November 4th 1902 from Natal, in which Hugh requests that as the war was now over he needed more money in his account at Cox & Co. African things were twice the price of things at home and he had previously written to Walker, but there had been no response probably because of the "Africans' inefficiency with such things as postal deliveries". He expected soon to be posted to Malta and after time there recuperating he would get four months home leave. Meanwhile, he was having no end of fun hunting wild animals, shooting, playing Polo and tennis and going to dances, but he found the colonial people uninteresting with little to say of any consequence. He later married Constance Sybil Tunstill of Reedyford House, Nelson and Thornton Lodge, Thornton Rust. They lived in Heysham Lodge, his mother having moved to Morecambe.[72]

James' nephew Jack Winn was also in South Africa in 1902 and in a letter to his Uncle marked censored, he asks for advice, and cash, in order to become an articled clerk to a busy lawyer who is about to become a Member of Parliament in Cape Town. He emphasises it's the best chance he has ever had, and with £300 per annum, he could succeed and repay his debts as soon as he qualified. A hand written letter duly arrived from the solicitor, Mr Percy E.R. Whitby dated 9th May 1902. He had offices in Australia as well as South Africa, but understandably he questioned Jack's commitment to work.

Jack's father, William Winn, who had taken over his father's law practice in Askrigg, was exposed as dishonest in a dramatic court case towards the end of the century. James who had always strived hard to be fair, understanding and, above all, scrupulously honest must have been mortified when his younger brother appeared in court charged with misappropriation of funds held in trust. When he became aware of the trouble he bailed his brother out of some of his debts, but as the full story emerged he set about helping his nephews to move abroad. All photographs of William and his family, except for a few when the children were small, were removed from the West Burton Winn's family album.

The much trusted managing clerk of the Askrigg practice, James Yelland, had served the family for some thirty five years. Reluctantly, he sent a

---

72  Christo Wright's daughter Nancy died at 4½ aged 5 Royd's Avenue, Morecambe which may have been Ann Agnes' home. As Heysham Lodge was a Wright property, Christopher Other may have bought the Morecambe house so she would have somewhere to live if she outlived her husband.

full legal document of four hand written pages to the Law Society calling for William Edmund Metcalfe Winn to be struck off the Rolls of the High Court of Justice. Yelland stated that he had been "thrust out for daring to discover the misappropriation of considerable sums of money" as well as for his temerity in claiming outstanding salary. His statement claimed that William was insolvent, carrying considerable debts and living on his "takings" from the accounts of local individuals and institutions. William had placed false values on properties as security on loans taken with Barclays Bank at around the time of the merger with the Swaledale & Wensleydale Bank. In addition, he collected rents on behalf of clients which he had pocketed. Some beneficiaries of various Trusts, managed by Winn, became sufficiently suspicious to instigate High Court proceedings which were held in abeyance at the insistence of the family. Winn publically implicated Yelland as the thief, to which Yelland responded: "A more vile proceeding and attempt to ruin the character of the family's old Clerk could not well be conceived." Yelland concluded his statement pointing out that the family of William Winn lived in apparent affluence, even keeping race horses. Bearing this in mind "various legal gentlemen and other persons of repute should be called to testify."

James Winn was bombarded with handwritten letters from the senior partner of Archer, Parkin & Archer in the county town of Middlesbrough on behalf of their client W. E. M. Winn. All were polite, but determined to cover his tracks and settle the debts incurred due to an addiction to gambling. James had been the main negotiator of the merger of the Swaledale & Wensleydale Bank with Barclays, and it can be safely assumed, he had to walk very carefully in protecting his family's name. To boot, he also held many public and institutional appointments and had his own reputation to protect. The matter was resolved and the guilty Winn moved to London. He was struck off by the Law Society and only returned to Askrigg to be buried.

However, some light relief came to James in those stern days of late Victorianism. One example was the celebration of the 100th birthday of Betty Webster, born in Muker in Swaledale on February 25th 1790. He sent a letter to Buckingham Palace with this information and, by return post, a reply arrived from Major General the Right Honourable Sir J. C.

Cowell KCB at Windsor Castle asking for legal verification. There was no formal birth certificate, only a record in the Muker Parish book of births, marriages and deaths of Elizabeth Webster which did not comply with the name originally forwarded to London, Betty Webster. The Vicar was of the view that girls registered as Elizabeth but called Betty should be so christened. All the correspondence from Windsor Castle is written in copper plate on crested vellum and one informs Winn that Her Majesty had approved the Vicar's view and commanded Cowell to write the necessary letter. In return James sent Her Majesty a photographic portrait of Betty Webster to which Cowell replied thanking him saying that Her Majesty was pleased with the likeness.

Another letter written in pencil, in a firm but shaky hand, came from one of Winn's Swaledale tenants, a Mr E Horn of Deer Park, Harkerside, Grinton. He complained about the state of his cow house as his calves had died from pneumonia the previous year and his recently born calves needed dry beds. He added that he had sufficient funds for the coming year as he had a very good five year old Shorthorn cow which was far too good for his poor farm, but which would suit a gentleman. It was to be shown at Reeth Show and would be on sale there. There is no record of the outcome, but one assumes the landlord fixed the roof and Horn sold the cow, possibly to James Winn.

In 1883, James was to take his wife on her first trip abroad. He was required to have a passport, a new introduction to allow government control over foreign travel. He duly applied to the Foreign Office who issued him with a large vellum document headed with the Royal Coat of Arms, numbered 20813, again handwritten in copper plate, and signed by Lord Granville, Her Majesty's Principal Secretary of State for Foreign Affairs and Lord Warden of the Cinque Ports stating: "To all to whom it may concern to allow James Clarkson Winn (British Subject) and his wife (*unnamed*) to pass freely without let or hindrance and to afford him every assistance and protection of which he may stand in need".

In 1890, Winn received a long letter from Joseph Moor, a farmer for 53 years, who was reaching the end of his days saying that he had one last request to make of Winn. He hoped if he drew Winn's attention to the matter of the decline of the annual Askrigg Moor July Fair which was in grave danger of failing completely, that Winn could do something to save it. The reason for the problem, he well knew, was because in July he always "got" his hay harvest helped by young men from Hawes "wroughting it" for him on dry days while on wet days they remained at their ordinary occupations. However these good men always stipulated they would never come on the Fair day, rain or shine. No longer were they so stipulating however. The reasons, Moor explained, were the alternative attractions to the traditional fair of cheap trips on railway trains and the band concert at Hardraw Force. There was another problem, the beer tents were suddenly being closed at 7 p.m. by order of the court of which Mr Winn was a member. The simple reason for this was that one evening in the recent past, quarrelling and brawling had taken place amongst some young men. Hence, the Askrigg policeman had requested that the local bench refuse the extension of licensing hours in future. The Justices did as they were asked. Moor then explained that not only did publicans erect beer tents for local farmers, the mines now did likewise offering hospitality to friends, workers and relations. His point was that if the licensed hours were only from 9 a.m. till 7 p.m. there was not enough time for tent holders to recoup their expenses as farmers could not arrive till after the noon at the earliest, having risen early to milk cows, feed calves and turn the cheeses, by which time the morning had gone. He had read in the papers that factory workers benefitted from work people's day holidays in industrial towns, but as local farm servants had no such facility apart from the Fair, it was their only chance of a holiday.

# Chapter 10

## Dyers & Bleachers and Ironmongers

The King family has a long history in Wensleydale and Swaledale. William Robinson King Senior (1819–1893) was born and brought up in Hull. His grandfather Henry had travelled there in 1744, forsaking the frugal rural life of farming and wool processing in the dales for a chance to profit from the town's growing maritime economy. The Kings were originally Stewards of Richmond Castle, beside the River Swale, who established themselves as wool buyers, dyers and bleachers in West Witton in Wensleydale supplying local spinners, knitters and weavers. In the mid-17th century, life was hard for rural business, especially farmers in the remote northern hills. The Kings were ambitious, intelligent and hardworking and, having acquired property, they were voting yeomen enabling them to become an integral and influential part of the commercial community of Wensleydale. Henry had been anxious to make his own mark in life, knowing he would be unlikely to do so either in farming or the wool trade. Around the coastal ports and the northern estuaries of Yorkshire there were booming fishing fleets, ship building yards and merchants in national and international trade.

In 1754, Henry saw an advertisement in the Yorkshire Post announcing the sale of an ironmongery and toolmaking business in the small port of Hull, 150 miles to the east of West Witton. No doubt, Henry discussed the possibilities with his father and his wife,[73] and it was agreed he should see if the business had potential. Henry needed no encouragement and he saddled up and rode off to explore the town, the port and the business in question. He had probably never strayed far from home before and his journey took him across the Vale of York where he must have marvelled at

---

73    Ann Calvert of West Witton.

the mixed farming and comparative prosperity of the farmers compared to his friends and neighbours in Wensleydale. As he approached York, there were fields of vegetables with huge groups of labourers harvesting and loading wagons. He then crossed the southern edge of the Wolds, which were then bare sheep walks, passing humble cottages lived in by poor labouring families. Settlements were few and far between, but as he rode over the southern edge of the Wolds he would have marvelled at the wide River Humber sweeping round and gleaming below; the flow crowded with craft of all types heading inland to town ports before the tide turned to carry loaded ships away out to sea. As he rode along the shore line, he was surrounded by a hive of activity in the boat yards and wharves where rope and sail makers busily worked. By the time he entered the town of Hull his anticipation of what was about to come was at bursting point. He knew he had to control his excitement as an accurate decision had to be made about diversifying away from wool dyeing and bleaching, and farming, to invest a considerable proportion of family wealth in a strange place amongst people he didn't know and in a business of which he had no experience.

After five days he returned home confident and excited at the prospect of owning the workshop and ironmongers business belonging to Mr William Southern of Church Lane, Hull. Southern had established a reputation as an expert craftsman toolmaker with a particular speciality in the manufacture of wood planes. In Hull docks and all along the banks of the Humber, a variety of wooden boats were being built with the tools of the trade: the saw, adze and plane. As the Empire expanded, Henry could see every reason to take the business and establish a sound future for the family in a growing economy. On the ride back to Wensleydale he could think of little else, he hardly noticed the work in the fields or the villages he passed through, and even during his overnight stop, near Thirsk, he sat by the roaring fire alone in his thoughts paying little attention to fellow travellers. He knew this would be the right move for him and his own family, but Hull was a long way off and people didn't travel much, hence he would be moving a good way off from the rest of his relatives. How he managed to raise the money is not recorded.

In those days, ironmongers were the most important and prosperous business in any High Street, stocking more individual items than other trades as well as offering a repair service for tin, iron, pewter, brass and copper goods. They sold lamps, oven ranges, tools, nails, screws, brushes, brooms, saucepans, kettles, ropes and wire. Their wares were suspended from the shop ceiling and hung on walls. Smaller items were stored in an array of small labelled drawers and the smell of tarred twine and rope pervaded the shop and warehouse. They employed men skilled in a variety of crafts who sat at benches in a wooden floored workshop behind the shop.

Southern had developed specialist mitre planes of wrought iron, beautifully dovetailed, which today are collectors' items. Within two years Kings Ironmongers and Tool Manufacturers of Hull moved into larger premises, adding a forge shop, a larger workshop and six cottages for senior employees, something few business men bothered to do at the time. The new premises were in the Market Place, a busy thoroughfare with people coming in to town from surrounding rural areas where the middle class economy flourished. Henry also saw another opportunity which he took by opening a furniture store, supplying all that could be asked for by people coming into the town six days a week. His third son Samuel joined him when he left school and soon became a partner with a remit to expand the retail furnishings business.

By 1776, Henry was exhausted by working seven days a week and often for eighteen hours a day. Samuel proved capable and equally hard working with a sound natural business sense. Henry had every confidence in him which allowed him to retire. The son was more gregarious than the father and when time allowed he walked round the town square talking with other men of industry and commerce. He also spoke to the mariners whose ships packed the harbour to load, or unload, cargo then heading away to other rivers and ports from where they gathered interesting information on new ideas and emerging markets both at home and abroad. He also studied newspapers looking for the next opportunity. In 1780, he read an advertisement from the Carron Iron Foundry in Falkirk which interested him. He sent word of his interest, and after an exchange of letters a date and place for a meeting were agreed. He met the owner of the company and they talked about their different business interests and discussed mutual ambitions. They agreed to develop commercial links to improve the output of the forging process in Scotland to meet the growing demand for King's planes and other tools around the world. Samuel's work load gradually increased and after much thought he decided he needed a partner to share the capital investment and management of the expanding business and increasing workforce. At one of his evening meetings in a Hull coffee shop, he met John Spence, a man in his late fifties, who had recently come to live in Hull having worked in building and construction in the new colony of New Zealand. He seemed honest and hard-working, they enjoyed each other's company and after considerable discussion, they agreed to form Spence & King, with John introducing additional capital to fund further expansion plans.

After nine happy years of working together, Spence died in 1790, leaving Samuel with the entire share capital as Spence had no heirs. The work load once more became very demanding, but the large workforce was managed by reliable and trusted foremen. However, the sales staff, business development and office supervision needed more attention than he could give. He invited a nephew from Wensleydale who had impressed him, another Henry, to join the family business which by then was one of the main employers in the town. Henry became a partner in 1806 taking up residence above the workshops and Samuel moved into a house some distance from the business. Henry married Jane Robinson whose father, William Robinson, was from the ancient wealthy family originally from Teesdale,[74] who lived at Edgley, a house a few miles from the King's home in West Witton.

According to the booklet 'The House of Kings', Kings of Hull employed 37,000 people in 1811 and over the next thirty years more workshop space was added. In Henry's capable hands, product development and improving technology increased manufacturing capacity. Water power was used to drive more lathes, forges and steam hammers. In 1843, he

---

74    The senior branch of the Robinson family had rebuilt Rokeby near Barnard Castle after it was sacked by the Scots following the Battle of Bannockburn. Earlier, a William Robinson had been a longbow archer at Agincourt and had come from Carleton-juxta-Snayth, a village west of Goole.

introduced his second[75] son, William Robinson King to the firm. He and Jane had followed family custom by giving William her family name, Robinson, as his second name to celebrate the joining of two respected Wensleydale families.

William Robinson King married Margaret Other,[76] sister of Christopher Other in Bedale Parish Church in 1844. His older brother the Reverend Henry King[77] officiated. William had returned to Wensleydale to find a wife just as his father had done. He was always interested in what his cousins were doing and on one of his visits he heard that one of them, Henry James King, was about to take a large rented farm on Lord Bolton's estate across the river from West Witton. The 2,500 acres included an area of medieval lynchet terracing created hundreds of years before to make ploughing and cropping easier for the working oxen and labourers to improve productivity. The farmhouse and buildings had been improved during the period following the Napoleonic wars when farm profits and rents had been high. Henry James King[78] moved to the West Bolton Farm in 1846. William congratulated him, but had no regrets that he had deserted the traditional bucolic family life for industry. He and Margaret returned happily to their business and Hull society.

In 1847, William Robinson King formed a partnership with a local businessman Robert Peach and arranged for his father to retire. The business would pay him an annuity, thus clearing the ground for his next planned expansion. Sadly, old Henry died in 1850 just missing the Great Exhibition of 1851 held in London's Hyde Park at which he and his son had planned to exhibit for some time. Had he survived he would have been proud to see his son collect a Bronze Medal for their latest wood plane, proudly stamped 'Manufactured by Kings of Hull, England'. William bought his father's shares from his mother and before he retired in 1866 he agreed to place 80% of his shareholding as the basis of a Stock Exchange Issue which met with great enthusiasm in the City of London.

---

75    His elder son had gone into the Church.
76    When Margaret died William married Jane Wade probably the sister of William Wade who had been his best man at his first wedding.
77    Rev Henry King became Vicar of Kirby Stephen.
78    In retirement he lived at Briar House in Redmire.

William remained Chairman of the public limited liability company. He died in 1893 having just passed the Chairmanship to his son of the same name.

Toolmaking stopped during the severe recessionary period of the early 20th century. King & Co. concentrated on their builders merchants, retail counters and the specialist supply departments working closely with architects and builders, supplying entire ranges of household fittings, heating and plumbing equipment and furniture to an expanding and flourishing population. The premises were mostly conversions of old buildings in which there had been a number of fires over time so a rebuilding programme of improvements to workshops and show rooms was undertaken just prior to WW1. In 1916, a German Zeppelin appeared over the city dropping its load of incendiary bombs, one of which made a direct hit on the main shop near Holy Trinity Church in the centre of Hull.

The First World War totally changed company strategy. The nation had been through a long period of recession over a decade prior to the outbreak of war. Hull's fishing industry nevertheless continued to thrive forming an economic buffer to the rest of the business community. Kings responded as new housing and modernisation came to a halt. While sales of furniture, kitchen and bathroom supplies declines, fabrication and manufacturing for government contracts boomed. Between the two World Wars King & Co. flourished once more while many businesses failed. It was a similar picture of recession that lead up to the Second War with military contracts profitably occupying the labour force. Normal trading conditions improved after the second war and King & Co. expanded by acquiring a small foundry in Darlington.

William R. King Junior died in 1921 leaving a thriving company of which he was very proud. He was mourned throughout the business community of Hull where he had practised as a solicitor. When he married Florence Muriel Theed[79], the Vicar of North Ferriby's daughter, he built The

---

79    Florence's great great grandfather was William Hey (1736-1819) who was a famous Leeds surgeon who founded the Leeds Infirmary. His wife was Alice Banks and her sister Isabella married a Hudson whose son Dr Benjamin Hudson married Ann Robinson from Edgley who endowed the Robinson Memorial School in West Burton built by her brother H. T. Robinson.

Mount[80] in West Burton where they lived until they retired to Folkstone in 1905. The modern housing development built in his garth has been called King Garth. He was a regular churchgoer and stopped to speak to everyone he met as he walked to the post office or village shop. On one occasion, which typified his generosity, he paid the fine of a small village boy[81] who had appeared before the Bench on which King served, for scrumping apples.

He was the first Correspondent of the village school, a post now called the Clerk to the Governors. He drew up a new Trust document for The Robinson Memorial Church of England School as his great uncle, H. T. Robinson, had died before the original deed was signed. William appointed new Trustees for the building who were also the Managers of the School. His successors were not legal men, and they failed to inform the Charity Commission of the appointment of new trustees. It has fallen to his great granddaughter, Jane Ritchie, to seek the help of Richard Nolan, a Cambridge University lawyer who had come to live in West Burton, to rectify the position. The School Governing Body hope to be appointed collectively as the Trustees, as only "the Vicar of the day," and "the owner of Edgley of the day," were deemed to be Trustees.[82]

During the industrial slump between the wars, King & Co. built new head offices in Hull which were opened with great ceremony by Her Majesty the Queen in 1948. The name of King had a national reputation for quality and good service, but British industry was about to change. In 1881 King & Co. had become a Limited Liability Company, adapting to changes in business development at around the time the Swaledale & Wensleydale Bank had been absorbed into the Barclay Banking group in 1899. Many ports around Britain's coast had been able to adapt to larger cargo and container shipping, but the River Humber had relied on its fishing fleet for too long, as had Grimsby, and as the fishing port of Hull lost its many small family-owned trawler businesses to large

---

80    The farmhouse that had previously been on the site was moved over the road to Moorside, now the Cat Pottery.

81    George Miller.

82    The Charity Commission decided in 2013 that the School site should be vested with the Official Custodian for Charities.

fishery companies, the Humber became strangely quiet. The King family retained their shareholding, but executive control in the company was passed to professional management. Two centuries of Kings in Hull had come to an end.

The last member of the family to play a role in the firm was Professor William Bernard Robinson King OBE who chaired his first Company A.G.M. on May 10th 1960. This was held as usual, at the Royal Station Hotel in Hull, where he announced with regret that the company had made a loss for the first time in its history. However, he went on, the Darlington business was maintaining sales while the industrial climate was generally one of depression. Hull was suffering from the dramatic decline of the fishing fleet which was leaving huge gaps in the domestic economy of thousands of families. In addition debtor level was high and, although the government had lifted post war credit restrictions, customers generally were not responding to this incentive by investing in new ventures.

# Chapter 11

# Bill King

William Bernard Robinson King (Bill) was born at West Burton on November 12th 1889 at 10.30 in the morning. His father William Robinson King Junior had married Florence Muriel Theed at Ferriby, near Hull, on the 11th February 1885 when the marriage service was conducted by the father of the bride, Rev. T. M. Theed, Vicar of North Ferriby, who later baptized their children.[83] Bill was baptized on 21st January 1890 having spent his first day out of doors on New Year's Eve 1889 when his mother started his Life Record Book recording every event of his growing up, no matter how small: from dates of injections, clothes shortenings as they passed down the family and of holidays in Hull visiting grandfather William Robinson King Senior, past Chairman of Kings Limited, who died in August 1893.

Mumps, scarlet fever, measles, whooping cough and influenza came and went, usually followed by periods of convalescence. For Christmas 1897 Bill was given a chinchilla kitten by his mother and the following year he was fitted for his first Eton[84] suit and received an egg box from his father so that he could display the bird's eggs he collected in springtime from the countryside around his home. He was proud of the variety of nests he found in the hedges, woods and on the moorland edge above the village. Each egg collected was neatly pierced either end with a black thorn and gently blown clean. He climbed high into trees stretching out dangerously to feel for eggs in nests sometimes jerking away as a disturbed hen took fright or occasionally pecked the intruding hand. The present 'Health

---

83    The Theeds retired to Leyburn and lived at Daisy Bank. Rev. T. M. Theed and his son-in-law shared an interest in wood carving.

84    A generic name for a type of young man's suit.

& Safety' culture would not condone the risk of allowing a small boy to go out on lone nesting quests, but the experience undoubtedly helped establish Bill's ability to tackle extreme challenges and danger in later life.

In April 1899, aged 10, Bill's governess Miss Andrews left and he followed his older brother[85] to a prep school in Keswick in the Cumberland fells. However, at the end of the summer term he left, "It did not suit him." The Victorian public school system was challenging for any young man and this was not long after Charles Dickens had come north to visit the 'hard' schools of Bowes which he used as material for his books Nicholas Nickleby and Oliver Twist. In October, he started at Mr Hough's School in Aysgarth, in the building at the top of Church Bank. When the school outgrew its facilities, the building first became a sanatorium for Tuberculosis sufferers and then a Youth Hostel before being closed at the end of the 20th century. It is now a book store. Aysgarth School re-established itself in Newton le Willows, near Bedale, and remains a preparatory school for leading public schools such as Eton, Winchester and Shrewsbury. The mural at the west end of St. Andrew's Church is in memory of Rev. C. T. Hales[86] and a school magazine shows a picture of the Aysgarth Middle Falls and the pool below captioned 'Our swimming pool'.

Despite Aysgarth being the next village to West Burton, Bill became a boarder. He was not very good at most sports, as he recorded in the small book that had now become his diary. He did though excel at high jumping. 1901 started with the death of Queen Victoria and a few days later Bill heard the broadcast of the Proclamation of the new King from St. James' Palace in London on a very crackly wireless. Bobbie started at his public school, Rossal in Cumberland, and became referred to as Bob. In April, Bill returned to school in Keswick as Mr Rankilon, who had been tutoring both boys privately at home, had joined the staff there. In June, by then exactly five feet tall, he learnt to swim and shortly after this learnt

---

85    Walter Henry Robinson King called Bobbie by his family.

86    Rev. C. T. Hales was the Head Master who oversaw the move to Newton-le-Willows. It is said that the boys, who sat at the back in the gallery, made too much noise during services, and pressure was put on the school to move.

to ride a bike. He was playing football and enjoyed being in the school team.[87] The King's Coronation was to be celebrated with a week's holiday in July, but King Edward VII was "poorly" so all was postponed until August 9th by which time Bill was already on holiday.

In 1903, aged 14, invitations arrived from friends' mothers inviting him to stay for this or that. His way of life was changing from the casual atmosphere of his family to the formality of most of his friends' parents' homes where any show of emotion had to be concealed and sons and daughters only spent time with their parents for a short time each day. Many of his contemporaries addressed their fathers as Sir, shaking their hands on meeting, never showing any love for one another. The King family was much more informal, with Bill referring to his parents as Mother and Dad. He had to be fitted for a dinner jacket, white shirt, stiff winged collar and black tie to be worn for dinner on these visits. He records attending dances, but not whether he enjoyed them. However, he was in no doubt that life was becoming exciting. In the spring he went to London for the first time and in the summer the family took a holiday in Scotland. In August he shot his first rabbit and made a very small table mat from its skin. During the October half term he shot and stuffed his first hawk after spending the day with the gamekeeper on the grouse moor above West Burton. These flying predators needed to be got rid of with the gun, he was told, to protect young grouse whereas today they are a protected species and fourteen year old boys can certainly not carry guns legally.

By 1904, he was five feet and seven inches tall and went to Uppingham, a public school in Rutland where, in the first term, he won the mathematical prize as well as an award for rifle shooting. The following year his mathematical prowess continued. During the summer term he was confirmed by the Bishop of Peterborough and in the holiday shot his first grouse from his new height of five foot nine inches while weighing in at 9 stones and four pounds. Brother Bob went up to Cambridge. In 1905, his parents left West Burton and went to live in Folkestone.

---

87  One of his skills, not recorded in this little book, was his ability to hypnotise hens by drawing a white chalk line in front of them. He used to place a line of hens across the narrow Front Nook, as the road is called, and another line across the Back Nook.

1906 was a sad year. On February 27th Bob died after being very badly burnt by benzoline which rowing teams rubbed on their hands to harden the skin. Having done this in preparation to row, he lit his pipe. There was a flash explosion and he died of shock almost immediately. The funeral was held in Cambridge on March 2nd. Bill noted in his record simply: "My brother Bob had an accident at College, burnt with benzoline and died from shock 1½ hours after." He never mentioned Bob to his grandchildren, but there is a memorial to Walter Henry Robinson King in the Chapel of Jesus College, Cambridge.

Being young, Bill made a quick recovery. By July he was feeling more cheerful when he was selected for the school rifle team to compete for the public schools' cup at Bisley. Academically, he continued to win prizes. He swam in the sea for the first time off the beach at Scarborough and his father bought a billiard table for the house at Folkestone. Uppingham became the centre of his life and prizes continued to be awarded especially for maths. He learnt to ride a horse, had lessons in physical culture and became a keen member of the Army Cadet Force. In 1907, he started on the long and testing process to get into Cambridge and succeeded. He went up to Jesus College with a first class exhibition award in October 1908, aged 19. The following year he was awarded his University half blue for shooting[88] and on the 27th of April 1911 he became a Freemason. His degree subject was Geology and in 1912 he was awarded the Harkness Scholarship as well as the Geological Survey Award which, before the coming of the Ph.D., was as high as any young geologist could go.

He was awarded a First Class Degree in the Natural Sciences Tripos. He had added Botany to his studies, in place of Physics, enabling him to identify fossilised plants. In his final year at Cambridge, Bill specialised in stratigraphy and he applied his knowledge and understanding of this subject to great effect on both World Wars. In 1912, while still at Jesus College, he applied to join the Geological Survey in London. He came top in the entrance examination and so was appointed to the Survey's only vacancy that year for a field surveyor.

---

88    Full blues were only awarded for rowing, rugby, cricket and football.

During the summer of 1912 he toured Holland and Germany ending up in Prague, little realising the trip would stand him in good stead in his forthcoming career. Northern Europe was not a happy place to be and it was obvious that war was on the cards. Back in Cambridge, academic work was interspersed by geological excursions with the Sedgwick Club to various sites around the country in the company of notable professors. Photographs of these visits can still be seen in the Sedgwick Museum at Cambridge. On 9th October 1914 the news from Germany was not good. Bill was surveying on the Welsh Marches and decided he should join the Reserve of the 7th Royal Welsh Fusiliers in Montgomery. By the 14th he was gazetted. He attended weekend camps and military training while continuing his geological work and an enjoyable social life. By the spring of 1915, the war that was "to be over by Christmas" was entrenched in the farmlands of France and Flanders with little hope of reaching a conclusion.

In April 1915, Major General W. A. Liddell, Deputy Director of Works at the British Army GHQ, requested the services of a geologist to help find water for men and horses and Bill King was chosen for the job. After some six weeks of preparation and briefing in London he was sent to France on June 16th to work for the Engineer-in-Chief. He remained there for the rest of the war apart from taking his leaves when work schedules allowed. He was the only British geologist on the Western Front and was joined by an Australian and a Tasmanian. By comparison, the Germans employed a Geological Team of over twenty.

In May 1916 Lt-Col. Tannatt William Edgeworth David arrived in France with the Australian Mining Corp which had been organised for Gallipoli. Col. David remained with the Corps acting as a geological adviser to the Controllers of Mines of the First, Second and Third Armies until he had an accident on 6th October 1916 when he fell 70 feet down a well near Vimy Ridge. David was a Welshman by birth. He was a born in 1858 in Cardiff and progressed to New College, Oxford where he read Classics graduating in 1880, aged 22. He became fascinated by geology and produced learned papers on the glaciation of the South Wales valleys where huge coal deposits were being exploited.

In 1883, he joined the Geological Survey Team of New South Wales and was responsible for identifying the Hunter Valley coal seam as well as a highly valuable and vast deposit of tin. In 1891, he was elected Professor of Geology at the University of Sydney and it was there that he started to wear 'the old brown hat,' a piece of headwear for which he became famous. In 1907 aged 50, he became interested in Antarctica. Ernest Shackleton invited him to join an expedition when he led the first successful ascent of Mount Erebus, an active volcano, as well as reaching the Magnetic Pole. Prof. David was awarded the King's Polar Medal and made Companion of the Order of St Michael and St George.

When the First World War was declared he was challenged and excited by the prospect of the part he could play. He was also resourceful and determined and had followed the progress of the Boer War in South Africa. This had alerted him to the huge potential of internal combustion engines in battle which would obviously be used in this latest war. Using his considerable reputation and influence, he arranged a meeting with the Minister of Defence in the Australian Government and raised the subject of tunnelling in the European conflict as being a crucially important weapon.

When Col. David had recovered from his fall down the well, Brigadier-General R. N. Henry, Inspector of Mines at GHQ asked him to join his staff and Col. David and Capt. King started to work together, eventually sharing an office. It says much about both men and their respect for each other, that they were not bothered about working for different departments within GHQ or their difference in rank. They concentrated on helping each other resolve practical problems. "I should like to take Capt. King with me" was a frequent request from Col. David when he set out to undertake any fieldwork. Col. David worked on preparing geological maps and organising test borings which were supervised by Lieut. Loftus Hills.[89] David also researched water table heights in relation to rainfall so that mine galleries could be dug without fear of them flooding. These had to be made in chalk above the water table. Capt. King concentrated on finding water and supervised many of the 414 borings for wells, making a comprehensive and detailed recording of them. The scale of

---

89    Assistant Government Geologist of Tasmania.

this war was enormous; the sheer numbers of men and horses, as well as a growing number of vehicles powered by internal combustion meant water supplies were vital. Without water all would come to a standstill: horses, men and motors.

Together David and King made a formed a formidable geological team, and were responsible for what Bill claimed, no doubt correctly, was the biggest bang of WW1 when nineteen mines were exploded simultaneously on the Messines – Wytschaete Ridge on 7th June 1917 at 3.10am. The nearest mine[90] to Lille, 11½ miles away caused the town to experience the sensation of an earthquake shock. Another mine gallery was started to attack The Pimple, a German stronghold on the northern end of Vimy Ridge. In this case mining was carried out in clay under 'no man's land' using a tunnelling machine called the Wombat, developed by another Australian, Col. Stanley Hunter, Professor of Geology from the University of Victoria. The Wombat had the advantage of being able to bore silently through clay or waterlogged chalk. The mine gallery was not in the end used as the Canadians took The Pimple by storm.

In September 1917, Bill King went to have a look at the remains of The Pimple after it had been taken, and he noticed that the conglomerate used in a concrete pill box contained granite pebbles. The Intelligence Staff were not at all pleased at "having to waste a day getting bits of concrete for a very youthful Captain from GHQ to examine!" However, Bill's sharp eyes proved that the neutrality of Holland was being violated as the granite pebbles came from the Rhineland. He was ordered to go to the Foreign Office in London and get "the big geological guns to confirm what you say!" The Dutch responded to the British Government's protest on 22nd November 1917 and a Parliamentary Paper was published in January 1918 on "Transport of traffic across Holland of Materials susceptible of employment as Military Supplies." According to F.W. Shotten, barge-transport of German materials through Holland ceased.[91]

---

90   Ontario.

91   Biographical Memoires of Fellows of The Royal Society Vol. 9, November 1963.

Bill became fondly known as 'Rocks King' by the Royal Engineers with whom he worked, and working with David he established himself as an expert on the science of warfare. The expertise of a geologist was recognised by the new breed of professional soldier and this was acknowledged when he was awarded the Military OBE and was twice mentioned in despatches. WW1 was a static affair fought long and hard from trenches that were the supply routes to the 'mole like' community providing food, water, medical attention and occasional moments of respite. Gallery mining and controlled explosions were adopted by both sides, but unless the geological planning was reliable it could be a total waste of time and men's lives. Col. David's sapper 'diggers'[92] had complete trust in the expertise of the two men.

During his home leave in June 1916, Bill married Margaret Amy Passingham, Dots, as she was called by her friends. They first met in 1913 when he and a fellow Cambridge geologist, Walter Campbell-Smith, known as Grizzly to his friends, were attending the British Association Meeting in Birmingham. During this trip to the Midlands they went to Grizzly's home in Solihull where, by pure coincidence, they met a friend of his called Beatrice Smallwood with whom Dots happened to be staying. The four of them met in a hat shop and it was there that Bill and Dots first set eyes upon one another. It was love at first sight, but the time was really far from right to make any commitments with a serious war on the horizon. They met as much as possible, and Bill took his new love to meet his parents at their home in Folkestone in October 1914. They became engaged and met again in Paris during short leaves from the front in June and September 1915 when Dots worked at Highclere Castle as a masseuse rehabilitating wounded service men. Massage was the precursor to Physiotherapy and didn't have the connotation the word has now!

At the outbreak of war, Lady Carnarvon, the chatelaine of Highclere Castle, near Newbury, suggested to her husband that their enormous home would make a practical and appropriate place for wounded officers to recuperate. His Lordship contacted the War Office and within days a

---

92    This is how the Australians came to be called Diggers.

team of men were brought in to move furniture, pictures and artefacts to make way for wards, medical facilities and offices. It was not long before other large country houses were offered, or requisitioned, for emergency hospitals around Britain.

On a short home leave Bill went to see Dots there and there are photos in both their albums of the two of them in the Highclere grounds. Dots became Mrs Margaret Amy King at a traditional country wedding in Eastnor Parish Church in Herefordshire in June 1916. The best man was a friend of Bill's from Cambridge who was also a friend of Dots from her days at Toft. He was a fellow geologist, Tressilian Charles Nicholas. The ceremony was conducted by the Reverend H. L. Somers Cocks and the reception was held in "Gran's lovely garden". The dinner the night before was at Bosbury House, the home of the Buchanan family[93] where Dots nursed their war-damaged son when she left Highclere. Her grandparents, George Augustus and Catherine Amy Passingham, had moved to the nearby village of Berrow after the death of their grandson, Dots' brother Charles, in Cambridgeshire. After George died, Catherine had moved to a smaller house in Eastnor.

After the Peace of 1918, Bill King was demobilised in 1919, and returned to Cambridge as a Fellow of Jesus College,[94] later becoming the Yates-Goldsmid Professor of Geology at University College, London.[95] Col. David returned to Australia and was knighted and decorated K.B.E., C.M.G. and D.S.O. When he died he was given a State Funeral, an honour usually reserved for only the highest ranking politicians. The two men collaborated with their report for the Royal Engineers on their geological work on the Western Front. They probably both dined out remembering the great excitement when the remains of a mammoth had been found during the making of a dug-out near Bapaume. The war had come to a standstill for the day in that sector.

---

93     Dots had met two of the Buchanan daughters when she was at school in Erfurt and had spent many summer holidays with the family in Scotland.

94     His daughter Margaret was christened in a silver rose bowl in Jesus College chapel. He became a Fellow of Magdalene College in 1922.

95     1931. Bill & Dots and their 2 daughters lived on the edge of Hampstead Heath.

Bill was fifty when WW2 became inevitable. In 1939, he was called up from the Army Officers Emergency Reserve and was given a Regular Army Emergency Commission in the Royal Engineers with the rank of Major and appointed as the geological advisor to the Engineer-in-Chief. Applying his experience from two decades earlier he returned to identifying water supplies, suitable ground conditions for airfields and provision of stone and gravel. Initially based in London, he was soon posted to mainland Europe.

The British Expeditionary Force's disembarkation on the beaches of Dunkirk was undertaken with a great spirit of confidence, but the enemy hit back hard and with unexpected power forcing the infamous retreat which Prime Minister Winston Churchill code named Operation Dynamo. When news broke of the total failure of the allied forces public morale sank, but surprisingly the careful release of information to the media gradually lifted public morale to a higher level than before. Bill was in France for Operation Dynamo and was immediately involved in the complicated evacuation, well in advance of the main force being informed, as preparations had to be undertaken before 331,000 men could be told what was happening and returned safely to home soil. Guns had to be deactivated, munitions removed or exploded, and a large number of vehicles that could not be shipped back, destroyed.

On the evening of May 20th 1940, Bill and some fellow officers were summoned to H.Q. for a briefing. Things were going badly, they all knew that, but it was worse than could have been anticipated as the entire invasion force was to retreat back over the Channel. Next morning at 05.45 hours as Bill's notes record, he and two other officers pulled out of their overnight camp with four companies of men and trucks loaded with ammunition for demolition targets. Their orders were to go to the Forest of Bailleul on the Belgian border beside the St Omer to Lille road and thence to Dunkirk. Two days of chaotic driving conditions with commands and counter commands coming through on radios followed. Everywhere there were confused and scared French people not knowing where to go for safety. Enemy positions were not known, the Luftwaffe were constantly on observation and destruction flights watching every daytime movement. Bridges were blocked or blown up, detours happened all the time. The trucks were thirsty beasts and fuel dumps that had not already been drained were hard to find.

Bill visited some emergency control points they had managed to identify over the radio and to reach some of them he "borrowed motor bikes or staff cars". What, in peacetime, would have been called theft did not come naturally to him, but he and his men were in an impossible situation and as he told himself "needs must". He led the convoy, which was grossly overloaded with high explosives, to a point near the beach head. He managed the operation, driving gingerly through hell on earth and for which he was awarded the Military Cross, an unusual distinction for a man over fifty. The citation read: "For bravery in convoying a large quantity of explosives from Boulogne to the departure beach while constantly under attack from the air and on the ground." His handwritten account modestly concludes *"Arrived Dunkeque 20.00 hours crossed on Sodality 05.00 on 24th."*

Back in England, he was posted to Northern Command to assess water supplies and ground conditions along the east coast around Hull. Working outwards in concentric circles, he created a complete inventory of the natural water resources in the area, identified as a possible invasion site, should the German Command invade from the northern shores of Europe. From 1941-43 he was attached to GHQ Home Forces, and he worked with planners on the invasion of France. He later explained in a lecture at the Military College of Science at Shrivenham that there were a number of requirements for the D Day landings:

"The landing area had to be within range of fighter air cover based on our own airfields. (Initially 80 miles, later increased to 100 miles.)

Beaches must be reasonably suitable for an actual assault.

The beach-head area must be suitable both for reasonable deployment and for the rapid construction of landing strips for servicing and fuelling fighters.

The availability of a good harbour after first few days. (Resolved by Mulberry)."

Normandy had a good hinterland suitable for airstrips, and did not have the surf found west of the Cotentin peninsula. General Sir Drummond Inglis, the Chief Engineer, told Bill that the D Day planners wanted to use Cherbourg as the bridgehead, but Bill insisted the geology was not conducive to the stated requirements. He also pointed out to the Command that there were "possibly more snags in the invasion beaches in Normandy than were dreamed of by the Intelligence Corps". These "snags" were faced by the US Paratroopers dropped behind Omaha and Utah beaches.

After considerable discussion, Bill's proposal for Normandy was acknowledged as the best option. The water supplies were good and the land over which they would advance was overlying limestone and the beaches were adequately weight-bearing. The broad and shallow approach beaches would allow large numbers of landing craft to disembark their cargoes of men and heavy machines. All that was missing was a harbour for the heavy equipment such as tanks, trucks, ammunition and ongoing supplies. A harbour was the major challenge.

The big push had been fixed for June 6th 1944, when the sun and tides would be just right once more to invade France. Churchill demanded that the best engineers were set to work to arrange an artificial harbour. He didn't know how, but it had to be done and there was no time to debate the whys and wherefores. The design team worked day and night, eventually coming up with what appeared to be a real long shot in the form of the Mulberry Harbour. They showed the PM their roughly drawn plans which he immediately understood as it was a brilliant solution. He told them that it needed to be built as quickly as possible and to solve design details as they did so. The engineers and sappers worked tirelessly and Mulberry floated into place on cue, constructed of six miles of floating concrete and steel, which flexed with the tide and during the invasion carried 2.5 million men, 500,000 vehicles and four million tons of supplies.

There was though an additional problem. As the appetite of the machines of war for fuel was considerable, a supply had to be transported from the UK refineries by road to the south coast and then across the Channel. Apart from the already crowded waters, there were constant threats from beneath the waves, and precious fuel could not be put at risk. The problem was solved using PLUTO.[96] Bill was consulted on this project in 1942 and asked to contribute his geological knowledge as to the nature of the Channel floor.[97] By 1943, Bill was being assisted by a former student, Freddie W. Shotten, who succeeded him as Geological Adviser to the Chief Engineer when Bill was released from the Army to become Woodwardian Professor of Geology at Cambridge University that same year.

Bill continued as a Senior War Office[98] Geological Advisor until 1953,[99] and was responsible for establishing a pool of geologists within the Reserve of Officers. He was also responsible for the 'Application of Geology' chapter of the Royal Engineer's text book on Military Engineering. There followed an academic career during which he lectured around the world and was acknowledged at every level of his profession. He held Honorary Doctorates at two leading French Universities – Lille and Renne. Although he was an able administrator, he took only a limited interest in research work. He was a brilliant field geologist and a good teacher and having served in two wars, he relished organising field trips with keen aspiring young geologists. He had a remarkable flair for finding fossils!

Bill King was a very modest man, and his Wensleydale neighbours were very surprised to learn of his achievements when they read his obituaries. He received the Gosselet Medal from the Societé Geologique du Nord, the Prestwich Medal from the Geological Society in France and the Murchison Medal from the Geological Society in London. These have been presented to the Sedgwick Museum in Cambridge. In retirement, in 1955, he continued developing geological mapping techniques, making frequent trips back to Cambridge, where he was a long-standing director of the Cambridge Water Company. On his autumn trips he always returned with a supply of cooking apples for Dots from the orchards surrounding the waterworks. Although he enjoyed staying at his London club to attend meetings of the Royal Society and other scientific bodies,

---

96   Pipeline under the Ocean.

97    After the War, Bill made a detailed study of the English Channel floor with the help of M. N. Hills.

98   The War Office was renamed the Ministry of Defence.

99   Bill King's archival materials 1946-55 are with the University of Cambridge Archives file #32/40.

he often went to Richmond to stay with his daughter's family and Jane well remembers seeing him walking briskly up the road from the station in his office suit. At home he wore 'plus twos' in the cold months and shorts in summer. As Chairman of Kings, he continued to make regular journeys to Hull.

He was a Fellow of the Royal Society with over 50 technical publications to his name and many Cambridge graduates acknowledged the benefits they had from his teaching. One young man to benefit from his friendship was Tom Martin, the son of the man Bill asked to take the Chairmanship of the Board of King & Co. when he retired. He also took the unusual step of acting as a referee on Tom's application to the Master of Emmanuel College, Edward Welbourne, a practice usually refused between leading academics. Bill asked Tom Martin Senior to accept the Chair of King & Co. in order that the company moved on from its traditional family culture. Although it had served the test of time, the company now needed more professional management. The invitation was accepted and immediately the problems of under-management were corrected by introducing new skills from Martin's company ARCO (Asbestos and Rubber Company, established 1844) in an attempt to lift financial performance at a time of huge industrial hardship for traditional family companies.

The King family farmed in Wensleydale in the 17th century originally having been stewards of Richmond Castle. They moved into many different activities, already well explained. For someone who became internationally renowned as a soldier, geologist and business man, Bill had not stood out from his contemporaries at school where he was a loner, having spent much of his boyhood roaming the family land where he was always happiest quietly observing nature. At Uppingham School it was the Natural History Society that occupied much of his spare time, along with rifle shooting for the school team. Bill retired home to Wensleydale where he and Dots had converted a cottage and farm buildings in Worton into a comfortable home. Their marriage was supremely happy, bringing together a unique mix: the sound traditions and standards of the Kings of Wensleydale, the bravery of the Celtic Passinghams, and the orderliness and determination to finish what you started of the German Gilligs. They had two daughters; Margaret and Cuchlaine. Both daughters were proud of their heritage and their home in Wensleydale.

Margaret Radegund King was born in Cambridge in November 1920. She read geography at Newnham College with Jean Mitchell as her Director of Studies. To her, the land she eventually inherited carried neither privilege nor position, but involved responsibility and care for all who dwelt upon it. From an early age she became friends with her father's tenants and their families, getting to know every corner of the land her forebears had farmed for generations. When she married, she made it her business to meet the local people connected with her husband's family. She developed a fascination for family history and first met Christopher Ritchie, her third cousin, when she was four in his mother's garden in West Burton, when he introduced her to his teddy bear Bobby. They next met when he visited her parents in Cambridge at the suggestion of his mother.

On graduating, she worked for the Geographical Section of the General Staff known as GSGS or MI4 at Eastcote, west of Harrow. After the war, she worked on the Dictionary of National Biography with the Oxford historian Margaret Toynbee. When peace arrived Christopher joined the British Council, that very British organisation which spreads the art, culture and way of life of Great Britain around the world, then still clinging to the traditional principles of Empire. Christopher came to stay with her parents in Cambridge in January 1948 and the next weekend he visited her in Oxford. At the end of his visit he proposed to her on the platform of Oxford Station on January 23rd. They were third cousins with a great deal in common. They married on the morning of April 17th 1948 at the Cambridge Registry Office wearing their ordinary day clothes, having arranged a proper blessing service in the afternoon at Magdalene College Chapel where Margaret wore white. In those days, the cost of a special licence to get married in a college chapel was prohibitive.[100] Charles Gillig's[101] sister, Emma Meschenmoser, who had somehow been traced by Dots, sent the dried fruit for their wedding cake from the USA.

Cuchlaine[102] followed her sister to Newnham College, Cambridge. She also read Geography being taught by a former member of Capt. Scott's

---

100 By the 1970's inflation resulted in weddings by special licence to becoming affordable.

101 Margaret's maternal grandfather.

102 Born in June 1922.

Antarctic Expedition. During the war, she joined the WRNS and was sent to Northern Ireland where she was attached to the Met. Office in Belfast. After the war, she went briefly to Durham University and then to Nottingham University in 1951 where she remained until her retirement. Cuchlaine was appointed as Professor[103] of Physical Geography in 1969, and earned an international reputation as a leading geomorphologist, specialising first in glaciation and then in coastal erosion. Her book 'Beaches and Coasts' has been a definitive textbook for generations of students.

She achieved her ambition to match her father's academic career, and like him was awarded a Science Doctorate by Cambridge University, entitling her to wear a scarlet gown at academic ceremonies. Given the male dominated environment of fieldwork research, it says much for her determination and academic reputation that she pioneered acceptance of single women being included in these expeditions. In the 1950s, when two members of a Nottingham University expedition to Iceland died in a blizzard, the expedition leader chose Cuchlaine to accompany him on the long and arduous trek to raise the alarm, trusting in her stamina and fortitude.

On her retirement to Wensleydale as a Professor Emeritus, Cuchlaine became an accomplished bell ringer at Askrigg Church, and for many years led guided walks explaining the geographical features of the Dales. She received a blood donor award for long service for the many pints she contributed. She loves to talk about all the places in the world life has taken her to, for both fieldwork and as a visiting lecturer.

Sadly Bill and Dots' happy retirement was all too short and Bill died in early January 1963, aged 73, from deep vein thrombosis having been admitted to the Friarage Hospital in Northallerton for the removal of a ureteric stone. He was stoical at all times and wrote to Dots from his bed shortly before he died "All's well. Don't bother to travel all the way to see me in this awful weather as I'm plumbed into all sorts of tubes."

---

103    A Professorial Chair was created for her personally.

His funeral was held at St. Oswald's Church Askrigg on January 28th 1963 and a memorial service was held at Magdalene College on March 2nd. His ashes were scattered on King land on Worton Edges above his farms at Cubeck.

# Chapter 12

# Celts and First Generation German Americans

Margaret Amy's genes were a mix of Welsh, Cornish and German. Her maternal grandfather John Passingham's family owned an estate near Lake Bala in Merionethshire, where they had held various positions of civic office for over 400 years. Their Cornish relatives however were somewhat different in that they were involved in the smuggling 'trade,' a traditional occupation amongst the coastal communities of Cornwall at that time. Possibly as a result of profits taken, the Passinghams on the south west peninsula had considerable landholdings. A memorial on the wall of Helston Church refers to family respectability during the 19th century when members of this branch of the family also held civic office[104] in the county. This branch of the family gave rise to some extraordinary individuals. One possessed the gift of second sight and heard the rustling of "dark bird's wings" in the bedroom wall as her children lay dying, as indeed many did. Mystic power in varying forms featured in future generations. Margaret's great aunt crossed the Channel and became a Trappist nun, but was mysteriously cast out of the order to die in Perugia in Italy.

The family had a colourful past and also a streak of unlawfulness and bravado. In 1794, a relative successfully took a lady to Shrewsbury Assize to recover a loan of £15,000 which she denied. This was an enormous amount at that time and the reason for it can only be a matter of speculation, but Passingham maintained that it had remained unpaid

---

104 "Jonathan Passingham of Hendwr in Merioneth, Esq. High Sheriff of that County in 1801. Formerly a Captain in His Majesty's 38th Regiment of Foot. Colonel of the 5th Cornwall Local Militia and Deputy Lieutenant of Cornwall. He departed this life at his residence, Bonython in the County August 17 1855 Aged 72 years."

for over twenty years. The relationship between the two parties was therefore in dispute and it was difficult to prove, but essential that he won because of the parlous state of his financial affairs. The Shrewsbury papers reported that he did indeed win. Eleven years later in 1805, Colonel Robert Passingham was sent to Newgate Prison for three years having "seduced a married woman and further falsely, wickedly and maliciously charged the husband with unnatural propensities and diabolical crimes, having himself violated their marriage bed."

Jonathan Passingham of Helston inherited family land at Heston in Middlesex through marriage to a cousin, Ellen.[105] Jonathan and Ellen were Margaret Amy's great grandparents and their younger son George Augustus was her grandfather. His elder brother Tremenhere, an ancient Cornish name, married Marianne Margaret Talboys, referred to as Aunt Peggy. They were members of an affluent, learned and cultural group in Cambridge. Trem was a renowned exponent of the music of Beethoven and enjoyed displaying his undoubted musical gifts on the piano playing to friends. In the group were also William Morris of the Arts and Crafts movement, Lord Tennyson and Burne Jones, a fashionable author of the day. Peggy's circle of friends included Lady Poynter, Lady Burne-Jones and Rudyard Kipling's mother. Trem finally met his end by falling from a window. At the inquest the Coroner censured Peggy as he must have felt that she may possibly have pushed him; a probability, but certainly not one that could be proved in court.

Trem and Peggy had eight children; their fourth son Guy became a parson, and their youngest daughter Mary Millicent, called Milly, married Cecil McLaren who was a Conscientious Objector in WW1 and deserted his regiment on principle. Whether he was brought before a court martial is unclear, but little was heard of them again and he was possibly shot as a deserter, but the family never talked of it, nor did they research the matter. The McLarens owned a well-known preparatory school in Summertown, Oxford in partnership with the Alingtons. Trem and Peggy's eldest daughter Ethel was, like her father, very musical and a gifted violinist. Living in the 'varsity town, her social life was almost

---

105    Her sister married Basire to whom the poet William Blake was apprenticed.

entirely amongst students, where she met and fell in love with a Japanese aristocrat, Hirokichi Mutsu, who went on to become a diplomat.

Ethel first met Hirokichi Mutsu in 1888 when he was a student at Trinity Hall; he having lodgings in her parent's house.[106] He was 21 years of age and found his Engineering exams very difficult, but he attracted Ethel who looked after him when he was ill. His father, Count Mutsu, would not countenance his son marrying a non-Japanese national, but when he died in 1897 Hirokichi sent Ethel tickets so she could join him in San Francisco where he was working in the Japanese Foreign Ministry as consul, and she happily became his mistress. He was later posted to Rome and then to Washington. He realised that in Washington he needed to be married to Ethel and finally got permission from the Emperor of Japan to marry her. They got married on 13th May 1905, the Emperor showing his approval by sending his Empress to the wedding. Ethel's name was changed to Iso Mutsu, and she taught the Emperor's children English. They returned to London, he as First Secretary at the Japanese Embassy, and Iso gave birth to her only child Yonosuke, or Ian, as he was known by the family, in 1907.

In 1910, they returned to Japan and lived in Kamakura where Ian's pronounced European looks got him into trouble with his contemporaries who saw him as a foreigner coming from a nation fast losing favour with Japan. He was therefore sent to school in Tokyo and Iso rented a house from the British Embassy. In 1925, it was decided that Ian should study in Britain, so Iso and Ian returned to England where the welcome was to say the least restrained. She was happy in her adopted country so she was pleased to return to Japan after a few months. Sadly, her health quickly deteriorated through a combination of cancer and Parkinson's disease and she died in 1930. Hirokichi died in 1942. Their extraordinary love story was published in 1994 entitled "Junai—Pure Love" written by Akiko Shimoju and published by Kodansha. Ian studied music at Birmingham University and married four times; his fourth wife being the daughter of a Japanese admiral. He was very pleased when Jane's brother Nicholas went to see them during a business trip to Japan. Ian disinherited his children

---

106    2 Station Road, Cambridge.

so he was the last Count Mutsu. Jane's grandmother remembered Ethel as, "having so strong an artistic temperament that one literally felt it, and one's values and time quite changed in her presence."

George Augustus, Jonathan's youngest son, wanted to go to sea, but his mother[107] refused to let him do so. At Oxford, in 1860, he attended McLaren's classes for training instructors for the Army Gymnasia. Recognising his natural athleticism, McLaren encouraged him to set up a similar centre in Cambridge which he duly did. Fitness and strength were fashionable with the students of the day and George Augustus was a good teacher. His love of mountaineering started when he accompanied one of his students on a climbing expedition. George was a very fit young man; he had no fear of heights and showed an extraordinary aptitude for balance and grip on sheer rock faces. He was invited to live with Trem and Peggy in the casual atmosphere of their Cambridge home surrounded by music and interesting people which was unusual at a time when strict Victorian attitudes pervaded nearly every section of the community.

George Augustus married Catherine Amy Staples, the daughter of an architect and gifted wood carver from a Devonshire farming family. She was extremely gifted in practical things such as bee keeping, honey production, butter making, fine needlework, knitting, gardening and the general business of farming. She also became interested in the occult[108] and supernatural and in later life, together with the wife of the Master of Trinity College, Mrs Butler; she founded the Cambridge Theosophical Society. Catherine was sometimes referred to as the "Devon Dumpling." He and Catherine were quietly married when they were both just twenty one.

They became close friends with a Dr Giles, a friend of Trem and Peggy's, who was very rich and lived alone in a large house, Milton Hall, just outside Cambridge. Whether the doctor had been married was not known, but Catherine suspected that he had had a wife who he committed to

---

107   Sir Henry Tate, of the Tate Gallery and Tate & Lyle fame had apparently wanted to marry Ellen.

108   In October 1889 she joined the Isis-Urania Temple of the Hermetic Order of the Golden Dawn.

a mental asylum where she remained for reasons unknown. The doctor built the young couple a house in his extensive grounds where George, amongst his various alternative occupations and interests, grew and sold grapes in the greenhouse producing an additional income of £750 per annum to add to his fitness training fees. His viticulture produced the equivalent of £15 a week which would have been equal to the income of a bank manager at the time. Dr Giles' patronage meant that George Augustus could give up running the Cambridge Gymnasium after two years. He could now concentrate uninterrupted on his climbing, game shooting and fishing, all of which he excelled at.

Amy's father and mother were unconventional and fun seeking, untypical of their time, adopting a way of life which they were happy for their children to follow. George Augustus was a strong gifted athlete with extraordinary physical and mental powers that suited him to become an outstanding mountaineer. He was of medium height, powerful, with exceptional reach and grip, and a shock of golden hair with searching blue eyes. He had natural instincts on a mountain. In 1872, he climbed the most notable Alpine summits at a rate previously unheard of. Shooting pheasants and partridges on Chiltern Hills and the Cambridgeshire flats, was far too passive as he missed the adrenaline rushes of the rock face so he returned to climbing, occasionally accompanied by his wife, who remained bivouacked in the valley as he took on high risk challenges on ice-covered rock faces. His most notable year was 1879 when he tackled the Weissmies crossing from Adler to Zermatt in Switzerland which remains today a rarely accomplished feat. This venture and others are recorded in the annals of climbing history and yet he was never elected a member of the Alpine Club for "reasons of a technical nature" probably because he was deemed to be 'professional' rather than an amateur athlete as he was known to have owned and run a fitness gymnasium business.

He retired from the mountains in 1883 after climbing around Zermatt where he sadly lost his guide and great companion Franz Andermatten "in his service" as George's obituary in the Alpine Journal recorded, without giving further details. Two years earlier, his other guide Ferdinand Imseng had died in an avalanche so he had lost both members of his climbing team. George was a life-long smoker, even while on the peaks and his breathing would almost certainly have been failing at heights over 8,000 feet, where the air becomes thin. He was a kind thoughtful man and a brilliant fisherman and once sent a small envelope to a friend of his granddaughter's which said; "My dear Jean, as I can't will a salmon onto your fly I send you a fly to put on yourself." It contained a beautiful fly he had lovingly tied for her.

Doctor Giles sponsored him on a world tour which cost £1,000 and he placed an additional £2,000 in trust for each of the three Passingham girls. Whether he did this in the event of their father having an alpine fall will never be known, but certainly this considerable sum proved very useful during the extraordinary lives of the girls in times to come. Amy was the first born in 1864 and she became the mother of Jane Ritchie's grandmother. Her two younger sisters were Inez and Adelaide. Adelaide got married to a Henry Saw[109] and had the marriage immediately annulled in order to access her money.

Due to Dr Giles' patronage, the Passinghams were well off, despite George's sometimes fragile economy due to his climbing adventures in Europe. Unsurprisingly, they had a large circle of friends, especially students, always ready for parties, dances and romance. The girls were not sent to school although at some point they attended a finishing school in Bournemouth. They were allowed to live unconventional free lives with occasional lessons in languages, maths and literature. They were spoilt both by their parents and the Doctor and received constant attention from throngs of rich and virile young men which made them all self-centred and wilful.

When Amy was 17 she became engaged to a student who quickly tired of his carefree irascible fiancée and took flight vanishing to somewhere in New Zealand before finishing his studies never to be heard of again. Amy's wild lifestyle continued unabated until at 19, she married a first generation German American, Charles Alvin Gillig.[110] He was 22 and had come to England aged 17, to work in his elder brother's business in

---

109   Henry Saw was a mathematician.

110   Charles Alvin Gillig was born in Baden, Germany and was taken to Buffalo in the United States as a baby where his father set up a wine importing business.

London. He was not a student so had to win her hand in competition with many other undergraduate suitors. They married almost immediately on the 10th January 1883, setting up home in Lea in the District of Lewisham, Charles working as a banker and Commission Agent in the Square Mile of the City. In October, their son Charles William was born and, for reasons that have never been explained, he was straight away entrusted to George Augustus and Catherine Amy (Gran) back at Milton to become their 'adopted son', which he remained for the rest of his life. They called him 'Chap' and he used their surname. They sent him to the new and controversial co-education public school Bedales, which was run on similar lines to their home at Milton with pupils of both sexes allowed to live, love and hopefully learn, with little authority. It worked for Chap and he achieved a sufficient academic standard to be awarded a place at Trinity College, Cambridge to read Land Management. From there he proceeded to Wye College, the agricultural faculty of the University of London, for a more practical grounding in farming. This combination was really far too academic for a career as a working farmer which is what he decided he wanted to be. Farming was in the doldrums at the time due to low prices for staple foods as a result of cheap imports from around the world. George and Gran could only invest in a small rented farm which could never have paid for their labours and certainly would never have shown a return on their investment.

The farm was near Toft which Gran took to like a duck to water. She worked with the cart horses, milked the house cow, made butter and fed the pigs on whey. However tragedy struck in 1909 when the unmarried twenty six year old Charles William Gillig was found lying near his gun in Toft Woods. He was dead. Inquests at that time were based on the minimum of evidence beyond the obvious. Just as when Trem's body was found below a first floor window, the number of people called before the court were few, and the evidence taken was elementary exploring none of the circumstances leading up to the death.

In Chap's case the coroner called the doctor who had gone to the scene. He described how the shot had entered the body horizontally at an angle, leaving an area of burnt skin, going over the heart and drilling through the spine, but in answering the coroner's question as to where the shot was found he replied that he had recovered it from within the body cavity. Chap was found laid face down with the weapon behind him which possibly indicated that he stumbled forwards as he walked and the reaction to the blast caused him to drop the gun as he lurched forward. Whether this was the weapon that killed him and as to its type, rifle or shot gun, the Press report did not clarify. The spent cartridge was in the gun and there was no apparent evidence of a scuffle. The coroner concluded, from the evidence before him, that suicide was unlikely due to the angle of entry of the shot and that therefore death was due to misadventure because of a stumble. The local community no doubt speculated, as they still would today, and talk went round the area that Chap could have been shot which seems unlikely due to the burnt skin indicating that the shot left the barrel very close to the body.

Nothing is known about his knowledge of his parents, neither of whom he had known. He must have been very surprised to meet his younger sister Dots in 1906, and there are lovely photos of the two together for the first time since they were very small children, both looking supremely happy. He had advertised in a local paper as looking for a farm manager's position. His sister was sure his death was an accident. Others have wondered if he was murdered. Unlike his sister, his surname was never legally altered, so his death certificate records him as Charles William Gillig. As a result of the tragic death of their much loved grandson, George Augustus and Catherine surrendered the farm and moved away to live in the village of Berrow, near Eastnor, in Herefordshire where George died aged 76 followed by Catherine on her 85th birthday.

Chap's sister, Margaret Amy, was born to Amy on April 16th 1885 at Lee[111] in Kent. Amy's maid Susan Cox, believed to have been only thirteen, was given virtually full custody of the new baby who grew to know her as Mummy's Sue. In November 1885, Amy and Gillig went to the USA where, presumably, she met her in-laws for the first and only time. Baby Margaret was left in London and on their return her parents moved to Blackheath. Later in life her grandmother told Jane that her mother had

---

111   52 Southbrook Road, Lee. Dots always maintained she was a Cockney as she was born within the sound of Bow bells.

hated losing her wasp-like waist line during pregnancy which was why her first marriage had failed.

According to Mummy's Susan, Charles Gillig was devoted to his wife and daughter, but Amy was unhappy. Whether he ever questioned her about the health and whereabouts of their son is unknown, but he worked hard returning home in the evenings often bringing Amy little presents. He had to make regular trips back to the United States which Amy probably didn't like. The trips would have been lengthy compared to today when executives go to New York and back in a couple of days. The marriage broke down. In 1886, he went to Chancery in London to agree the guardianship of his two children in favour of his wife, which was followed by a Deed of Separation for Chap.

What Amy got up to is a mystery, but from the way her life developed, and bearing in mind the freedom she had grown up with, it is almost certain that she would have had a busy social life which caused her rejection of Chap which was very much disapproved of by her parents and sisters. She went home to her parents in Milton but by 1890 she had fallen out with them and moved to Kenilworth in Warwickshire without Chap, to stay with her Aunt, her father's sister Gertrude, where the next man in her life appeared. Edward Armitage was the Chairman of a well-known engineering company in London that amongst other things developed the Pilgrim Car. The company stopped car manufacture at the beginning of WW1 to develop machine tools and engine parts. As little Margaret started to learn to talk it was clear she was tongue tied and unable to speak properly. Aunt Gertrude's husband was a doctor and arranged for her tongue to be cut, enabling her to become clear and fluent in her speech.

Amy desperately needed her freedom as she had Armitage in her sights and needed a divorce which was no easy matter in late 19th century England. Having made enquiries about the matter, she decided to go to South Dakota which was reputed by those who knew about such things to be an American State where divorce was allowed for desertion and cruelty and not just for infidelity. She travelled under the name of Westbrook, so there was no trace of her departure. Having married in England her certificate of marriage was something she had to distance herself from as it would be more difficult for an American divorce to be challenged in England. It was a high chip game which she intended to win.

She boarded the SS Egyptian Monarch in the Port of London on April 27th 1891 as Mrs Amy Westbrook, 26, lady, accompanied by Miss D. Westbrook, female child aged six, accompanied by Miss Susan Cox, nurse aged 19. They occupied three cabins and had thirteen pieces of luggage between them. The party were registered as settlers. The other passengers were either settlers or Ranchers returning home having bought cattle in Britain to improve the stock on their vast prairie farms. As SS Egyptian Monarch was a cargo ship, cattle men were employed on the ship when it was transporting animals. The ship could also carry 40 saloon passengers. At that time, the upper classes crossing the Atlantic usually used the large luxury passenger liners sailing from Southampton while the ports of London, Glasgow and Liverpool were used by migrants from all over Europe who had previously crossed the North Sea from Northern Europe as well as British people seeking the new life of the 'American Dream.' Susan looked after Margaret, who had been renamed on the passenger list as Dorothy Westbrook and that is why many of her friends in future years called her Dolly or Dots, as it was a name that stuck. There can be little doubt that Amy would have stood out amongst the motley passengers. During a storm, the Captain of the ship celebrated Dot's sixth birthday by having a special cake made. Dots' remembrances of this journey only record this kindness and a sash her mother wore later in Denver. It seems that fear and worry blocked everything else out.

On arrival Amy wondered, subconsciously perhaps, whether any of the Gillig family had wind of her arrival. She had her plan and the three of them set off for South Dakota travelling by train in rough carriages used primarily for moving the essentials of settlement and returning with crops and animals surplus to the needs of new communities in far-away places. This was not the usual way for Victorian ladies to travel, but Amy was determined. She had thoroughly prepared her every step towards freedom and her new man. After a long train journey they arrived in Yankton on the Missouri River, the capital of The Dakota Territories until 1883 when the town of Bismarck became its capital. South Dakota was Sioux territory where Col. Custer had his famous last stand, and Yankton had grown into a sizeable Midwest town since the coming of the railway and the search for gold in the Black Hills. Before the railway, Yankton had been an important staging post for the Missouri river steamers. The surrounding country remained the domain of the Sioux Indians; buffalo meat from the ranges was the staple diet and men, women and wagon trains were heading out in all directions to stake their claims. Many kept on heading west, following the sun, once they had seen and stood on the challenging soils of South Dakota.

Having established a 90 day residency in the town, Amy headed to the Courthouse to file a brief form with her name and address and that of her husband with the Circuit Court of the State of South Dakota.[112] According to the report of a later court case in England, Charles responded with a cross petition from New York State, no doubt pointing out that she had deserted him, not the other way round. Dots told her granddaughter that Amy had abandoned her son, her husband and eventually herself. Despite a search of South Dakota Circuit Court Divorce records through the internet, no actual record of the divorce has yet been found.[113] However the case was referred to in a résumé of case law on Migratory American Divorces – 'Their International Status'. Judgements seem to have depended on the domicile of those involved. The report states: "...it was decided that she had, infact, acquired a bonafide domicile, and that her divorce was valid, and her second marriage was valid."

In March 1892, a news item from Yankton to the Minneapolis Tribune reported "MRS AMY GILLIG. She is Missing and Fears for her Safety are Entertained." The article refers to her as the divorced wife of Charles A Gillig, President of Gillig's United States Exchange, London. She had told her lawyer in Yankton that she was going to New York for four weeks and hadn't been heard of since 1st December. The article ends "Foul play is feared." Dots remembers them going to Chicago before travelling back west to Denver but doesn't mention the trip to New York in her remembrances written in the mid-1950s. Amy was however, not back in Milton, Cambridge as reported in the Sacramento Daily Union on the 7th

---

112    South Dakota became a state in 1889.

113    Amy claimed in Court in 1906 that she had been granted a divorce on 23rd November 1891 but produced no evidence.

March 1892. Nor do the articles explain who in London was looking for Amy or why.

When the validity of her divorce was later challenged in 1906, Amy told the English Court that she had at some point written a letter of farewell to Edward Armitage which he took delivery of in the West Indies, on his way to Tasmania to visit his brother, which means that she knew his movements. He replied from an unknown port with a proposal of marriage which she said she declined. It is highly unlikely that Amy had ever intended to remain in Yankton to become a cookery teacher although that is what she told the Court. Sometime later, according to Amy, Armitage wrote again; this time from Mexico, proposing once more, and suggesting that Amy travel there to marry him as he was ill. She told the Court that again she declined. However they were married in Denver Colorado on July 1st 1892, Amy using her assumed name of Westbrook. Her marriage was certainly not legal even if her divorce was.

Edward Armitage was the younger son of the Vicar of Casterton in Westmorland who had left him £9,000 in his will. The Armitage family came from Leeds. Edward's granddaughter and Jane are both certain that Armitage was not on the SS Egyptian Monarch travelling under a false name, remaining convinced that he arrived in Denver from Mexico. By any stretch of the imagination this is a long and peculiar route from England to Colorado. He would, however, have been constrained by the railway network of the early 1890s. Their view is possibly confirmed by the fact that Dots never remembered him as being one of the few fellow passengers and Susan Cox would no doubt have seen through any disguise. She came from Milton and knew Amy's parents so could have been pressured to tell the truth later. But had he a beard on embarking on this adventure and removed it when he reached his eventual destination in Denver? We can speculate, but we will never know the truth although if you judge the position on Amy's form, truth was not her strong suit. There is nothing to suggest that Armitage hadn't believed she would get a divorce but he must have known her name was not Westbrook as he had visited her at her Aunt's house in Leamington Spa when she was Mrs Gillig.

Dots and Susan were despatched back to England before Amy and Edward Armitage were married, for her to attend a Roman Catholic school in Boscombe, near Bournemouth, where she was entered in the name of Dorothy Westbrook Armitage. She recorded that she found this very confusing as all her names were then new. Understandably, she was a quiet, withdrawn, serious little girl. She found out later that 'Westbrook' was her great great grandmother's maiden name. Elizabeth Westbrook had married Jonathan Passingham of Heston, Middlesex.

Amy announced to the family in England that she had successfully arranged her divorce and that all in her life was well once more. What she didn't tell them was that she had married Edward in June 1892 under the name of Amy Westbrook. The marriage took place either in St John's Church Denver, or possibly the City Hall. Even then the City Hall had a golden dome demonstrating the huge wealth of the new city that was the centre of the U.S. beef industry and the reason why so much of country's railroad system was headed for Colorado Junction where huge feedlots finished cattle bred on the prairies that were eventually sent to enormous slaughtering facilities in Chicago.

Dot's Roman Catholic education proved unsatisfactory as far as her mother was concerned. In 1893, aged eight, she was sent away to Switzerland to live with a family with eight children to go with them to the local village school. Susan remained as Amy's maid and eventually married Armitage's gardener. There is no known reason for selecting a Swiss family, or how they were found, nor did Amy appear to consider the difficulties of learning a new language with a family that didn't speak English. The stress of her chaotic life brought on a bout of serious pneumonia from which Dots nearly died. Once back to good health she was returned to England to accompany her mother and stepfather on a long voyage to Tasmania to fetch home Edward's invalid brother, James Auriol Armitage. The journey, there and back, lasted ten months and Dots always remembered how the two long voyages and the quiet isolation of the island colony was the first time in her short life that she had felt really happy, if still insecure.

On arrival back in England Dots was despatched to Kingskerswell, Devon, near to her maternal grandmother's home, to live with a Mrs Thompson, a lady of straitened circumstances presumably with some family connection. She didn't go to school and shared private lessons with young Leslie Thompson. During a walk one day she heard her new 'keeper' telling a friend in the village shop that as she was so hard up she was considering poisoning Leslie and then herself. Dots' life of worry, insecurity and chaos returned. She would have to be poisoned before Leslie, would she not? She wrote to her mother, but it was some time before Amy rescued her by which time she was beside herself thinking that her time was about to come. Her thirteenth birthday (1898) was celebrated by yet another move, this time to school in Erfurt, Germany. Again, she was alone and unable to speak the language. Unsurprisingly, it didn't work out. She couldn't understand the teachers who had no sympathy for her, but she became friends with two Buchanan sisters whose family were at the time living in Bootle. Amy was invited to stay with them and became a lifelong friend of their younger sister Jean[114] who later became godmother to Dots' daughter Margaret. Eventually, Dots returned to her stepfather and mother's home at Greenhills, Tilford in Surrey. She shared a governess with a naval family who were very kind and loving to her, including her in all their family activities, but very soon another plan was hatched. She was sent to St. Leonard's School in St Andrews,[115] Scotland to study for the entrance examinations to Leipzig Music Conservatoire.

The family always wondered how much Dots knew about why she was forced to go to such a variety of schools in different countries and entrusted to complete strangers. She attended her first lessons in Scotland two days after the death of Queen Victoria in 1901. She was homesick, for where would be hard to guess, and we know her mother had forbidden any correspondence by members of the family, or from any acquaintances she had met on her way around the world. This appears to have been a happier time for she passed her exams to go to the Conservatoire to study music.

Amy was in trouble again. She had no children during the first eleven years of her marriage to Armitage, but then suddenly they produced a family of five. In 1905, at the time her second son was born, she heard that

---

114   Mr Buchanan later moved to Bosbury House in Herefordshire where Dots nursed his badly wounded son Robbie at the end of WW1.

115   Dots met her friend Beatrix Smallwood neé Wade, whose family lived in Solihull, when she was at St. Andrews.

Charles Gillig was obtaining a Decree of Nullity on the marriage he had entered into with Carrie Osgood on the grounds that he was a bigamist as his divorce had not been legal. Charles had married the recently widowed Carrie Osgood in 1899. He had proof of Carrie's adultery with another banker Augustus Frederick Miles. Amy sought leave to intervene but this was not allowed so she took him to court to prove her divorce and to ensure the two Armitage boys[116] were not illegitimate. A court case started to roll with the eventual outcome being that the judge found in favour of Amy because Gillig had cross petitioned using the laws of New York State thus recognising that a divorce was being sought. Whether there was a Masonic connection between the Judge and Mr Armitage or whether he just felt sorry for him no one knows; but it does seem very surprising that she won with no proper paper evidence of either a divorce or a marriage in her proper name. She didn't pursue costs and remained married to Armitage. Photos of him show a very sad, worn man who must have wondered about the wisdom of marrying Amy.

Charles Gillig's family were hard working and had originally gone to the United States in the mid-19th century from Baden Baden where they were brewers, probably to escape the increasingly restrictive social and economic regime of Bismarck. They established a successful business importing German wines through a company in New York State, later expanding and diversifying to become financiers. The family were early settlers who through their success, along with other similar families from Europe, helped finance the Statue of Liberty, built to welcome and encourage all who followed them into the new world of freedom. In 1877, Henry Gillig, Charles' elder brother, established a finance company in London and by 1880 the American Exchange Europe in the Strand was providing banking facilities to Americans passing through London, possibly to invest in their homelands, but more likely to encourage others to follow their success. At the time, many of them had made vast fortunes

---

116   The third Armitage son, Everard, married a Hungarian Baroness who escaped with her mother during the 1919-22 Hungarian Revolution over the rooftops, and crossed the border into Austria hidden in a hay cart. They only escaped being stabbed with pitchforks by border guards as a loyal young man accompanying them caused a diversion, losing his own life by so doing.

and were bringing money, and sometimes daughters, back to become part of London Society hoping to attract cash strapped titled families into dollar rich marriages which were the final seal of success to an émigré settler family. Some large and notable British estates were rescued in this way from almost certain collapse during the hard times of the mid and late 19th century.

Charles Gillig became a permanent resident in England. His job was to make contacts and, being young, he met many people from the flourishing middle classes some of whom were at Cambridge where he had met his wife. He made political connections and through these he was asked to arrange a visit to America for Mr Gladstone, the first by a British Prime Minister. His other claim to fame was the production of his 'London Guide' published by Rand McNally which informed American visitors of everything they needed to know during their stay in the capital and further afield around the country. It sold for 28 dollars and at least 15 editions were printed.

After some time the Gillig Bank in the Strand became the United States Exchange known as 'The American Rendezvous', offering account holders accommodation, similar to the traditional gentlemen's clubs in St James', where luggage could be stored and where they could live and entertain during their stay. Charles Gillig took over the Strand offices in 1886 as sole proprietor of The United States Exchange and became general manager of Charles. A. Gillig, Giles & Company Bankers Limited. As the 19th century drew to a close things were not well in Europe. Germany was making trouble for other European nations and as a consequence far fewer Americans were crossing the Atlantic. Charles' travel agency business was totally focussed on clients from the United States and the war would probably have bankrupted him. His personal life was miserable and Charles had told his doctor that he was sleeping badly. Perhaps, if he still had an English wife and family all would have been different. On March 12th 1915, Charles visited his solicitor's office in Marylebone and wrote a will leaving his remaining assets to his brother, Henry Francis Gillig. He requested that he be cremated at Golders Green Crematorium after which his hot ashes should straightway be cast to the wind and, finally, all related costs of his worldly departure were to be kept to the absolute minimum.

On Tuesday 16th March 1915 at 10.15 p.m. the Hall Porter at the main entrance to Westminster Hospital, Henry Long, watched a man in a heavy black overcoat approaching along the gas lit street towards the main hospital entrance. Henry imagined this was a doctor he had not seen before, checking on his patients as was the custom for surgeons after operations. The man stopped to study the hospital notice board. Long raised his tophat and bid him "Good evening, Sir" and returned to his office inside the foyer. Almost immediately he heard a loud bang which at first he thought was a car wheel puncturing, but it was followed by a loud groan. He rushed out to find a body, a gun, an umbrella and a bowler hat rolling away down the steps. It was the late and very depressed Charles Alvin Gillig. The Coroner summed up the inquest by saying that he had obviously chosen the hospital steps "in case he failed in his endeavour". He was therefore a considerate man. A copy of his new will had gone to a friend, James Parton, marked Private, with a message: "Love to Harry and all friends." The final verdict was of death during temporary insanity.

In May 1906 Dots, by then aged 21, changed her name by Deed Poll to Miss Margaret Amy Passingham, but as late as 1963, by then Mrs Margaret Amy King, she still had to give legal confirmation to an insurance company proving her change of name was indeed official. Dots lived for a short while with her grandparents and brother at Toft. When her brother Chap died and her grandparents moved to Berrow, she went to London to train as a masseuse. She came seventh in the final examination in her year. The skill of massage had yet to turn into physiotherapy.

When Amy heard that Dots had agreed to marry Bill King she started what turned out to be ineffective legal proceedings to put a stop to any such idea on the grounds she was far too young. She tried to do exactly the same to her Armitage sons, threatening to cut them off from their inheritances and telling people, including relatives, all sorts of untruths about them. However, she could do nothing, and Dots became Mrs Margaret Amy King in June 1916, while Bill was on leave from the battlegrounds across the English Channel. Amy died in 1921, aged 65. Dots and her eldest step-brother agreed that they had always loved their mother and that she really had tried to reciprocate their love, but was prevented from so doing by her over-powering and consuming selfishness and jealousy. However on her death bed, the last name her mother had mentioned was that of her eldest daughter.

# Chapter 13

## The Scottish Ritchies

Christopher Ritchie's paternal family came from the north eastern corner of Scotland that protruded out into the North Sea, north of Aberdeen, living in a place called Old Keale near Fraserburgh. In the 17th century, this was exposed country where the living came hard. John Ritchie of Old Keale, in the parish of Tyrie, was born in 1650 and died in 1736. His wife, Mary Davidson, bore him six children. This was the time of industrial and rural revolutions in England, the Scottish Borders and north to Perth, but in Aberdeenshire life was about meagre self-sufficiency, fishing, boat building, spinning, weaving and farming. Further west, the English Red Coats were clearing up the Frasers and other revolutionary clansmen after their victory at Culloden. It was a time of speculation about the future as wars, revolutions and continual streams of rumours about new developments and political unrest caused quiet humble people such as John and Mary to become anxious for their family's safety. They encouraged their children to head south where life was better and from where the British Empire was beginning to turn the globe pink. This news came from seamen returning to northern ports from the Port of London.

When George Ritchie was seventeen he followed his brother Alexander south, and headed to the River Thames working on a large boat out of Aberdeen, loaded with barrels of herrings, rough woven tweed, whisky and timber bound for London. These ships carried a limited number of passengers who could volunteer to work as crew, thus travelling free. On arrival there he left the boat and found accommodation in Rotherhithe where he later died, aged only 27. He was buried in Deptford as a dissenter from the established church. When he was 20 he had met and married Mary who had born him five children. She joined him in his grave thirty nine years later. Their eldest son William was an entrepreneur who traded as a timber merchant, supplying the booming shipbuilding business. His success was such that he moved to rural Surrey, away from the busy commercial riverside community where the stench of the Thames and its constant drift of sewage pervaded every moment. However, both he and his wife Hannah were returned on death to the family burial ground in Deptford. They had fourteen children: a set of twins, nine singles and three who died at birth. William died aged 75, Hannah predeceased him aged 55.

Their second son William, born in 1775, married Sarah Pitcher, the fifth surviving daughter of Thomas Pitcher, a shipbuilder from down river at Northfleet. When in 1835 William's business became precarious, it was called into administration by the London County Council, whereupon Sarah promptly renounced her involvement. William Ritchie & Sons had speculated on a large shipment of cheap Norwegian timber at the time Napoleon was finally beaten which caused shipbuilding across the country to fall into sudden recession for the first time in British history.

They had six children and their third son Alfred married Janet McCall,[117] the granddaughter of a wealthy Glasgow merchant. Her father had moved to Liverpool and later built a house near Penrith. Alfred and Janet lived in Greenwich until she died. Alfred managed to be appointed administrator of his father's failed business. He turned the remnants of the business round and then sold it to great advantage and moved away to Minchinhampton[118] in Gloucestershire with his six children from where he invested in Ham Mills in Stroud. He died aged 67. Alfred and Janet's eldest son, also called Alfred, was born in 1844. He became an intuitive successful businessman and a member of the growing upper middle class society of the County of Gloucestershire and served as a Commissioner of the Peace. This appointment of respectability was further endorsed when he married Elizabeth Mary Grieve. The Grieves were Scots from near Peebles, the most notable being Dr John Grieve who was a physician to Catherine the Great of Russia. After her death in 1793, he was invited back

---

117   Janet's maternal grandfather Robert Liston was elected Moderator of the General Assembly of the Church of Scotland in 1787.

118   Alfred and his children lived first at Burleigh House, Minchinhampton and then moved to Ham House, Brinscombe.

to the Russian Court by her son Paul, becoming his First Councillor of State. He died in 1805 whilst serving Tsar Alexander, and has a memorial in Bath Abbey. Elizabeth's grandfather, first cousin to Dr John, had moved to Monmouthshire and the family lived in Abergavenny and Llanvair.

Alfred and Janet's second child, Marion, was born in 1846. Together with her first cousin Dr Annie McCall, a niece of her mother's, they founded the Clapham Maternity Hospital and Marion became its administrator. She was exceptional in her understanding of, and dealing with, patients who came before her. This was at a time when unwanted pregnancies had frightening consequences. The aim of the two women was to minimise emotional trauma by having a special ward for these unfortunate girls keeping them away from other people while the futures of their new-born were decided.

Alfred and Elizabeth had two sons and two daughters. When Alfred died in 1884 aged 40, their mother took her children to live on the Continent as it was cheaper, and the boys finished their education in Lausanne. Elizabeth[119] then went to live in India, as her daughter May had married Rev Edmund Richard Clough, Canon of Nagpur.[120] Albany Herbert became a violinist and moved to Seattle. Janet never married. She lived with her mother in Raniket, returning to England to live in London when her mother died. Jane remembers being told Aunt Janet had been chased by a tiger when on her bicycle! Alfred Julian, called by his second name, met Ina Winn, as Georgina was called, when she was on holiday with her parents and Julian helped carry her suitcases.

On July 1st 1908, Georgina Maud Winn, 31 years of age, daughter of James Clarkson Winn, married Mr Alfred Julian Ritchie of Gloucestershire, 32 years of age, a partner in the firm of tea merchants Cox, Ritchie & Co. Mincing Lane, in the City of London. The bride's father was entered on the licence of marriage as gentleman, with no mention of his professional status, and the groom's late father as a manufacturer. The wedding took

---

119   Elizabeth was always referred to as 'Granny in India' by Jane's father.

120   Their daughter Eileen Marion Elizabeth Amy Clough, known as Betty, was John Ritchie's godmother and used to recount stories of 'skinning the New Year in' after a tiger hunt. She was always given the responsibility of skinning the nose.

place on a Wednesday at St Andrew's Church, Aysgarth. Mr Yeates, a friend of the groom from London, was best man. On the day following the celebration, the Winn servants and tenants were entertained in the decorated and illuminated grounds of The Grange at West Burton, and on Friday the school children were similarly amused. At the main reception following the marriage, the guests feasted on an eight course wedding breakfast of Hors d' Oeuvres, Consommé, Salmon and Lobster, a five meat main course with potatoes, peas and salad followed by tarts, sponges and desserts. Margery Burrill was a bridesmaid. The Bridegroom's mother didn't attend the wedding as she had previously booked her passage back to India.

Julian and Ina lived at 237 Cromwell Mansions in Kensington before WW2 when they moved to West Burton. He was a tea merchant in the City before the Russian Revolution after which his business ceased trading as almost his entire trade was with the upper echelons of Russian aristocracy. During WW1 the family lived in Sidmouth[121] where their youngest son Christopher was born, before moving to Weston super Mare.[122] Julian had a difficult relationship with Christopher who was frightened of him. He was understandably hurt when his pet fantail doves were eaten by his parents during the food shortages of WW2. He rarely talked about his father to his children.

After the closure of the tea business Julian established a business trading in Malayan rubber. That also failed and in financial desperation he pressured his three sons to give him the £1000 inheritances they had each received from their grandfather, James Winn. He found rural life difficult having no interest in shooting, fishing or farming. He did, however, once invest in a pedigree shorthorn cow as he coveted a silver cow his wife had presented to the Wensleydale Agricultural Show for a champion animal of that breed. His cow won for three consecutive years allowing Julian to keep the trophy which was given to Denys Gardiner, the family accountant, on Ina's death. Julian was however interested in ghost hunting, but unlike his daughter Muriel, he never actually saw one.

---

121   At a house called Kanandi. There is a seat on the Promenade in memory of their Nanny Brookes.

122   Their house Clarence Croft no longer exists.

To boost his lack of confidence he applied for an entry in Burke's Landed Gentry, which was accepted, and he had a Ritchie crest created. Margery was very impressed when an Indian Prince was a guest at The Grange, West Burton. The two men had met through the rubber trade and a trip to the Dales would have given the visitor a new perspective on British life.

Julian was a strange man who didn't always get on with his own family[123] or his children, but once on an outing to the London Zoo he wrote NORA with his stick on the mud caked side of a water buffalo, standing quietly by the bars, for a little friend of Christopher's which much impressed her. He was also a mountaineer and climbed the Matterhorn, aged 15, which was at the time a record as he was the youngest person to have done so. The climbing gene seems to have been influential as Jane Ritchie's youngest brother Timothy has also inherited a love of the Alps and climbing which he shares with his forebears Julian Ritchie and George Augustus Passingham.

Julian died in 1948 following a sudden heart attack when he fell onto the drawing room fire and was seriously burned and lost his sight. He was sent to Shotley Bridge Hospital. When he returned home he told his son Christopher that a little green man came and sat at the end of his bed to talk to him which comforted him, but there was nothing that could be done. Ina Ritchie died in 1956 as the result of a fall received two weeks earlier when she visited the Rose & Crown in Bainbridge for tea during a drive out. She had inherited farms in Wensleydale, Walden and Littondale and her tenants mounted a guard of honour at the funeral along with providing six coffin bearers. In the traditions of her family she had been a stalwart of the community, on the church council and a keen contributor to, and supporter of, all local events, always in the formal Victorian style of her childhood, wearing hat and gloves.

---

123    He fell out with his Aunt Julia because he was rude about Aunt Marion. His Uncle Clement's daughter Margaret (Jane's Cousin Daisy) kept in touch with her great nephew Christopher, and Jane used to visit her in her flat in Sussex Gardens on her way across London from Paddington to King's Cross. Daisy collected snuff boxes and musical boxes. When she died Jane was given some money by her companion Phillipa Gregory-Smith, allowing Jane to help her mother and Uncle Gerald pay for the electrification of the Aysgarth Church Clock.

Julian commissioned the Pedigree of the Ritchie Family extracted from the records of the College of Arms which was accredited by them on completion. The work is handcrafted and bound in a blue hardboard cover of twelve inches by eighteen. On the introductory page there is a handwritten inscription, by Julian, giving both his London and adopted West Burton addresses, and confirming the College of Arms accreditation, stating that the information came from the original family history inscribed by the College of Arms circa 1830. There is also a hand painted Coat of Arms with the motto 'Ring True.' The crest is a muscular hand gripping a buckle and cow bell. The heraldic shield includes three calves to denote the Metcalfe descent, two wavy blue lines to represent the Walden and Bishopdale becks which ran through his wife's land and the white rose of Yorkshire. He also had the family motto engraved on the inside of Ina's wedding ring.

The family record commences when the nation was entering the Industrial Revolution with six children born to the first Ritchie's of Old Keale. In beautiful copper plate each of their descendants is recorded with place and dates of birth, marriage and death. The Pedigree covers 17 vellum pages in the centre of which are shown likenesses of the senior male of each generation from William son of John and Mary to Alfred Julian (1876-1948) who carried the family name through to the 20th century. On the penultimate pages the descent of the Other family is defined from Thomas of Thornborough, date of birth unknown, but who died in March 1658 and his wife Elizabeth who died in 1657. It clearly illustrates the breeding from the mid-17th century through to the union between Thomas Other and Jane Lister.

The end pages describe Julian's four children and their descendants through to the generation born in the last half of the 20th century. His three sons all devoted their careers to their country; Alfred and Gerald as professional soldiers and Christopher serving in the army during WW2 and in peacetime as a key member of the British Council until his retirement. Three of Christopher's children were given second names to commemorate the four dominant families in their line: Jane Other Ritchie, Nicholas King Ritchie and John Passingham Winn Ritchie. Timothy was given the second name of William after his grandfather, Bill

King. Christopher wasn't very keen on his wife's Robinson connection so none of his children were given that name, despite the fact that much of the wealth of the King family came down the Robinson line.

Julian and Ina had four children: Janet Muriel born in 1909, Alfred James Patrick born in 1911, Gerald born in 1913 and Christopher Julian born in 1916. This generation was born just before and during the horrific First World War, and no one at the time could have realised that this would be the generation born to fight the Second. At the outbreak of WW2 the children were respectively 29, 27, 25 and 22. They were known to each other respectively as Fatty, Doc, Jappy and Op.

Muriel suffered a personality change after contracting Sleeping Sickness in her teenage years. The sweet character of her childhood became brusque and the feminine little girl with curls became manly in appearance. At some point she stayed with her cousin Lottie Wright, who lived in great state at Halton Park in Lancashire near the Crook of Lune, where Muriel spent time on the home farm learning about cows and sheep. It was there that she got the taste for a lifestyle way above her means which ultimately proved her undoing. After a while she felt she had learnt enough from practical farming and used her one thousand pound bequest from her grandfather, James Winn, to go to Wye School of Agriculture, part of London University. She left Wye at the outbreak of war and moved home and proceeded to bulldoze her mother into letting her manage their home farm, adjacent to The Grange.

Muriel took a keen interest in the land inherited by her mother from the Winn, Other and Stackhouse families and enjoyed being part of the local farming community. She and her friend, Mollie Fisher-Ambrose lived at Grange Farm. She pressured her mother into buying her a herd of pedigree Ayrshire cows and her flock of sheep that died from a double strength dose of sheep dip. The two women led a troop of Girl Guides and ran the village's voluntary Fire Brigade until the recruits, all men, got fed up with constant fire practices. Eventually they refused to turn out, logically thinking that air raids over their little village tucked into the Pennine hills were most unlikely. After the war Muriel hoped to join the Metropolitan Police, but she didn't pass the selection process. Instead, she trained as a nurse in London in the 1950's, and received a Queen's Award. She had caused her mother to finance her short farming career so that there was very little money to pay Ina's death duties. She also abandoned Mollie who moved into The Grange to become Ina's companion.

During the war Muriel had spent every waking hour working amongst country people. She despised animal cruelty and took considerable risks to help anyone, and particularly any animal, in trouble. One very hard snowy winter's day she heard of an old couple stranded in their sparsely furnished farm house away up in the hills in Walden, remote from the village, and they had neither food nor fuel. She harnessed her horse to a sled and trudged there, through deep drifts, to deliver the essential animal fodder and food for the old folks. On another occasion, she castigated a man for goading a horse with a heavy load of wood in the Market Place in Leyburn. Her outrage aroused both comment and favourable support from onlookers at the time.

Muriel was good with her pen and she was awarded an English Speaking Union Prize for an essay. As the war drew to its conclusion, talk of land nationalisation was well advanced once more, although Westminster was beginning to feel uncomfortable about the cost of compensating hundreds of private land owners. Muriel took up her pen and wrote a piece for the Royal Economic Society Journal in 1944 entitled: "Relationships of Landlord and Tenant". Although too long by today's standards, it convincingly made the unpopular point that the traditional system of land tenure was in trouble. She had experienced the paternalistic system of the more traditional estates in the area where the farming community was quite content paying reasonable rents, but she had heard of men who had become wealthy from wartime profits buying land and placing sport, privilege and privacy before all else at the expense of their farming tenants by demanding unaffordable rents. Following the war, taxation on traditional wealth, especially that held in land, was already high. The rural economy was out of balance. Traditionally, estate owners supported local shop keepers and tradesmen who, in their turn, often gave credit to financially stretched farmers knowing that they would eventually be paid. Times were critical her article said, and she asked the question: "would the post war period be any better?" She veered on the side of caution, coming out against change and in support of subsidising home food production, and thus the consumer. This is exactly what happened with the introduction of the radical 1947 Agricultural Act three years later.

Under the terms of this Act tenant farmers were given security of tenure, for the first time removing the uncertainty of a landlord or his agent giving them notice to quit virtually without reason, or informing them of an unaffordable rise in rent. Under the Act, capital grants, guaranteed prices and production subsidies combined to make farming far more secure than before. Muriel's contribution cannot be judged, but her opinions were well presented. Whether her article was read by people able to influence and correct what was a potentially disastrous situation for Britain's food security, we do not know.

In more peaceful times Muriel loved to show Light Sussex poultry, taking prizes at local shows as well as at the Royal Agricultural Society of England Show when it was in Darlington and York after the war. Sadly, before she retired, she lost faith with the people of Wensleydale and, following a period of mental illness, decided to live in Northamptonshire near her eldest brother, Alfred, who had retired to Stoke Bruerne on the Grand Union Canal. When Alfred moved to Cornwall she followed and managed to buy a small holding at Lower Manworthy in Devon. She had farmed, or nursed, tirelessly all her life in her own fashion, but her eccentricities had taken over and she imagined her new farm would naturally be all tranquillity with fields full of contented animals. The dream quickly became a disaster as continuous expense and rising debts took their toll. She refused to accept that farming a different soil, in a different climate and in a strange place, without the essential financial support of her mother, would make it impossible to make a living from the small, wet and under-capitalised farm. She wrote to her brothers hinting that she needed financial support, which was initially forthcoming, but the begging became accompanied by rude demands. The family realised this was a limitless black hole of debt and advised her to retire. At first she flatly refused, but a sale was eventually her only way out. She had given away family furniture, pictures and heirlooms to pay debts and had nothing left.

Janet Muriel Ritchie died on the 23rd June 1984 in a nursing home in London. On 11th August there was a short memorial service at St.

Andrew's Church, Aysgarth when her niece Jane addressed the small congregation: *"Tonight we are here to represent the many people who will always remember Muriel Ritchie. She was an able woman with great strength of character who always threw herself wholeheartedly into anything she did, whether Farming, Nursing or running the Girl Guides. Happier to be a giver than to be a receiver; she was in many ways extremely generous with her time and her energies. I was brought up on stories – now almost legends – of her taking a horse and sledge to rescue an elderly couple snowed up one winter; of her berating a carter in Leyburn Market Place for ill-treating his horse; and she gave a small niece a china angel to protect her from burglars, and a pot of strawberry jam whenever she came to stay. She was not always an easy or indeed a very well person, but in many respects she was somebody of great genius. She was awarded the English Speaking Union Essay prize one year, she was a Queen's Nurse and she won prizes at the Royal Show for her Light Sussex hens. She is perhaps best remembered as "a good talker" as a Teesdale farmer described her to me recently. Certainly my happiest memories of her are listening to her in full flood laughing as words poured forth, with her listeners unable to get a word in edgeways. The legacy of the many years she lived and worked in West Burton she left to those who knew her, is a fund of colourful stories about a person, who, once met, was never forgotten. May God bless our memories of her, and her's of us."*

Muriel's brothers were very different. Alfred James Patrick Ritchie became a professional soldier joining the North Staffordshire Regiment in 1931 aged twenty, and during the war was Adjutant of 1st Battalion of the Staffordshire Regiment and awarded a military MBE. He was captured in Burma, imprisoned by the Japanese and, like most of his fellows, he was tortured and had his finger nails drawn which ranked fairly high on the pain score tables that were kept by the prisoners. When released he was sent to Gibraltar to recover both mentally and physically before returning home. After spending his leave at home, and with the Iron Curtain ominously being created, he transferred to the Royal Corps of Military Police to become a Provost Marshall at a variety of commands including Bengal, Gibraltar and with NATO forces in Berlin prior to his retirement. After his mother's death he married Mollie Fisher-Ambrose in 1955. He was by then a full Colonel.

Mollie's parents had been killed in the first war and she was brought up in a Dr Barnardo's orphanage. Her real name was Mary Medbury, but she used the names of her Barnardo's 'sponsors' Miss Fisher and Miss Ambrose. She changed her name by deed poll before she got married. She pretended she didn't know when her birthday was although she had a birth certificate of sorts recording her date of birth as 5th May 1911. She wove a sort of fantasy series of memories which Jane listened to but didn't really believe. She was clever, passed exams and read English at London University despite being dyslexic. She met Muriel at a Girl Guide Jamboree, and came north to help her run Grange Farm during WW2 before becoming companion to 'Mrs R.' as she called Ina. She thrived on stories that raised her self-esteem, once telling Jane she had been responsible for getting the telephone box installed outside the old school and chapel in Walden.

When Alfred retired he was presented with a trained Doberman police dog called Deutsch, reflecting his keen interest in military dog training which had been part of his responsibilities when serving in Egypt. He got on well with his niece and nephews, particularly his nephew John. Jane had been driven to her christening at St. Andrew's Church, Aysgarth by his Gurkha driver who had given her a set of children's cutlery with teddy bears on the handles to mark the occasion. He and Mollie lived briefly in The Grange at West Burton after his mother died, but to Mollie's chagrin, Ina had left her property, including the Grange furniture to be divided between her four children. As there was very little money to pay death duties, and Alfred was still on military pay, The Grange had to be sold. They moved briefly into Peel House, the former Police House built by James Winn and then kept a couple of rooms for their own use in Grange Cottage.

However, Alfred may well have realised that although he loved Mollie very much,[124] living in West Burton was perhaps not the best solution. Mollie was thought to be snobby once she became Mrs Ritchie, which is not how her husband was thought of. When Alfred fell out with one of his tenants he decided to sell up and move away with Mollie and his donkey Sally, to Stoke Bruerne, Northamptonshire on the Grand Union

---

124   He called her Pootle.

Canal. There they became interested in the working community on the canals. He helped establish the Waterways Museum, made a substantial investment in a small fleet of working barges and bought a narrow boat called Lupin for his own use. Mollie learnt the traditional canal craft painting skills of the Roses and Castle design found on canal boats. They later moved to Mullion on the Lizard in Cornwall where they had a lovely bungalow called Carag Luz overlooking the sea, before moving to a little cottage opposite Mullion church. Alfred died in 1993 and Mollie in 2007.

Gerald Ritchie went to Aysgarth School at Newton-le-Willows and was always described as "a very kind brother" by his younger brother, Christopher. Gerald also became a soldier. He married Elspeth Warren, the sister of one of Christopher's Cambridge friends. They met on a skiing holiday where they were both injured and got to know each other sitting it out at the hotel. They were married during the war and he was awarded the Military Cross for bravery while serving in the Parachute Regiment. In the family archive there is a letter he wrote to Muriel following the D Day parachute invasion at Pegasus Bridge during which a piece of shrapnel pierced him just below the shoulder, saying it had been "a party I wouldn't have missed for the world." He explained vividly how his small company were packed into a Dakota transport plane towing a plywood glider full to capacity with troops and how, when the "prepare to jump" red light went on, the doors opened and France lay below him in the moon light pockmarked with the shadows of craters. The green light suddenly glowed. He was first out. For a moment his mind went blank as he hit the freezing air. Then he drifted down looking at the grey foreign landscape beneath. He made a bad landing on very rough ground. Quickly unhitching his 'chute harness he set off to the rendezvous point noticing there was a horse grazing in the field, which chased him. He recorded how this equine aggression made him think that this was definitely a German horse. Gradually his battalion assembled waiting in anticipation for further orders, and excitedly exchanging the experiences of the past hour. For nearly all of them this was a first time battle experience and they had come straight from basic training on English heaths to be dropped at high speed onto war torn French soil. Eventually, Gerald assembled as many of his group as possible in a lime quarry by a cottage from which the residents, a poor labouring family, nervously emerged to greet the scruffy camouflaged soldiers with painted faces by shaking their hands. There were "Bonjours" all round, but as Gerald pointed out, at 2.00 a.m. "It was neither the Jour nor was it very Bon."

Machine guns rattled, planes flew overhead, a squad of commandos appeared and, suddenly, they heard the skirl of bagpipes. Gerald felt safe at the sound. The countryside at dawn reminded him of Gloucestershire, but that thought soon passed as the stench of explosives and dust filled the atmosphere and his lungs. Broken gliders lay everywhere. Surprisingly there appeared to be few injuries. Those were to come. He had hoped to meet up with his best friend, but didn't. He found out later that none of the air crew from his Dakota was seen again and it was assumed they were shot down over the Channel on the return journey. His second in command was found dead four days later, the Colonel was killed and his obituary appeared in the Daily Telegraph on the day he was writing to Muriel. Having arrived to fight they found that retreat had become the order of the day. The original letter is now in the Imperial War Museum. When Gerald left the Army he retrained as a Probation Officer and moved to Wiltshire.

The youngest member of the family Christopher Julian Ritchie was, like his brothers, educated at Wellington College,[125] a school with a military tradition founded on money accumulated by stopping a shilling from the pay of all ranks as a memorial to the victorious Duke of Wellington following his death. Christopher went up to Magdalene College, Cambridge to read Classics when he was just nineteen in 1935. After the war, in 1946, the Master of Magdalene wrote a retrospective assessment of him as part of the entry procedure to the Civil Service: "Major Christopher Ritchie was in my college from 1935 to 1938. He was placed in the second division for the Second class in the Classical Tripos and in the first division of the Second Class Tripos (Part 2). He showed high qualities of industry and character: thoughtful, with a cultivated taste, he was very pleasant to deal with and was always willing and courteous. I consider he would make an admirable Civil Servant, especially in the Foreign Office, where

---

125    Christopher's Old English Sheepdog Lolly went with him and was looked after by the Housemaster and his wife. Lolly learnt to ignore Christopher if they met on the stairs during school hours.

he will perform his duties most faithfully." This was praise indeed from a man such as the Master, A. B. Ramsay, a highly regarded academic who had seen hundreds of young men pass through the gates of Magdalene to enter careers at the highest levels, especially in politics and the powerful Civil Service (which had lead the nation's aspirations in building the Empire for two hundred years before the second war when it was at its mightiest.) After 1945, those times were changing.

In February of that year Christopher received his Classics Master of Arts degree in the Cambridge Senate House and an excellent career lay ahead with the British Council. On 17th April 1948 he married Margaret Radegund King, daughter of Bill King. So the genes from the union of Thomas Other and Jane Lister, 145 years earlier in 1806, were brought together once more. Many of their joint predecessors originated from Wensleydale. Christopher's mother, Georgina Winn, was the granddaughter of Christopher Other and his wife Anne Stackhouse. Christopher Other's sister, Margaret, had married into the King family.

Christopher's early life had not been easy. His father had bullied him and sent him to a prep. school he hated. Julian wanted him to go into the Foreign Office, but his application was unsuccessful. His personal ambition had always been to become a country solicitor hoping to work for Hugh Maughan in his Middleham practice. He succumbed to TB on leaving Cambridge, just as the war was about to be declared, and any hopes for his future career were put on hold. He recovered quickly but, on joining the army, his lungs were found to be damaged thus making him ineligible for a commission. He joined the ranks and experienced an unknown life style. He was sent on demolition missions working on crude alterations to large country houses that had been requisitioned for military purposes. He was upset to be ordered to destroy such things as classical stairways in stately homes. On one occasion, preparing a military hospital in a grand mansion where they were temporarily stationed, they were pulling out wonderful panelling to burn to keep warm. While there he remembered meeting a nice nurse who, he told his children, did nothing all day but nit examinations of his fellow soldiers' hair. He also used to tell his family how he spent much of these early months of the war peeling potatoes. However, it all changed when he was posted to India, where he was promoted and sent to Staff College. He spent the rest of the war in India and Burma.

When he received his BA (Hons) he did so at the same time as a friend who became a vicar and officiated at his wedding, the Rev. Francis Clarke. The organist was Tommy Evans, another friend, and it was he who produced a poem which had been written by Christopher, and long forgotten, characterising Francis and the very out of date social attitudes of the time:

## The Vicar of Hobby-cum-Hoop

> When the Master of Magdalene said, "Clarke you must go!"
> I applied to the Bishop of Wells and Truro.
> The Bishop of Truro he asked me to dine,
> (Really that cork, and Australian wine!)
> But impressed with the way I handled the soup,
> He made me the vicar of Hobby – cum – Hoop.
> Of course the Court Circular mentioned my name,
> And the "County" consulted the peerage to prove
> I was no more vicar, but one of The Clarkes.
> (Three castles in Ulster and various parks.)
> So the local nobility came in a troop
> To call at the vicarage of Hobby-cum-Hoop.
> Of course I must hold the communion at nine
> But I frequently go to the Castle to dine.
> And dear Lady Hobbledehoy is really too kind
> (Charming woman and so refined.)
> So really I think that I made quite a scoop
> In accepting the living of Hobby-cum-Hoop.
>
> So though I'm neither a Dean nor a Don
> I no longer look back at the days that are gone
> For Easter may come and Advent may go
> (The organ won't play as there's no one to blow.)
> The flowers on the alter may wither and droop,
> But I'll still be the vicar of Hobby-cum-Hoop.

Today this is outdated verse as class, land, titles and paternalism have lost their meaning, but just after the war those were the mark of a dying class structure as these brave young men of war clung to their 'old ways'.

At the end of the war, now with his commission, Major C. J. Ritchie, Royal Army Service Corps, required another reference for his application to Whitehall's elite apart from the retrospective one from his college. He asked Brigadier Luff D.D.S.T. 12th Army, South East Military Command to oblige. He agreed and pointed out that he had a five year connection with Ritchie and always found him well above average in education, with all round efficiency, good general deportment and bearing noting especially that he had been promoted from second lieutenant to major very much faster than was usual even in war time. He was clearly a candidate for promotion to an appointment calling for exceptional tact, possessing great self-confidence and initiative. This was, in his words, quite exceptional in a junior officer. The Brigadier was well satisfied with Ritchie's promotion which confirmed his integrity and loyalty to King and Country. He had no hesitation in recommending Christopher for the Civil Service. He had served in both India and Burma and preferred not to have his military career mentioned after he was appointed to the British Council.

He was awarded an OBE ten years after he was married, having been in charge of the Establishment Division of the Council and Director of the Fellowship Division overseeing the education of over 5,000 overseas students through his work. The British Council had particular links with Commonwealth countries and an overseas adult student was often invited to Christmas lunch by Christopher. The British Council's education programme should not be undervalued as it generated significant goodwill towards the British. In the late 1960s, Jane remembers a game of croquet on her parents' lawn at Boston Spa. "This is the only country in the world where you could find an Israeli and an Egyptian playing a friendly croquet match together" one of the guests told her.

Christopher and Margaret started married life living first in Kew and then in Richmond, Surrey where Jane and her siblings were born. When the daily journey from Richmond to Bond Street tube station began to pall, Christopher insisted on being demoted and he moved to the British

Council Office in Leeds where he was also responsible for offices in York, Hull and Bradford. They bought a house in Boston Spa, between York and Leeds. Wherever they lived they made regular trips home to Wensleydale. In 1960, Cowstonegill, the derelict farmhouse in Walden they had restored was sufficiently habitable for the Easter holiday.[126] It was later used for one of the James Herriott Vet TV episodes as it could easily have passed for a 1950's setting. Although he worked in an atmosphere far removed from country life, to him the moors and the call of the wild remained his first love.

> Oh for the call of the grouse from the heather,
> Oh for the wind that brings wild weather,
> When the rain clouds scud over the stone strewn hills
> And the mist rolls down from the tops of the gills.
> When the becks swollen high with recent rain
> Then I and my dog tread the moors together.
>
> Oh how much have they missed, who have not heard
> The weird storm cries of a moorland bird,
> The curlew's wail, and the plover's shriek,
> Echoing across the moorland bleak.
> Up rose a pack of grouse from my feet
> A Blackface ewe gave an anxious bleat,
> As over her head down wind they whirred.
>
> Oh to tramp the moors with one's dog,
> When the weather is wild and threatening fog;
> To follow the sodden tracks through the ling,
> To watch the moorfowl with lightening wing
> Seek the cover of down land from the gale;
> While the cruel rain smites one's face like a flail
> And the snipe drums over the peat strewn bog.
>
> C. J. R. date unknown, but it's his 'call of the wild'.

---

126   There were dried cowpats on the bathroom wall and Alice Thompson's chickens were still trying to nest in one of the candle holes.

When Christopher retired, he and Margaret converted the Old Hall Stables at West Burton from being used as a cow house into their eventual home as they realised that retiring up Walden was not really practical. Christopher was particularly pleased to be back home in the village he loved so much, amongst people who had known him since he was a little boy. Margaret found the move more difficult as she loved being up Walden but she gradually quietly assimilated into the community. After Christopher's death in 1977, she and Jane got to know the younger generation when they started a Sunday afternoon craft club. Old Hall Stables remains Jane's home today. The view down the quiet village green, the school opposite, the young generation playing on the green, folk coming and going: it was the culmination of a lifelong ambition to return. The community had created and maintained the surrounding countryside on the flank of Penhill overlooking village life which was grazed by sheep kept by farmers, many former family tenants. This was just one of thousands of villages from which the Nation's fighting men and women had drawn strength and whose people had created a strong British influence around the world over centuries.

There were post war tensions, not least in India, where Christopher had been for most of the war, but it remained the purpose of the British Council to maintain influence through the promotion of British culture and education which was what his career had been all about. He had served in a war, the second to end all wars, which it hadn't, but the world of the '50's, '60's and '70's had become more peaceful than the fifty year period leading up to WW2. His final career honour was when he was made an Honorary Doctor of Letters at the University of Bradford, which he was initially reluctant to accept as he was not a fan of Bradford University's Chancellor, Harold Wilson. Christopher had worked closely with Leeds, York and Bradford Universities in the interests of the overseas students so he eventually accepted with good grace. He died at home from a heart attack on August 24th 1977 aged only 61. Wensleydale never had the true benefit of this man who was one of its sons and who had so much to offer the community he had returned to. Margaret gave herself to that same commitment as she, through her father's lines and her mother's example, had been brought up so to do.

Christopher and Margaret had four children. Jane Other Ritchie was born at 29 Cambrian Road, Richmond, Surrey on April 1st 1949. She was educated at Sesame Primary School, Putney High School, St Mary's Calne and Newnham College, Cambridge. She was awarded her M.A. from Cambridge in 1970. Their eldest son, Nicholas King Ritchie was born 6th December[127] 1951. He followed his father to Wellington College and Magdalene College, Cambridge and was awarded his M.A. in 1974, becoming a merchant banker. He married a diplomat's daughter Nina Mason.[128] John Passingham Winn Ritchie was born in 1954. He also went to Wellington and trained at Oxford Polytechnic to become a Chartered Surveyor for the Valuation Office. He married Margaret Ellison, a widow with two girls. In 1960, Timothy William Ritchie was born. He also went to Wellington, then to Oxford Polytechnic to study Estate Management. He married a solicitor's daughter from the West Midlands, Bernadette Anne Edwards, training in fine arts with Bonhams, initially specialising in carpets. He now has his own fine arts valuation business, based in Bristol.

From their Aberdeenshire roots, the Ritchie family spread around the world. The Rouge Dragon Pursuivant of Arms, attendant to a Herald at the College of Arms, verified the Ritchie entitlement to a coat of arms by tracing the family roots back to 1625. He noted: "the name is one of a small Highland Clan, with its own tartan, associated with the family Adams. After Culloden in 1745 some the family removed to London and the River Thames".

Margaret died on Boxing Day 1999, having been a widow for 23 years. Her family, her dogs, St Andrew's Church at Aysgarth, the Parish Council of Burton-cum-Walden and its community were the centre of her life. As one of her neighbours said at the time, "she would always go that extra mile." As a school governor, parish clerk, church warden and supporter of the West Burton Methodist congregation she was involved in all aspects of traditional English village life. She inherited tenanted farms and a group of her tenants carried her coffin into St Andrews's Church,

---

127   6th December is St. Nicholas' Day.

128   Nicholas & Nina have five children: William Heath, Edward Thomas, Christopher Timothy, Jonathan Mason and Lucinda Alice.

thence to the family grave where she was lovingly lowered into the upper layer of the double decker plot above Christopher. Margaret had been a keen genealogist and local historian and had researched the history of Wensleydale and her family back to Henry VIII's Dissolution of the Monasteries.

# Chapter 14

## Four hundred years of rural change

From the end of the 15<sup>th</sup> century, land ownership, which had been the power base of the Crown, the aristocrats, their squires and supporters, entered a period of change. In Wensleydale, much of the southern side of the Ure valley had belonged to the Crown. In 1628, Charles I had incurred substantial debts and his creditors were pressing so he sold his Pennine land to the Corporation of the City of London. By 1656, the City decided to sell the tenants on this land their freeholds, a rare occurrence, thus creating an area of small voting yeomen. The land to the north was held mostly in smaller estates, although there were larger blocks belonging to such families as the Lowthers, who became the Lords Lonsdale; the Scropes; Metcalfes, originally stewards of another small block of Crown land; and the Powletts, a female line of the Scropes later the Lords Bolton.

Valley land was progressively enclosed, whilst on the open ground running up to the moors communal occupancy had become the norm. By 1600, 90% of the fertile valley land was farmed in field systems, as against strip systems, which would have been rare in many districts. The moors and surrounding high pastures, known as allotments, were originally grazed by monastic flocks, but the Reformation heralded the end of large flocks supervised by monks and shepherded by local folk to whom they had taught flock management skills. The weavers of mainland Europe, who traditionally took the 'Golden Fleece', suddenly had to go through new negotiating processes with a domestic wool industry comprised of thousands of small farmers and dealers. There were disputes over rights to graze and the numbers of stock often held on unidentified areas of pasture. To maintain some form of order communities introduced beast gates, later known as gaits,[129] which were fixed units of livestock that could

---

129   Sheep gaits are defined as so many ewes and their followers.

run on defined areas. The indigenous sheep had been carefully bred by the monks and gave rise to the Wensleydale and Swaledale breeds running on the moors and in the Dales today. Over time they became hefted, as ewes taught their lambs where to return to feed and find shelter.

The importance of the uplands lay in their natural resources. Some were reserved by the freeholder such as an institution, the Crown, or an aristocrat and would have included the forestry, mineral and sporting rights, but the grazing, peat deposits, brushwood, stones, rocks and bracken were held in common. By 1700, 5,300 acres of valley land at the top of Wensleydale, with common rights onto the ling (heather), was farmed by 93 families, an average of 57 acres each. Mining was running down, wool had not held its premium, but cattle numbers were increasing.

Much of Britain's expansion abroad was funded by landed families who invested in shipping from coastal ports and rivers such as the Thames, where around 2,000 boats were emptied and loaded daily with the essential goods of Empire. The attractive returns from investing in shipping and cargoes, both into and out of the country enticed some landowners to sell land. Farming yielded poor returns in the form of rent, and minerals were all the time fluctuating in value, but shipping seemed to offer a solid and certain return. The boats bound for Africa with supplies were unloaded. Then they moved a labour force, in the form of slaves, to the sugar islands of the Caribbean returning home with sugar, rum, molasses and gold from the plantation owners, many of whom were British. As the Empire matured, slavery came to an end and returning ships replaced them with increased tonnages of cereals brought back to British flour mills from America, Canada and Australia at well below the cost of home production which had a disastrous effect on arable farming and ultimately rents.

The fortunes of farming fluctuated with some land agents fixing rents at unrealistic levels, refusing to recognise the realities of the cheap food policies of government. Pastoral areas such as the Pennines, the South West moors, the Welsh Marches and the Scottish Uplands were largely unaffected by these economic swings, but in the 19th century freezer ships were introduced to deliver cheap supplies of butter, cheese, lamb, beef and wool from the Southern Hemisphere to Britain.

As mining went into decline hundreds of working men were left unemployed, and, if they remained without work, they were forced either to emigrate or to draw meagre support from the Poor Law funded by a local tax on farming. Consequently, farmers found it preferable to find work for idle hands to do in the form of wall building, to meet Enclosures agreements, road building, roof thatching and manual farm work in preference to making use of the new implements being introduced to reduce farm labour. Home wool prices fell, flocks became smaller and cow numbers increased introducing a new enterprise; farm house dairy production of cheese and butter. The cows calved in spring onto the lush Dales pastures resulting in a flush of milk which was made into cheese. As the yields and quality fell in the autumn, milk surplus to domestic requirements was turned into butter. Most farmhouses had windowless, cheese rooms on the north side that were always cool and where dairy produce was stored, waiting to be sold at the market or to dealers in butter and cheese.

Cheese was wrapped in thin linen covers and butter was sold in firkins, light wooden barrels, holding half of one hundredweight. There was trouble at one point when the firkin makers of West Witton[130] were accused of reducing the depth of containers thus reducing the net weight of butter sold. It was quickly proved that they were working in league with local farmers thus being paid more for less. The merchants solved the problem by introducing check weighing. Traditional trust was becoming a thing of the past.

Weekly markets in Leyburn and Hawes were attended by merchants from the Yarm area forty miles away. They bought dairy products from many farmers and returned with their loads to trade and deal by bulking up even larger loads to go to ports on the River Tees for onward shipping to London. The Cistercian monks had developed the original Wensleydale cheese from sheep's milk, but by the start of the 18th century most cheese was made from cow's milk thus boosting local farming incomes. The carters transporting dairy produce returned with groceries, flax for linen manufacture in the water mills, iron, tar, timber and salt.

---

130    West Witton was a centre for firkin making.

*Bill King and Dots Pasingham when engaged at Highclere.*

*From left to right: Prof Barrois, Professor of Geology at Lille University; Captain Bill King and Col. David after Lille had been freed by the Allies in WW1.*

*Bill King's portrait at Magdalene College, Cambridge by kind permission of The Master and Fellows. Bill is holding a rock boring from the sea bed of the English Channel.*

*Prof Cuchlaine King ScD.*

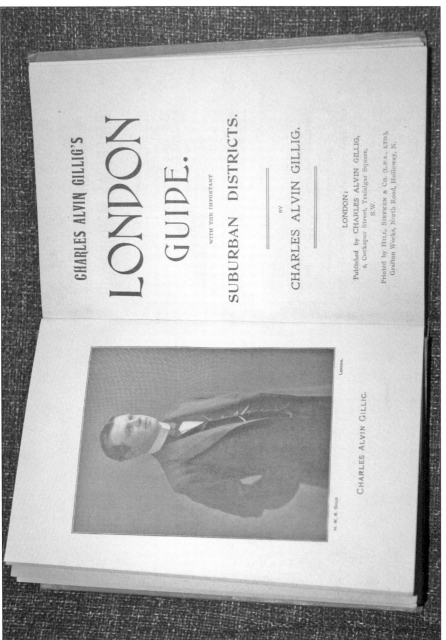

CHARLES ALVIN GILLIG'S

# LONDON GUIDE.

WITH THE IMPORTANT

SUBURBAN DISTRICTS.

BY

CHARLES ALVIN GILLIG.

LONDON:
Published by CHARLES ALVIN GILLIG,
2, Cockspur Street, Trafalgar Square,
S.W.

Printed by HILL, SIFFKEN & Co. (L.P.A., LTD.),
Grafton Works, North Road, Holloway, N.

H. W. R. CHILD

CHARLES ALVIN GILLIG.

LONDON.

*Charles Gillig*

-183-

*Ball at the Grosvenor Gallery hosted by Henry F Gillig, (presumably held on 4 July) from Frank Leslie's Illustrated Newspaper 6 August 1887*

-184-

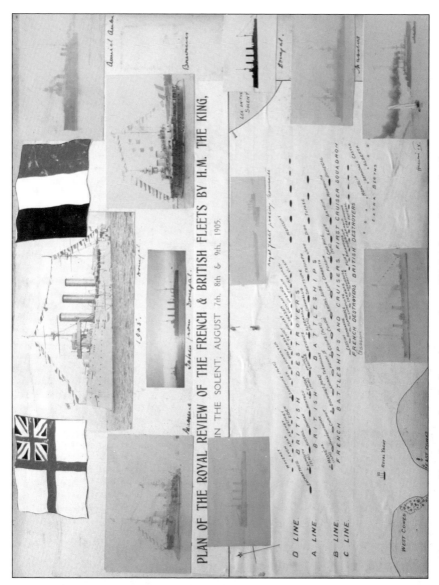

*Dots' scrapbook showing review of British and French Fleets 1905.*

*Dots and Amy Armitage with Cognac at Greenhills, Tilford, Surrey.*

*Dots and Chap meeting for the first time.*

*Portrait of Dots.*

*Dots and Jean Buchanan with car SP 198.*

*Shooting Party in Scotland with the Buchanans. Dots second from right.*
*Jean Buchanan extreme right.*

*Dots on holiday. She is to the right of the right hand car.*

*Page from Dot's scrapbook whilst at the Highclere 1914 including photo of Lady Carnarvon.*

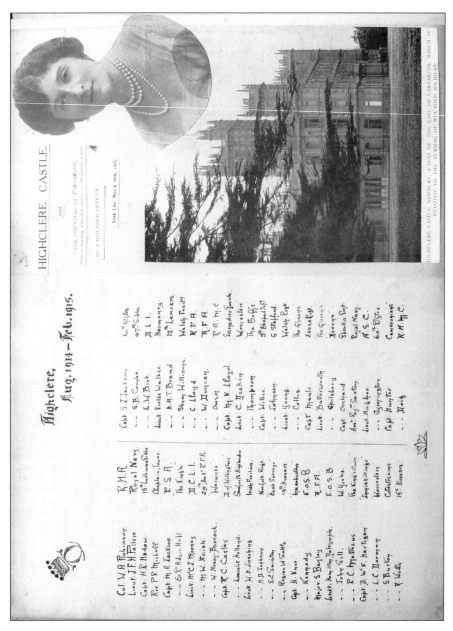

*List of injured army officers August 1914 – February 1915, Highclere.*

*William Ritchie (1775 – 1835).*

*Janet Muriel Ritchie.*

*Left to Right Christopher, Alfred and Gerald Ritchie.*

*Jane photographed by Ramsay & Muspratt, Cambridge, 1950.*

*Jane's family at Worton 1960's.*
*Back row left to right: Dots, Margaret, Timothy, John, Jane and*
*Christopher; Front row: Bill and Nip, Nicholas and Caramel.*

*Photo taken in Barnard Castle after the announcement of the Falklands*
*War. Margery did up the hooks and eyes on Jane's sun-top and bought a*
*cauliflower from the market whilst the photograph was being taken!*

*Jane Ritchie with Mark and Tom Lynas, May 2006.*

*Jane with Nanŭk and Sally. Photo taken by Ronnie McDonnell for Mollie Ritchie.*

*Interior of The Work Place.*

*The Work Place entrance.*

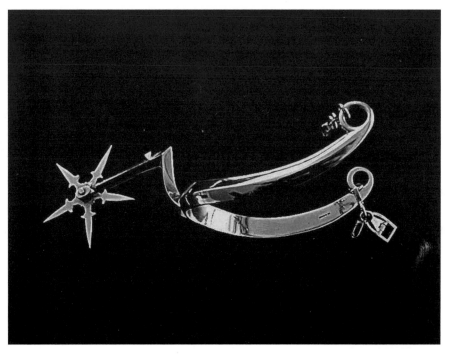

*Replica of the Charlton Spur.*

A survey of farm holdings carried out in the early 19th century emphasised the importance of common rights in the hills and dales. Manorial Courts[131] which resolved manorial disputes, appointed farmers and professionals to sit in judgement. In one area of 506 acres of meadow and pasture, with access to a common, there were 1,143 sheep, 338 cattle and 46 horses. In other words an acre of meadow (cutting grass), or pasture (grazing grass) was carrying 2.2 sheep, 0.75 of a cow and 0.09 of a horse. This was before the days of fertiliser and would be regarded as very intensive grassland farming today. However it illustrates the role of the common grazing as these animals would have spent much of the summer on the moor or fell.

Horses were the sole source of power for carting produce on and off the farm and the only transport for the family to market, church or chapel either ridden or driven, saddle or harness. Tough ponies of around 15 hands, similar to the Dales and Fell ponies of today, were most common compared to the larger Clydesdales and Shires of the arable country further east although they would have been seen in the Dales hauling heavy loads of minerals, timber and produce.

It is possible that some farmers on the Pennines followed their fellows on the North Yorkshire Moors where the Cleveland Bay horse became popular in the 19th century. This was originally a cross between the typical English hunter and the heavy horse. They were bay in colour, over 16 and up to 17 hands high and capable of being ridden, driven or going between the shafts. They could be used on smart occasions in a carriage, gig, post chaise, or trap. Her Majesty the Queen currently leads a programme of breed improvement of Cleveland Bays, stabling a team in the Royal Mews which are used for ceremonial parades.

The Enclosure Acts were introduced in the 17th century and developed with some urgency between 1800 and 1850 as Napoleon tried to cut Britain off from its supply of imported food. Each enclosure required an Act of Parliament to be approved in Westminster where Parliament was gradually becoming more democratic as people such as William Cobbett, fought for and won rural seats in the House of Commons. In 1881, the last

---

131    In the north Manorial Courts were known as Courts Leet.

Enclosure Act was passed in Wensleydale around Cotterdale and Staggs Fell on Abbotside, covering an area of nearly 10,000 acres.

Lord Lonsdale sold much of his Dales land to the Wortley family from West Yorkshire who had considerable interests in coal on their own estate near Sheffield. The non-aristocratic Metcalfes who had over invested sold much of their Dales land to their tenants. The Duke of Bolton reduced his land holdings, some of which had come through marriages to the Scrope and Powlett families. The complex Lordship of Middleham, in which some of the families in this book had interests, was dispersed to tenants who then became yeomen farmers sometimes without sporting and mineral rights. The Other and Lister families purchased mineral and sporting rights over some of these yeomen's farms, notably in Coverdale.

As the 21$^{st}$ century dawned, Margery Freeman passed away. A great deal had changed in her century. Villages, almost entirely occupied by families with a rural way of life when she was a girl, were now dominated by commuters, the retired and holiday visitors. Farms were much larger employing fewer people. The cattle in dairy herds had gone from traditional brown breeds to the black and white of the Friesian which had first appeared in the dales in the 1950's. During her active life the cross bred lambs from the horned ewes on the moors were sired by Teeswater rams and called Mashams, and by the time she had reached the age of sixty the breed of crossing rams had changed to Blue Faced Leicesters with their progeny called Mules. These sheep, sold as gimmer lambs were to become, and remain, the main harvest of the hills as breeding ewes to go to farms in the Midlands and South of England. Margery and Jane's relative, always known as Uncle Wiley (his son married one of Christopher Other's sisters), was one of the originators of the Masham cross bred and successfully promoted them by exhibiting and winning prizes at the Great Yorkshire Show.

# Chapter 15

## Two young men

Our looks, personalities, temperament and intelligence are defined by chromosomes carrying a multiplicity of genetic markers. When an ovum is fertilised, the two sets of chromosomes link at random, with the result that every foetus carries both dominant and recessive genes. Therefore an individual's character, or physique, cannot be foreseen and a break back to traits from a generation long passed can often appear. A sudden mop of black hair in a family that is predominantly fair haired, or blue eyes where brown have always prevailed are examples. Margery Freeman and Jane Other Ritchie, second cousins twice removed, had similarities such as fallen arches, a love of cats and an unusually intense interest in their families and the locality in which they dwelt.

Margery's maternal grandparents were very down to earth people. Her maternal great grandfather, a farmer, was almost certainly from thrifty peasant stock and her maternal great grandmother was the gipsy girl about whom so little is known. Despite considerable research, no genetic record has been found of the girl taken back to Gale Bank Farm by widower John Kirk. Margery recorded her name as Ellen[132] Nagley, one not recognised by the Gipsy Council. She probably had jet black hair, dark skin and an empathy with nature and music. We know that this nomadic race can carry hereditary genetic traits resulting in short life spans, which certainly was not the case with Margery. Her father, Charlie Burrill was a solicitor and her mother came from a medical family.

Margery was at home with nature from an early age, interested in hunting and fishing with an understanding of the activity in farming and forestry

---

132   Records show her name was in fact Elizabeth.

around her home. During her trips with her grandfather on his daily rounds visiting the sick, injured and infirm she met local people and made friends and acquaintances. After a home education she went away to the Royal College of Music and left as a promising violinist and accompanist, able to write and conduct music, which she put to good use in the local musical societies and celebrations, but took it no further. Travel abroad appealed to her yet there is little to indicate that she travelled much in Britain[133] although in her home clime she knew every beck, moor, meadow, fell top and river bank. Neither did she suffer fools gladly. As a magistrate she took a hard line on crime, but showed compassion in cases brought before the bench due to poverty or unavoidable circumstance.

From her writing a lot can be understood. Her little red poetry book describes her personal experiences and innermost feelings at an important time in her life. Her freelance articles, mostly rejected by editors, were far removed from the standards of her poetry, but her regularly published articles commissioned by the Field Sports magazine, were of a higher standard and demonstrated her expert knowledge of things happening in field, covert, river bank or pool.

There is another little red book entitled "Things I want to remember", written in her upright scrawl in grey ink with a thick nib. These previously unread pieces illustrate her incredible interest in all things natural and some of the contents would offend people today. It is undated. The first notes are taken from a book by Paget entitled The Rose of London which is a comprehensive explanation of the sport of falconry. Next, after three blank pages, comes hunting in the time of Richard III, explaining the rituals and art of stag hunting including a unique glossary of the chase with details of the kill which takes eleven pages, concluding with three on wolf hunting pointing out that the last such hunt took place in the reign of Queen Elizabeth I. There follow ten bare pages and then five of notes taken from the book entitled 'Middleham Moor' by Hugh Maughan, the solicitor from Middleham, who acted as managing agent for a number of local estates as well as overseeing the management of Middleham Moor.

---

133  Margery and Reg occasionally went to Scotland with all expenses paid by Margery.

This little note book, measuring six by three inches, in a way formalises the sort of experiences and knowledge that would have been passed down through gipsy families over generations while sitting around a fire or in a hoop cart at night fall. Her other interest, of which there is little evidence in her archive, was archaeology. She had sufficient knowledge to be invited on several occasions to join Leeds University digs in the Dales.

As the limitations of age increased, Margery's interest in her wider family grew. However no mention is made, amongst the mass of family trees she scribbled on a variety of pieces of paper, of many details of her own family. One would have thought that local gossip, over generations, would have made the appearance of a gipsy girl at Gale Bank Farm, all those years before, an essential part of folk law to be passed down and captured in the memories of future generations. People in Middleham and Leyburn were unaware of Margery's ancestry.

Neither Jane nor Margery had children of their own. Although Jane's working life involved working with young people, Margery would never serve on the Juvenile Bench because she was not a parent, although she did write as if a parent in one of her short stories. Reg didn't share her interest in nature and rural pursuits, and unlike Jane, Margery had very few close friends. However, both women had one special boy in their lives. In Margery's case it was a young boy[134] whose family had bought a house in Redmire. The young man was initially interested in learning how to fish with a fly, but Margery soon found she could share her extensive knowledge of country wisdom and field craft with him. Her detailed writing about hunting, shooting and fishing reveals an extensive knowledge and understanding. She was pleased to have met someone with whom she could share this knowledge and her love of the river, wood and moor.

When Margery's husband died, she decided that Elm House was too large and too much work for her to cope with alone. Northgate, the house in Redmire she had previously rented when her brother got married, was for sale and this time she bought it. She was pleased to move back to a house and garden she knew. Margery made plans when her young

---

134    Margery always referred to him as "the boy".

friend visited her during the school holidays. Salmon and trout, grouse, pheasants and rabbits, she had a fund of information on their habits and habitats. She had followed the Wensleydale Harriers to hunt the hare on foot, and when younger she had followed the Otter hounds. When in her nineties, she told Jane that she thought the days of hunting were passed. It is to her credit that she was able to take that sort of social change in her stride.

Her detailed knowledge of the role of gamekeepers is perhaps surprising. She records the annual operation of burning heather when gamekeepers used a pole with a large flap of heavy linoleum on its end with which to beat out the burn when it reached a particular point, usually at the end of a patch of long old heather and before it reached the younger shoots. This took place in late winter before the grouse hens started to nest. In spring the keepers had their rounds trapping the egg thieves: stoats, weasels, hedgehogs and raptors. They took note of nesting sites and popped the odd bunny for supper, or for the dogs. The final act of good moor care was to make sure the shooting butts were in perfect order with turf on top and swept out inside. Then, at last, came the 12th of August preceded by much talk and excitement amongst the shooting fraternity, wondering whether the late spring had kept numbers down, whether so and so would, as usual, lose his temper with his springer spaniel, which normally happened.

In her younger days Margery had attended the shoots organised by her brother. On the early shooting days of the season, guests were long standing friends and fellow moorland owners. The keeper had a special game cart pulled by a pair of Dales ponies which carried five people and the 'bag' neatly hung by their necks in pairs, known as a brace. The number of days shot was only determined when grouse populations had been assessed after two or three days of driving and flanking. The art was to stop shooting to leave at least one hen per 50 acres. During the first season beaters covered ten or more miles daily, pushing grouse forwards to the guns over distances of up to a mile. The head man watched his long line of up to thirty men, making sure they stuck to the line avoiding no obstacles, wading streams and scrambling over rocks. Beaters called flankers, made sure that birds attempting to fly away left or right from the line of guns were pushed back by the appropriate noises and movement of men flapping paper feed bags on the edges of the beaters' line. From grouse shooting it was a simple move to more mundane pheasant shooting as the principles were similar.

Margery's first love, however, was fishing with the fly. With great thoroughness, Margery subjected the young man to the Freeman method of learning river fishing. Having got the feel of a light pliable cane trout rod he had to cast his line to alight the fly, for training purposes a small piece of cotton wool, accurately on dinner plates dotted around the lawn. Initially he was tasked with hitting a plate twenty feet away and gradually moving away to twenty yards, casting to left and right, allowing for the breeze and developing a delicate touch. Margery then became a fish and attached herself to the line and taught her pupil to gently and skilfully bring the fish towards the bank to be netted. Too hard and the line would break, a snag on the line might well lose the fish, so he had to learn the art, or the 'feel' for when a fish swam fast downstream. Too hard a pull and the quarry will be gone. Finally, he had to learn the skills of tying a fly and gutting his fish. It was not simply learning about the river, for in summer they drove up Coverdale, or over into Swaledale, to admire the landscape and for Margery to reminisce about the past. Margery was doing for her young friend what her grandfather had done for her. At Margery's funeral, he delivered the eulogy, and raised many smiles as he described his fishing lessons on Margery's lawn and their days together in the Dales countryside.

Jane Ritchie's equivalent young friend is the great grandson of Tressilian Charles Nicholas (known as Tress), former Senior Bursar of Trinity College Cambridge, whose family had been close friends of both the Passingham and King families for many years. Amy Passingham's sister Adelaide had gone to a finishing school in Bournemouth with Tress's mother, and when he went up to Cambridge to read Geology his mother told him to visit her friend's parents at Milton. He walked there only to find they had gone, but luckily someone in the Post Office knew the family had moved to Toft. Tress later went and met the Passinghams and Jane's grandmother Dots, who used to play the piano for him when he visited. He was given George Augustus' old bicycle which made getting around town much easier. George had bought himself a new one with gears!

Tress got to know Bill King through the Sedgwick Club, the Cambridge University club for geologists. He always described Dots as his second oldest friend,[135] and with the birth of his great, great grand-children it is a family friendship spanning seven generations. Jane appointed herself honorary godmother to two of the great grandchildren: Mark, who stayed with her in what they jokingly called the 'Staindrop Hilton' and his older sister Jenny.

Mark's father worked for the Geological Survey and was sent on placements all over the world, taking his wife and children with him. Mark, his sister Jenny and their two younger siblings lived peripatetic lives which created interesting gaps in their education. The constant inter-continental moves interspersed with visits back to homes in England was, to say the least, unsettling. The family eventually settled in Majorca with the intention of following a dream of self–sufficiency based on growing exotic fruits to export back to the U.K. It was a disaster for despite having an understanding of soils, rocks and climates they picked the wrong small holding in the wrong place, with the result that their crops were largely a failure.

Mark couldn't settle in Majorca and wanted to sit his A levels in England. He explained his predicament to Jane at his great grandfather's hundredth birthday dinner given by Trinity College, as his aunt's seating plan fortuitously sat them together. After dinner Jane sought out his father and told him that if there was no other option Mark could stay with her at her home in Staindrop, County Durham to study for his exams at a local school. She thought no more about it until, two weeks later, there was a knock on her door and Mark's father stood there saying he had come to see if she really had meant what she had said? Well of course she had.

One of Jane's business colleagues once said; "Most people would give their eye teeth to live with Jane". Mark was about to find out whether that was the case or not, when, in the summer of 1989, Jane welcomed him, aged 16, into her life for two years. The venture was successful, but the outcome could never have been foreseen by either party. They agreed to both make a written record of their adventure together, and Jane struck

---

135    His oldest friend had been to school with him and lived in Palermo.

to a bargain she had made to teach him to drive and help him to argue better than she could herself. In return, Mark would work hard to achieve really good results in his A levels and pass his driving test. In her record of that first year, she started by saying that she knew it was not going to be plain sailing, but that she was certain it would be positive, enriching and that at the end she would have a sense of achievement, adding that she must allow herself space and protect herself from thought overload.

Mark's great-grandfather Tressilian Nicholas was part of the academic hierarchy of Cambridge and maintained a close friendship with the King and later the Ritchie families. Confronted with a teenager in the house, Jane found home life very different from her day job. She had had bred into her a set of standards that were not those of the current generation. Mark objected strongly to wearing a tie for school. Jane bought him a black one telling him he would need it one day for his great grandfather's funeral. She was impressed with the way he remembered to write a thank you letter to the Uncle and Aunt who he had been staying with.

He liked rice but not potatoes and wanted gravy or sauce with food to make it easier to swallow. He had arrived very short of the right clothing, but during a weekend at her mother's home in West Burton, Margaret Ritchie presented him with a variety of good outdoor attire. Jane gave him a silk dressing gown which, much to her surprise, he immediately took to wearing in the evenings. Her mother was charmed by him, especially when he offered to take the dog for a walk which established a warm relationship between them which pleased Jane. The two became very fond of each other and when Jane's mother gave him £5 for half term spending, he asked Jane how a pensioner could afford such extravagance. It never occurred to him that she had a widow's pension from the British Council.

On leaving university, Jane worked amongst school leavers and understood their charms, abilities and problems so within days of Mark's arrival she was getting an impression of her temporary companion. He bullied her when he wanted something, not luxuries or food, but for work that he could do on the word processor, which was something new to him. He wanted to be able to touch type suggesting to her that perhaps, one day, he would become a journalist. He liked reading and, contrary to his father's opinion, he had many interests. Jane was somewhat surprised though when he announced he didn't much like writing about himself.

Gradually letters arrived from relatives, homesickness took hold and Jane heard him crying one night after he had gone to bed. There was nothing she could do as no amount of kindness on her part could compensate for the absence of his family; she just wasn't family. Mark often asked her to repeat things, giving her the impression that his hearing was not as sharp as it should be, and he said, more than once, that he had difficulty picking up the strong Teesdale accent when he went to the chip shop; where incidentally, he found the chips were not to his liking. They were crisp and his preference was for soggy ones.

Jane has never owned a television, which Mark found extraordinary. He asked, even demanded, they should get one, but Jane refused. However, when they went to his family's store of spare furniture on a friend's farm near Nottingham to collect things for his sister to take to university, he found an old black and white set. Jane bought him the Independent newspaper each day and pointed out the columnists she thought he would enjoy reading and, then in the evening, they could discuss, and possibly argue over, his reactions and opinions.

Jane was pleased he was becoming part of a circle of young people from school, especially when he was invited to a party in nearby Egglestone. Possibly as a result, she was even more pleased when he washed his hair, but was then somewhat perplexed when he refused to dry it. Ever conscious of her new responsibility she wondered, at one point whether she might be overfeeding him and realised she was without liquid paraffin in her medicine cupboard to relieve any associated problems. Ever observant, she also noted that Mark had written to his parents and his great grandfather, and she wondered exactly what he was telling them about his temporary home and way of life.

He started his last two years of secondary education at Teesdale School in Barnard Castle with understandable trepidation, but seemed fairly happy, and when he announced that English lessons were including poetry, Jane responded by fostering this obvious enthusiasm. She shared his love of the rhythm of words and produced an example in his honour which sadly he didn't keep. Jane did.

> From Majorca a modern Milton
> Came to Teesdale and the Staindrop Hilton.
> A down at heel Neville in hat and coat,
> Mark Tressilian Lynas has lost his mote.

The Staindrop Hilton was a reference to the Bangkok Hilton, a notorious prison featured in a film starring Denholm Elliot and Nicole Kidman which Mark and Jane had watched at her mother's one weekend. Margaret Ritchie thought that Mark looked like Neville Chamberlain in her father-in-law's best black overcoat and a black trilby Mark had bought himself. He caused her a lot of amusement when he went mushrooming so dressed, moving at speed with the coat flapping as he spotted another mushroom. 1989 was a very good mushroom year and vast quantities were deep frozen only to be lost in 2001 when Jane moved into her mother's house and the deep freeze was inadvertently switched off. Jane explained to Mark that a mote was a biblical reference to prejudice.

To Jane, the relationship was just as fascinating and challenging as it was for Mark. Her observations, in those early days, included being surprised that he liked going to her mother's house at West Burton for the weekends so much. He became interested in the Teesdale Fell Rescue group and joined them on the hills, frequently in the guise of an injured walker, to test the skills of the search and rescue dogs. He had to learn the Highway Code before he could attempt his driving test and took this with him to study while he waited for the dogs to find him. Jane could not understand why he so desperately wanted to convert his new friends to his type of music. She thought it strange he couldn't work out how to stop the bus when going to school although he always got off at the right stop on the return journey. Only years later she found that he preferred to walk to the earlier stop in the morning in order to catch the bus with his friends.

As he settled in he undoubtedly put pressure on Jane's quiet well organised home life. Although his parents had written to her in the early weeks, she was surprised they had not corresponded with their son. In

September, Mark's sister Jenny arrived back in England to attend Essex University, and wanted to collect various items from the family furniture store near Nottingham. Jane could not see how Jenny was going to manage this without her help. So Jenny appeared in Richmond where her boyfriend's family dropped her off on their way to take their son to Teesside University. Jenny stayed with Jane and Mark until they took her to Colchester via Nottingham.

On the 26th September, Jane recorded she had cut Jenny's hair while Mark was out laying bricks at the nearby Deerbolt Young Offenders Unit on a school visit. In the evening her cleaner, Elsie, came and chatted while her blind husband was at a meeting of the Antediluvian Order of Buffaloes (the Buffs) in the Wheatsheaf pub in Staindrop. A friend of Jane's also arrived and a rather bizarre evening followed. Jenny decided Napoleon's horse[136] was called Jeffery which was a reference to Wendy Cope's parody of the poem: "For I will consider my cat Jeffery" in her anthology Making Cocoa for Kingsley Amis. On September 27th Jenny dyed her hair black and on the 28th went off to Middlesborough to see her boyfriend. After a weekend at West Burton, Jenny was taken down to Colchester, the car loaded with things she had purloined from her parents' furniture store. Jane and Mark stayed a night at Bar Hill, just north of Cambridge, on the way home so that they could visit his great grandfather in Trinity College the next morning.

In October, a friend of Jane's, who used to attend the Durham University 'Milk Round'[137] recruiting on behalf of his firm, came to stay. They had met through a mutual friend when he was in the army stationed at Catterick. Friends of his rented a cottage near Winston, a village outside Staindrop, and were moving out so the landlord was looking for a new tenant. Jane had wanted to move from Newton Aycliffe into the country and took up his offer of an introduction, which led to her move to Westholme. When not posted abroad he used Jane's washing machine usually late at night

---

136  Although Napoleon's most famous horse was called Marengo, Jane's mother maintained one was called Nicol as Napoleon had named the German pumpernickel bread as Pain pour Nicol.

137  Universities then held annual recruitment fairs attended by major employers of graduates.

telling her "you've not lived until you've washed at midnight." It annoyed her that he refused to let her finish the job by ironing the clothes thus denying her the satisfaction of 'doing a job properly.'

The visit was a mixed experience. When Mark had been told about it he had surprised her by saying he hoped she wouldn't become too emotionally upset as he couldn't cope with tears. Jane was pleased the two of them got on, but recorded in her journal," I still care about him in a very protective way and although I'm not "in love" with him, I do love him and miss him when he's gone." The three of them read several of Wendy Cope's poems with great enjoyment, but Jane was sorry her friend refused to let her give him a copy saying he had changed and become cynical. She recorded, "hadn't he always been like a bear with a sore head?"

Mark had a friend he wanted to come and stay, but understandably Jane felt she really couldn't take much more youth in her life than she already had. There were complaints that Mark was being rude at school and although she understood his reaction to a situation he had found himself in, she pointed out that he had to learn to understand and manage the attitudes of people different from himself. A long discussion followed! His economics teacher asked the staff in the school office to be more tolerant.

When Jane's old dog had reached the end of her life Jane braced herself for the sad final journey to the vet, but what would Mark's reaction be? After he had left for school, she left a note for him to find when he got home. She would have time to cry before facing him. To her relief and joy, as she walked in, he gave her a big hug and asked if she was OK? They decided to go more or less straight away to a local dog rescue centre and pick a new companion. The little bitch they agreed on was called Tigger and cost £10. Mark paid £5 for the front end, as he didn't like what came out of the back.[138]

*On the 9th November 1989 the Berlin Wall was breached marking a new era for the youth of East Germany in particular and for the world as a whole.*

---

138   Mark's parents later gave Jane the back half of Tigger as a thank you present for having Mark to stay.

Mark's grandfather, Tressilian, died two days later on the 11th November. The funeral was to be in Cambridge. The drive down country from County Durham was dismal, the roads were crowded, there was a thick fog and they were fast running behind time so Jane turned off the A1 at Norman Cross going via Ramsey, the Forty Foot Drain and Pidley. To her surprise, Mark took the map and navigated eastwards, across the Fens, avoiding the traffic on the approach roads to Cambridge. They met Mark's great aunt Jean and her husband under Trinity College's New Court archway on their way to the mortuary where the body lay. Mark's grandmother, Lo, had left Jane a message to dissuade Mark from going to see it. He had not needed much persuasion.

King's Parade was closed in honour of one of the great men of the University. The cortege proceeded from Trinity College to St Edward's Church which was full of flowers despite the announcement in the Daily Telegraph to the contrary. The retired Senior Chaplain of Trinity Hall, who had been a close friend, referred to Tressilian simply as "my kind friend". Jane recorded how she would always remember following the coffin down St Edward's Passage after the service looking through the fog to a stone cross on the ornamental screen of King's College, the apricot coloured flowers on the coffin lifted high by the bearers; the shop on the right was brightly lit and full of multi-coloured golfing umbrellas, in stark contrast to the grey, cold dampness of the November afternoon.

Mark didn't travel back with Jane as he wanted to stay with his parents for the evening and to return the following day. This caused a row, as instead of returning north by train he travelled by coach as it was cheaper, but it took longer. He finally arrived in Darlington at 10.00p.m. Jane was furious as she wanted an early night having driven 400 miles the previous day in awful conditions, but he refused to understand why she was so cross. Her anger is expressed in her record: "Time has not the value money has as far as he's concerned."

At the end of Mark's first term, Jane helped him pack two large bags with shopping for his parents: books, seed tags, Marmite and a Christmas pudding, and a small case for his own few possessions. Her record ends there apart from an entry recorded the following year referring to another visit once more triggered by the 'Milk Round' that had been disruptive to Jane, Mark and the dogs as it broke their established routines. By then a Bernese mountain dog puppy had joined Jane's household. The three drank a bottle of Roccadelle Macie Chianti Classico and the label is significantly preserved in the record.

By November 1990, Mark's university entry form had been completed and Jane speculated, privately, that: "on a good day he'd probably get 2A's and a B or, perhaps even 3 A's, but on a bad day who knows?" Cousin Margery gave Mark a trunk to take his things to Edinburgh University. Mark was scathing in his contempt for such an old fashioned practice. When he and Jane arrived at the Hall of Residence there were trunks being unloaded from all the cars. "It really gets up my nose that you are always right!" was his response. He still has the trunk in his roof space still serving its purpose as a useful storage container.

At Christmas, a year later, Jane received a card:

*Dear Jane, I chose this card for Christmas and the New Year to thank you for all the wise advice and hospitality you have given myself and my sister over the years. When I'm famous I'll mention you on T. V.! Love, Mark.* He was going to be a writer.

The idea of sitting the two together at that centenary party had worked remarkably well, for Mark went on to write books, appear on television and become involved in the politics of global food security. He had passed his school exams with flying colours and gone on to Edinburgh University where he realised his abilities, interests and, ultimately, his ambitions: the environment, the world, its people and their future became his domain. Jane smiled when he told her that his flatmates did not have the same standard of washing up as he did.

Mark is now a prolific writer and commentator in the controversial world of environmental policies. He is a Visiting Research Associate of the School of Geography and Environment at Oxford University. His book Six Degrees, dealing with the dilemma of global warming, won the Royal Society prize for scientific books and became a hit for the National Geographic Society T.V. Channel and has been published in 22 languages.

He became advisor to the Maldives Government on their project to become carbon neutral, but after three years the President, Mohammed Nasheed, was overthrown by a military coup and the idea floundered. At one point he contested the case for nuclear power, but having gone back and thoroughly reviewed the alternatives he became supportive. After attending the World Conference on the Global Environment in Copenhagen 2009 he wrote an article that received varying reactions around the world when he wrote: "We have just seen a disastrous shift in geopolitics. This will be China's century as they have just demanded total freedom of action in their environmental policies. After all the hype and hope and the mobilisation of thousands a wave of optimism crashed against the rocks of power politics."

In 2013 Mark was invited to speak at the Oxford Farming Conference, the premier annual meeting place of UK agriculture. He had been a leading objector to Genetic Modification, but he told his audience, he had reviewed all the evidence and decided he had been wrong. The result was quite remarkable with both sides joining in worldwide arguments and debates. In the course of a 45 minute paper he moved the G.M. position on a long way and he will probably be able to claim to have placed the first brick in the wall of overall acceptance of the technology throughout Europe. Mark had come a long way from his temporary home in Staindrop where he had learnt the discipline of living within conventions and to have the ability to question and rationally discuss ideas and propositions, then to take action and make things happen.

When Mark brought his future wife to meet Jane for the first time she asked, in her usual direct way, when they were going to get married. Mark said they couldn't find an engagement ring Maria liked as she wasn't very keen on gold, consequently there was no date arranged. As Mark told the guests at their wedding, "Jane promptly stumped off upstairs and came down with a sapphire and platinum ring." She asked Maria to try it on to see if it fitted which it did. Jane asked for it back and handed it to Mark who then proposed for the second time. Maria once more accepted and Jane gained another very dear friend. Their first daughter, a little pink baby girl born on Valentine's Day, was named Rosa Jane in her honour.

# Chapter 16

## Jane: charity and vision

Jane Other Ritchie was born at her parent's home in Richmond, Surrey on April 1$^{st}$ 1949 with her grandmother Dots in attendance. Dots had of course had the most extraordinary upbringing, being treated very oddly by her mother. When Dots' first daughter was born, the doctor in attendance said she must be very happy now she had a handsome husband and a beautiful baby. Dots replied that she also wanted a granddaughter. At the time of Jane's birth, the medical profession was modernising, using wartime experience of new drugs and techniques. She was the precious first born, with an indulgent granny who wanted only the best. Desensitisation injections were fashionable amongst the pregnant mothers and grannies in Richmond, as they were said to clean up any allergies small children might have. The family doctor, John Dancy, was approached on the matter and responded with a long letter explaining why he was against these as yet unproven techniques which were already getting a bad reputation in the profession with suggestions they were being exploited amongst wealthy parents. Already some people had been made worse by the practice, in fact, some had died. Therefore the idea was never followed through and the relieved doctor said later, "A new form of drug, anti-histamines, is now available to deal with allergies as they appear." In a funny quirk of fate, Jane later met John Dancy's granddaughter when they were both pupils at St. Mary's School in Calne, Wiltshire.

Jane and her brothers grew up in quiet post war Richmond on the fringes of the County of Surrey and Greater London. The River Thames wound its way through the town, its banks bounded by graceful Georgian buildings. Richmond Hill, not the one where the famous Lass lived, ran from the town centre up to the main entrance to Richmond Park which remains an authentic Royal deer park, but with hunting excluded, of course. The Ritchie house was just one away from a small pedestrian access gate into the park, not far from the main Richmond Hill gate opposite the Star & Garter Home[139] for seriously wounded soldiers, sailors and airmen of two world wars. In fine weather these men would sit on Richmond Terrace in a variety of wheel chairs and were a constant reminder, especially to curious children, of the consequences of conflicts on human beings.

Her father bought a short lease on 29 Cambrian Road from a Mr & Mrs Codrington, descendants of the Admiral of that name who was Captain of HMS Orion during the Battle of Trafalgar. When the lease expired the family became council house tenants of Richmond Borough Council. Old Mr Codrington gave Christopher a dress sword that had belonged to his ancestor for safekeeping. On the death of her mother, Jane and her brothers decided to sell the weapon during the centenary year of the Battle of Trafalgar. The Admiral had been very much in favour of naval ratings having higher wages, but failed in his demand to Parliament for an extra penny a week. So he resigned from the Navy and managed to win a seat in the Commons where he was successful in raising the pay of naval ratings. Hence in London, there are several pubs named the Admiral Codrington. Jane gave her share from the sale of the Codrington sword to the RNLI in memory of those people who worked tirelessly, after the battle of Trafalgar, to save lives in the great storm that followed. Rear Admiral G. H. Evans who retired to West Burton, thought it strange that instead of having an ivory handle as a captain's dress sword of that period should have had, it was covered in shagreen.[140] Perhaps Admiral Edward Codrington had had sweaty hands?

During the summer and Easter holidays of her childhood the family headed north to Wensleydale, visiting both Ritchie and King grandparents. On the death of his mother, Jane's father inherited three small farms and a derelict farmhouse in Walden which they renovated with financial help from Dots. Holiday visits took on a new meaning with everyone sharing the work of the house and the turf-hidden cobbled yard. The older children had to do a daily square yard of weeding to expose

---

139   The Star & Garter Home moved to Surbiton in 2013.

140   Fish or eel skin.

the cobblestones before being allowed to escape to Cross Farm, above the house, where they were welcomed by their friend Alice Thompson, whose two younger daughters, Margaret and Joan, patiently let them tag along with whatever farm work they were doing. Jane's brothers learnt to shoot rabbits which were then skinned by their mother and cooked. Jane's parents didn't believe in waste so every possible rabbit recipe was prepared during the holiday which put Jane off rabbit for life. They fished for trout with worms on hooks which was not very successful as the river bank was overgrown and the line always seemed to end up entwined in the lower branches of trees. Jane never learnt the knack of killing the few they did catch. Many hours were spent bashing away at thistles in the surrounding fields. Thistles seriously upset her father, although they didn't seem to cause his tenant much concern.

When grandfather Bill King was alive there were glorious days out for picnics, always with a fire surrounded by beck stones on which they boiled the kettle for tea and cooked bacon. For Jane's parents, much of the time of those precious holiday weeks in summer was taken up improving the old farmhouse, organising repairs and improvements to the three tenanted farms. Christopher spent most of one holiday battling to get two thirds of the farmers in Walden to sign up to electricity installation. He could understand their resistance to modernity as tradition ran deep. Frugality was the byword and farmers could see few advantages only never ending expenses and bills for washing machines and other unnecessary luxuries their wives would want. However Christopher knew they must eventually be persuaded to move into the modern world in order for their farms to survive.

As she approached thirteen, Jane went away to St. Mary's School at Calne,[141] Wiltshire; a school with a reputation for a good rounded education. She enjoyed it much more than her previous school and gained a place at Newnham College, Cambridge, following the example of her mother and aunt. Although her father was in some ways rather Victorian in outlook, he was totally supportive of girls having the same standard of education as boys, but as a Classicist he didn't think much of Geography

---

141   Then home to the Harris sausage factory.

as her chosen subject! He told her that it was important she trained for a career so that if she got married and her husband died or divorced her, she would be able to work to support her family.

Throughout her school career Jane worked hard, but was not a natural academic being more interested in people and practical things. As there were three Janes in her class she was called Other. She didn't excel at anything, but was chosen to tell a fellow pupil who smelt, that she needed to do something about personal hygiene! Her first ambition, as a little girl was to be a shepherdess, like the ones on the sofa material at home, holding a crook with ribbons, a crinoline skirt and a dog. When she learnt this was only a figment of someone's imagination, her quiet ambition was then to follow in her mother's footsteps: to get married, have a family and a dog.

She went up to Newnham College, Cambridge initially to read Geography, but after two years she switched to Archaeology and Anthropology. During one Social Anthropology lecture, the lecturer said he didn't think people made bargains with God any longer which was a common and well understood practice in the past, and he asked if any of his audience had done so. Jane was the only student to put her hand up. He proceeded no further as that was not the response he had expected. Had he done so, he would have been told that Jane had already informed God that if he wanted her to get married then He'd have to find her a suitable husband and thus, instead of hunting for one herself, she would work as hard as she could at whatever she did and, in the process, make as many good friends as possible. Like her grandmother Dots, Jane has made numerous friends. Over the course of her career in County Durham she benefitted from having three bosses who allowed her the freedom to work independently as hard and as creatively as possible.

In her last year at school she and her fellow students were advised to visit their University Appointment's Board in their second year at university so as to have time to think about their careers before the pressure of exams started. Jane dutifully bicycled off to discuss her career possibilities. Three visits were arranged for her. First she met a Factory Inspector in Leeds, then a Hospital Administrator in York and finally a Careers Officer in Cambridge. She wasn't sufficiently interested in equipment and machinery at the first and didn't want a training that entailed moving around an administration network which left the Careers Office. When she visited they were busy relocating their office and were worried about the future of the adopted office cat. Her mind was made up and she decided that was a good place to start. If she didn't like the work it would anyway give her the chance to find out about other opportunities.

West Yorkshire Local Education Authority awarded her a postgraduate grant to train as a Youth Employment Officer, as Careers Officers were then called, at a training centre at Swanley in Kent. Jane was somewhat disappointed that this was not the Garden of England she had heard so much about at school. Instead, it was a developing suburb gradually swallowing up redundant commercial glasshouses with broken panes and rotting cabbage patches. She wanted to work in the north of England and applied for a job vacancy advertised in the Times Educational Supplement by Durham County Council in their sub office at Barnard Castle. She posted off the application, telling God it was up to Him whether He saw fit for it to arrive safely and successfully. It did both. The interview panel was made up of Councillors one of whom, in all seriousness, asked Jane to come and dig his garden, in the hope she could find some valuable antiquities based on her degree qualification in archaeology. She noted he had overlooked anthropology. They offered her the job there and then; she was surprised and hesitated. "Come north Pet!" was the same Councillor's exhortation. It was easier to say yes, than no, so she started as a Careers Officer in Bishop Auckland in August 1972.

The post war decline of traditional regional industries was really biting in County Durham in the early 1970s. In 1976, the Labour Government was in power and Jane was able to put a philosophy she had thought through to the test. It was quite simple: misunderstanding, whether international, national, local or between two individuals was wasteful, unnecessary and, above all, harmful. She therefore set about clearing up existing misunderstandings on her patch in South West Durham. She established an organisation to link employers and schools to get the message across to young people approaching their working lives that an understanding of English, Maths and basic Science was essential if they wanted to become part of the local industrial work force. The organisation was given the rather cumbersome name Durham Industry Commerce &

Education Association in order to be inclusive. This became shortened to DICE and Tony Breckill from Black & Decker designed an appropriate logo depicting a DICE. Jane used bright yellow paper resulting in her letters being referred to as Jane's yellow perils.

Shirley Williams was Secretary of State for Education at the time, a committed reformer, who launched The Great Debate on the future of education. This took the form of a series of conferences at strategic points around the country all attended by the Minister. The first was held in the Civic Centre of Newcastle City Council in February 1977. Jane's boss, Dermot Dick, the Principal Careers Officer for County Durham, attended this first debate and cited DICE as an example of innovative good practice. The focus for the debate was entitled, "Educating Our Children" and covered four main subjects: The curriculum details for the 5 to 16 age groups, the assessment of standards, the education and training of teachers, and finally school and working life. These became the basis of DICE discussions over the next decade.

Sixty five companies and organisations became members of DICE along with thirty nine schools. By 1986, nine years on, only thirty of those companies were still in existence. Jane faced the facts. Mechanisation and the decrease in demand for traditional skills effectively meant a change of tactics. She found similar challenges in rural areas to the west of industrial Durham where change was also evident. She had been appointed District Careers Officer for South West Durham in 1973 and worked from Bishop Auckland where industrial and rural County Durham met. After a year living in Newton Aycliffe, Jane lived first in a hamlet just outside Winston and then in Staindrop, the large historical village near Raby Castle. From her scrapbooks it is clear she worked seven days a week and, even when shopping in Barnard Castle on Saturdays, she met 'her youngsters' and enjoyed hearing about their progress and problems.

Jane remembers that when she was coming to the end of her time at St. Mary's she was considering her future and she could only think of becoming a nanny because of her experience of looking after her youngest brother. Her father told her not to be such a cabbage, she had brains to use. She asked the Head Mistress, the inimitable Miss Gibbins, for her advice. Miss G, as she was known to her pupils, referred Jane to the powers above, "Jane dear, the Good Lord decides what you will do. You merely have to do it."

Jane understood why girls, living in the rural parts of her patch, wanted to become a farmer's wife. Jane thought this both reasonable and sensible, as in her view, a farmer's wife was a job in itself. She had seen how the Thompson girls had run their father's farm. However, to her surprise, her views were reported by the Guardian newspaper, appearing in the Naked Ape column much to the amusement of the Director of Education who sent her the cutting. In 1982, work in a trade was the first career choice for young men, with the armed services coming second. How different from the 18$^{th}$ and 19$^{th}$ centuries when mining and quarrying in the western dales employed thousands and farming relatively few. By the mid-20$^{th}$ century, the industrial prosperity of eastern County Durham derived from ship building, steel manufacturing and coal mining was waning; traditional mining and quarrying in the Pennines was largely forgotten, apart from road stone; and the tradition of apprenticeships was considered outdated.

There were some successes amid the frustrations of trying to develop career opportunities for young people in this depressed region. One that stood out for Jane was the glowing academic career of 18 year old Eileen McLellan, from West Auckland, who attended the King James I Comprehensive School in Bishop Auckland. A very able girl in all respects, she was offered places at both Oxford and Cambridge. Jane took her to visit Cambridge and as a result Eileen chose to read Natural Sciences at Clare College. Her Head Teacher actually complained that she had missed two lessons in order to visit Cambridge, so when the local Press featured her success, Eileen very fairly thanked Jane publically.

In 1989, Jane became the Business Link Development Officer for County Durham. In making the move she was advised to keep a low profile, but anyone who knew her passion for, and commitment to, improving the lot of the next generation would have smiled for she was no shrinking violet. She set about establishing the Durham Business Education Executive (DBEE), which later became the Education Business Partnership (EBP). She researched the priorities of the members coming from businesses and schools across the county. She recorded 33 ideas from which she and her committee then selected four. British Steel, Cummins Engines and Glaxo had together developed a Junior Leaders' scheme which was adapted into a Business Ambassador scheme, drawing on experiences from an Industry Year project in Staffordshire. By 1991 DBEE had 62 Ambassadors from 39 companies in County Durham. This scheme was eventually adopted across the North East Region benefitting thousands of young people.

Jane Ritchie had a reputation as a determined person with few equals especially when projects were funding-dependent as they nearly always were. DBEE called on her to put her money raising skills into play. The Royal Society of Chemistry was probably surprised to be approached by Jane, but after an explanation they responded and persuaded the chemical giant ICI on Teesside to invest seed corn funding for a Primary Science Caravan to introduce primary school children to Science. This would require £30,000 annual running costs. The Regional Development Agency, One North East, recently formed by the Blair government, granted matched funding for the project. Jane later went into battle to obtain as much as possible for her Education Business Partnership (EBP), and after applying for a seven year grant she was more than pleased to receive a five year award.

Jane was a founder member of the National Education Business Partnership Network becoming its first Secretary following its launch at her alma mater, Cambridge University. In 1999, the DBEE received a Quality Kitemark which gave Jane an excuse to get a footpath at the school where she worked repaired in preparation for the important inspection visit. Such practical achievements have always given her great satisfaction. Looking back she has many happy memories of managing an Education and Business Partnership, and was very proud to have been referred to as "that bloody woman" by a senior Training Enterprise Council (TEC) employee. When the town of Darlington was separated from County Durham, the Chief Executive asked her organisation to remain as their EBP. This was an enormous honour and reflected how much Jane and her team were valued.

On three occasions, Jane collided head on with the world of quangos where political correctness and rank were always challenging. On one occasion making her opponents back off by threatening to picket the TEC offices with her business friends and partners. 1999 was her 25$^{th}$ year working in education business partnership and she celebrated with a 50$^{th}$ birthday party for friends and colleagues, very few of whom failed to accept the invitation. Her staff received a carnation for each year they had worked with her and she toured the room explaining why each guest had been invited.

As she was approaching retirement, Jane was awarded the MBE in the 2002 New Year's Honours List 'for services to careers and young people'. As by then she lived in North Yorkshire the award was listed under her home county, not County Durham where she had earned it. She didn't want to travel to London as she had been through that experience when she had attended her father's OBE investiture. Her memories of Buckingham Palace and the long slow-moving queue of recipients made her worry that her back could easily seize up with all the standing. At her father's investiture she had been a small girl and had been shocked that no one had offered even a cup of tea to the patient waiting recipients. To her delight, Jane found she could receive her award from Lord Crathorne, the Lord Lieutenant of North Yorkshire, the following summer. She decided to share the celebration with Cousin Margery, and His Lordship obligingly carried out the simple award ceremony in Brentwood Lodge, Leyburn, the council run care home where Margery was spending her final years. He took great trouble to meet all the staff and residents who attended what was an unusual and simple ceremony. The informality of the occasion gave him the opportunity to publically commend his Cadet who was highly delighted to be presented with a copy of the St. Andrew's Recipe Book which Jane and her mother had compiled in aid of church funds. A lamb and ginger recipe really took the young Cadet's fancy.

A decade before in 1992, Jane had developed the concept of a specialist centre for the Technology Enhancement Project which would help children understand that in the workplace Maths, Science and Technology were closely linked, and a career involving any one of these subjects would often need evidence of an understanding of the other two. She had met too many young men who told her they liked metal work or technical drawing, but didn't see the need to have a good knowledge of Maths and Science.

# Chapter 17

## "Give Jane the rest"

Margery Freeman died in 2004 just before her 101st birthday. She was nearly blind and very deaf in one ear. She was by then deprived of all she enjoyed; racing on the telly could neither be seen nor hardly heard, the enjoyment of gardening, walking the moors and fishing the rivers were simply fading memories. Most of her few close friends had died. She became increasingly frugal, dressing in much-mended old clothes, despite having a considerable untouched portfolio of stocks and shares from the sale of her assets after the death of her husband. Until her final years she enjoyed regular meetings with her stockbroker,[142] watching share movements and discussing new possibilities and the ways of the money market. Her accountant in Leyburn, and her solicitor in Richmond, jointly managed her affairs and had been appointed as her attorneys and executors.

At 96 her executors were concerned whether she really understood the consequences of her will. They arranged to sit her down to ask if she really wanted to leave most of her money to a cats' home. Many years earlier Margery had told Jane's mother that she intended to leave her money to a cats' home, and Margaret and Jane were both amused at the idea of super fat indulged moggies lounging in luxurious chairs in sunlit warmth for evermore. After some discussion with her executors, Margery decided at that point to give a 'big helping' to both a cats' home and to the Royal Naval Lifeboat Institution in memory of her late husband, and she agreed to rewrite her will.

---

142    Richard Whiteley of Cawood Smithie now Cardale Asset Management Ltd.

Her direct relatives, and those of Capt. Freeman who were known to her, would now benefit along with local churches, chapels, organisations, several friends and acquaintances. She left her farm in Redmire to Jane on the understanding that she would look after it. She took Jane round Hogra telling her the ancient names of each field and adding background information which had come down the family over two hundred years. She was horrified when she found a pipeline had been laid across the land without her permission. Jane hoped she would take the matter up with her Agent although she knew it was unlikely as Margery avoided direct interpersonal conflicts as much as possible.

Mrs Freeman's ideas of the value of money were stuck in a time warp and consequently her bequests were in small amounts compared to the residue she left. After two meetings with her administrators she become bored, and later complained to Jane that she didn't want to give any more to a particular individual. Jane assured her that it was her money to do with as she wanted, and left it at that. Later Jane learnt that having made some 40 bequests she had announced in a tired voice that she'd had enough and instructed her solicitor to "give Jane the rest". Margery told a great niece that she had left Jane enough to go on a cruise. Sadly that is probably what Margery would have liked for herself to remind her of those days when she travelled to Tasmania and Australia, but a cruise was certainly not on Jane's wish list.

When Stephen Garget, Margery's solicitor, went to see Jane after Margery had died, she handed him all the small change she had found in the room in Brentwood. He took the thirty or so pence, put them in his bag, then looked at Jane and solemnly informed her that, after making the forty bequests, Margery had left the residue to her. Jane imagined this would settle the outstanding bills. Garget paused, and then made her nearly fall off her chair when he said "That will be about nine million pounds". She was shocked and, for a moment, quiet. Garget too was silent realising the news had come as a total surprise. Jane's immediate reaction was to tell him "Well at last I can build the Industrial Learning Centre."[143]

---

143   The working name for The Work Place before it became a reality.

Jane had never been motivated by money and never needed to be, but she was really motivated by her dream of what became The Work Place. There was no question about it, she could now make that dream come true. The money and reclaimed tax, already paid, was placed in a charity. Given Margery's love of the family home at Redmire, with all the history of her Other forebears, the charity was called the Elm House Trust. Jane had long held the belief that if one is lucky enough to receive a windfall, it should go to the first thing that came into the mind, thus avoiding temptations of self-centred spending.

After her extraordinary meeting with Stephen Garget there followed a sleepless night as she turned over her immediate reaction to the news. Three times, since 1992, she had attempted to bid for funding for an industrial learning centre which had twice failed due to constant changes in government policy, but it could now be built. The third bid however was still in progress when she heard of her good fortune, but it had stalled as her bid for capital funding had been turned into a revenue bid by Sedgefield Borough Council without her knowledge. The Gatsby Foundation's support for the original concept of the Technology Enhancement Project, based on the need to understand the inter-relationship between maths, science and technology had been the starting place for her original vision. The predicament of young people with limited employability skills was an added driver to create a learning resource that would become a highly visible sign of understanding and recognition of the importance of learning and skills, attitudes and attributes. Most important of all, Jane hoped the centre would be seen as a contributor to wealth creation in an area which had experienced appalling industrial decline over many decades. Work Related Learning would certainly make a huge difference to the lives of young people and, ultimately, to the industrial economy in the North East.

Jane's family upbringing, her early life at St Mary's and then at Newnham College in the rarefied academic air of Cambridge University had made her a caring person with a tendency to formality with good manners and a strong work ethic. Her King relatives had moved from Stewards of Richmond Castle to farming and manufacturing, and then to military, academic and professional careers. Her Ritchie line was rooted in

Aberdeenshire producing traders who, over the generations, went from boat building and timber trading on the River Thames, to mills in Stroud, tea and rubber trading in the City of London, to the military and the Civil Service. Both families retain connections in Wensleydale today through property which has been in the family for generations bringing them back home on a regular basis. Jane has fulfilled her ambition to get back home to West Burton but it took her until she was forty to accept that she was not going to follow in her mother's footsteps and have a family of her own.

Jane entered her second career following the death of her Cousin Margery. The Elm House Trust was to hold the inheritance with a Board of Trustees comprised of the stockbroker who had managed Margery Freeman's portfolio over many years and Jane's middle brother John who could, somewhat justifiably, have easily resented the fact that his sister had inherited the lot; but he didn't and gladly took his seat. A specialist lawyer from Rollitts was appointed to take the Trust through the complicated process of establishing full charitable status and, by complete co-incidence, Jane found that a Dr Rollitt had been on the Board of King & Co many years earlier.

VOLT, the Vocational Learning Trust, was formed as a separate charity to build, own and manage The Work Place. First a site had to be found which was strategically sited to be accessible as possible to communities from where 'learners' would come. Jane wanted to ensure that the final building would be one of quality therefore the site and then the design must be right. Her intention was for striking architecture, an exciting interior design and an atmosphere far removed from the typical school that would inspire young people to think, achieve work related skills and understanding. She hoped they would appreciate a quality experience and be better prepared to follow worthwhile and rewarding careers.

The Elm House Trust committed £4.5 million to the project, but this had to be increased after Durham County Council withdrew their grant application for an additional £1M from the Regional Development Agency. However a second bid for £600,000 was later successful and paid for equipment and provided for the initial revenue expenditure. Jane had to make further capital available for an external evaluation, which was the only time she was reduced to tears during the process. She headed for the site office of the main contractors, Clugston Construction, for tea and comfort. The Site Team had become firm friends and several of them remain so.

The decision on the final site took a strange twist when Triturus, the Great Crested Newt, appeared on the radar of the environmental officer conducting his site inspection. Surprisingly this small amphibian has its own EU legislation requiring all building and development sites within 100 metres of a known newt, to be granted a licence by Natural England, as English Nature was then called. A naturalist's comprehensive report therefore had to be commissioned. There was no doubt that the Aycliffe Business Park was strategically right and there were various options across the designated area. The first site was deemed to carry a flood risk requiring £400,000 to resolve, and this was before any newt investigations took place. Eventually the present site was agreed and the amphibian search began. When the proposed entrance had to be moved slightly, another newt consideration was required and a tree came into the firing line which could not be cut down until after the nesting season. By a miracle it disappeared one weekend before any birds took up residence, leaving Jane with a wry feeling that one of the site team would have a nice warm winter with plenty of logs. Eventually, and after considerable payment of fees to 'newtologists', the site was deemed to be totally newt free, and the safe haven that had had to be identified in the event of any newts having to be re-housed, was not therefore a requirement. Human rights pale into insignificance in comparison to the rights of amphibians.

A Construction Design Team had to be commissioned: architect, project manager, quantity surveyor, mechanical and electrical engineers, civil and structural engineers, landscape architects and the main contractor. While Jane was waiting for probate to have direct access to the charity's funds, Durham County Council agreed to lend her £30,000 in exchange for their Estates Department appointing the professionals. The Construction Design Team understood and took for granted the tremendous strain construction sites carry in their wake for all concerned. Every day brought challenges usually requiring a number of disciplines to come together to reach a solution. As the Mechanical Engineer explained to Jane, "professional disagreements go with the territory", but he added, it was nearly always possible to sit down afterwards in a pub for a jar. However when Jane looks back she realises how much everyone took care, as far as possible, to protect her from the various disagreements.

As the project reached completion Jane was very touched to hear that Clugston Construction had nominated her for the Construction Industry's Client of the Year Award which placed her in a category along side large corporations in cities and towns around the country. She was thrilled and surprised to win the North East heat and to be the national runner up overall. This was a compliment to everyone involved in The Work Place Project and the unique relationship between the people who did the work and Jane herself. She was on site regularly to inspect progress and attended site meetings. Clugstons followed H&S requirements by issuing her with her own reflective jacket, clearly marked with their company name and the regulatory hard hat marked 'The Gaffer'. Their site office became in her words, "A place where I was offered friendship, patient explanations of problems and, importantly, care. They were always aware that I was a totally novice client developer."

When all was complete Jane wrote a short booklet entitled 'Drawings Rule OK?'[144] It had never occurred to her when she set forth just how important the drawings used on large-scale building projects became once they had been agreed. If it wasn't on paper it didn't happen, at least not before a replacement was agreed, or the original properly altered by the professional concerned and signed appropriately. She quickly found that drawings could put common sense out of the window when two plans, of different features in the same area, conflicted simply because one contractor failed to agree to exchange his work with another.

To her frustration she found that re-siting a wash basin entailed moving a light switch which required new plans to be drawn. Her design objectives were purposely unusual. Jane wanted a mathematical feature[145] in the courtyard to test young minds. These were forgotten as they were not on any drawing. Consequently work already completed had to be taken up

---

144   Jane had previously written a booklet called Building The Work Place.
145   To demonstrate Pythagoras' theorem – the 'Square on the Hypotenuse.'

and the surface re-laid, requiring yet more plans. The Fibonacci curve of tulips and daffodils were wrongly sited and left off the grass banking. Jane hopes that at some time in the future children may add their own floral curves to these banks where they were originally intended.

Ground source heating, rain water harvesting, well thought out light access, unusual materials and startling design features – such as the intriguing spiral staircase, resulted in a 'state of the art' building which was both fit for purpose and achieved within the original budget. The architect drew a line at see-through sewage pipes, but Jane did manage to have 'cow kennels' turned into offices with full height walls so that the staff could protect their privacy.

For students attending courses in The Work Place there is an opportunity to see and understand the complexity of the building which is controlled by a computerised Building Management System. Although a relatively small building, The Work Place reflects identical technology to that in the skyscrapers being erected all over the world, the building of which offers challenging career possibilities to young people. New technology inevitably brings with it health and safety questions and these mounted all the time. Jane is a patient and tolerant person, but even to her some of the demands of the Health and Safety Executive seemed inane. The legal requirements emanating from new technologies raised challenges she had never considered at the outset. For instance, ground source heating draws its warmth from a considerable distance around the site therefore if a neighbour places an additional system too close they become poachers. An awareness of adjacent developments below ground level needs to be included in future legal development agreements.

The Northumbrian Association awarded Jane the Hotspur Award in 2009 allowing her to keep the replica Charlton silver spur for a year. The spur is awarded annually to someone who has "through bold endeavour" done something to benefit or raise the profile of the North East. Other recipients include Brendan Foster, The Duchess of Northumberland, Lee Hall, Anthony Gormley, Alan Shearer and Sir Bobby Robson. Accepting the Award, Jane asked for the following to be read out at the House of Commons dinner *"I am very honoured to have been awarded the Hotspur Award for bold endeavour by the Northumbrian Association.*

*Having checked my Shakespeare, no doubt Harry Percy's actions could have been described as foolhardy or worse. I am not sure that trying to swim through 'Turkish Delight' for over 30 years has been particularly brave, but I hope that I share his honest approach and sense of fairness; and I have learnt to understand why people rebel against the status quo. It has been a real privilege to spend my working life trying to serve the young people and businesses of County Durham and Darlington through education business partnership; and the North East Region through the Business Ambassador programme. Hotspur was a 'doer', and I doubt in real life he had the time for the long elegant speeches Shakespeare gave him. This Region needs more practical doers and a greater understanding of what it is to BE enterprising in the public, as well as the private, sector. One of the greatest compliments I have been paid was to be called the grit in the oyster. I have more patience than Harry Hotspur and I thank you for recognising my endeavours and hope that The Work Place will be of real lasting benefit to the North East Region."*

When she received the Spur at Washington Old Hall she said"......*I feel a sort of 'unknown soldier' in view of the illustrious list of previous recipients......Whilst I am very proud to be recognised for 'endeavouring' – the word comes from the French – en devoir – to have to, implying a duty, I am not at all sure that I can claim any of the boldness attributed to Hotspur by Shakespeare in Henry IV Part I. Being enterprising and a Belbin[146] Completer is not the same as being impetuous or risking one's life. Building The Work Place was simply doing what I had been asked to do by my employer – Durham County Council. The last Director of Education[147] in England had told an audience assembled at Durham Cricket Ground for County Durham's Education Business Partnership's 10th anniversary that I would succeed in building an industrial learning centre, and I remember feeling as though I had been set an impossible challenge.*

---

146    Meredith Belbin is a British management theorist who developed the theory of 9 Belbin Team Roles and the Belbin Team Role Inventory personality test.

147    Keith Mitchell

*Education Business partnership (with a small 'p') contributes to national competitiveness and is essential if young people are to understand both the concept of economic competitiveness and the skills, attitudes and attributes that are needed in the workplace. The Work Place is an outward, visible affirmation of my belief in the importance of education business partnership to the wellbeing of the North East. It is designed to be a hub for work-related learning for the region and consists of a number of flexible spaces within which young people can undertake learning and understand the relevance of that learning to life after school.*

*Endless meetings and bid writing is a modern form of brain drain with precious little to show for the vast cost of time and travel and use of intellect. Too little time and energy is left to be a proper change agent – which is why education business partnership develops so slowly. No one, including leaders and managers has enough time to think let alone actively listen. Far too much wisdom and experience is never recognised or tapped into. I would like to see an award for partnership on the lines of the Queen's Award of Industry to recognise working together for the common good.*

*The North is a wonderful place. Full of people who endeavour, who are as loyal as Hotspur to their kinsmen, who become treasured friends and colleagues; but unlike Hotspur, we rarely go that extra mile and revolt. Direct action got him killed by the future Henry V. I am not advocating we attempt to resolve issues as Hotspur did; we just need to be bolder, more effective lobbyists. Asking all MPs and senior Civil Servants to read the Audit Commission report 'People, Places & Prosperity'[148] would be a start. Thank you for recognising the value of a public servant who has simply put her money where her mouth is; the building of The Work Place is taking a risk as schools may be reluctant to pay for using it, but education business partnership needs to be championed and young people and North East employers are both worth the endeavour."*

---

148   The Audit Commission accused Government Departments of rolling out funding to the regions without any joined up thinking. It was not surprising the report concluded that the fall out was a mess of the order of Humpty Dumpty, wasting valuable resources in the hopeless task of trying to create a holistic solution.

When Jane was planning the opening of The Work Place she came up with a dedication which summed up her concern for, and commitment to, the young people she had enjoyed working with:

> "FOR THE CHILDREN OF COUNTY DURHAM TO SHARE
> WITH THEIR NEIGHBOURS IN THE NORTH EAST
> AND NORTH YORKSHIRE"

Pupil representatives from all County Durham Secondary Schools were invited to the official opening and Jane explained that she had deliberately chosen the word 'children' as she thought this was one of the most beautiful words in any language. Not one to believe in waste, she decided to put the family crest her paternal grandfather had had designed to good use and added that to the dedication. She felt she had done her best to 'Ring True'.

It is sad to have to report that as this book reaches its conclusion, The Work Place has failed in its intentions and Jane believes the young people of County Durham have been let down. She has done her utmost to create a new environment for communities that have faced enormous change in employment opportunities since she started work in the early 1970s. She worked for local government for her entire working life and tried to overcome the consequences of the huge industrial change. She was continually frustrated by the lack of joined up national policy. Where does The Work Place fit into the new economic climate? Central Government remains dithering on the subject of new skills education and has disregarded the exceptional resource of the building. A Junior Minister visited but was re-shuffled out later in the week. A non sequitur no doubt, but very frustrating after all the background briefing that had been prepared.

The Careers Service is no more, and there is currently no government funding for Education Business Partnerships. Jane is sure the wheel will turn full circle in time as politicians cannot resist making continual educational changes. Since 2010 the concepts of Localism, Sustainable Communities and The Big Society have collided with policies from the Department of Education, the Department of Health and DEFRA to name but 3 Departments. Learning to listen is as important as learning to read, write and arithmetic. Politicians seem to find this skill as hard to learn as the proverbial camel finds getting through the eye of a needle.

# Postscript

*Although my vision for The Work Place is currently not being met, the building is being put to good use and it is meeting the charitable purpose of the Vocational Learning Trust. It is a beautiful building, very well cared for by its two Caretakers Tommy and Dave. It is important to move on and graciously pass the baton to others to go forward and manage the resource as they see fit. The Trustees of the Vocational Learning Trust and the Directors of The Work Place (Aycliffe) Ltd receive no remuneration, and have given, and continue to give, generously of their time and talents.*

*I have achieved my personal ambition of getting home to West Burton, the same ambition as my father. Cousin Margery's legacy has enabled me, with the help of others, to preserve West Burton Village Green in the ownership of the Parish, and to extinguish all vexatious manorial rights in Burton-cum-Walden. The Elm House Trust has supported a range of community projects in Wensleydale and its tributary valleys and will continue to do so.*

*Jane Ritchie*

# Sources (as far as they are known)

City of London Library

Romantic Richmondshire, Speight 1897 Ed Audrey Segal 9<sup>th</sup> edition

Dictionary of National Biography

Whitaker's History of Craven

Visitation of Yorkshire 1564

Dugdales's Visitation of Yorkshire 1665-6 Surtees Society

County Families of Wales T. Nicholas 2<sup>nd</sup> edition

Foster's Yorkshire Pedigrees

Foster's Visitation of Yorkshire

Yorkshire Pedigrees Harleian Society

Tyssen Library Pedigrees

History of Richmond by C. Clarkson

The Genealogist

Thoresby's Ducatus Leodiensis

Whitaker's Deanery of Craven 3<sup>rd</sup> edition

Burke's Commons

Burke's Landed Gentry

Memorials of an Ancient House – A history of the Family of Lister or Lyster by H. L. Lyster Denny

Some Old Families – A contribution to the Genealogical History of Scotland by Hardy Bertram McCall 1889

Memoirs of my Ancestors by H. B. McCall

William Bulmer's Directory of the North Riding of Yorkshire 1895